THE SALTWATER FISHERMAN'S BIBLE

Revised Edition

THE SALTWATER FISHERMAN'S BIBLE

Revised Edition

ERWIN A. BAUER

Doubleday & Company, Inc., Garden City, New York

BOOK DESIGN BY SYLVIA DEMONTE-BAYARD

Library of Congress Cataloging in Publication Data

Bauer, Erwin A.
  The saltwater fisherman's bible.

  1. Saltwater fishing.   I. Title.
SH457.B38   1982   799.1'6
ISBN 0-385-17220-6   AACR2
Library of Congress Catalog Card Number 82–2388

CONTENTS

1

TARPON

For several miles the rum-colored tidal Parismina River of Costa Rica flows through a dense lowland jungle. In places the river is only a dank tunnel under a canopy of dark-green forest. The bag-shaped, three-to-six-foot-long nests of Montezuma oropendolas, large tropical relatives of orioles, swung from overhanging trees and exquisite multicolored tanagers and toucans darted over the water in our path. At one point the sound of our outboard flushed a band of howler monkeys, and their rumbling chorus followed them away through the jungle. Despite all of these exotic sights and sounds, Dick Kotis and I were not prepared for the spectacle we found in a widening of the river—in a murky, brackish backwater called Laguna California.

The place was literally alive and choked with fish. A man might spend his life in search of such a place and not find anything to match it.

Wherever we looked, the water was seething. Everywhere schools of silvery fish rolled to the surface. Some wallowed and others leaped clear. All were tarpon, and big ones, from 40 to 100 pounds or more. Our boatman, Calixto Lopez, cut the motor and we drifted into the center of

the mass of fish. It was a sight to make anyone, and especially a serious fisherman, feel weak in the knees.

With unsteady hands and light casting rods and reels, Dick and I tossed a pair of surface plugs toward the nearest school and immediately a tarpon sucked in Dick's lure. It was not a hard strike, but when the tarpon tasted the hook it catapulted out of the lagoon twice, so quickly that it seemed to be two different fish. Before Dick could even catch his reel handles, the tarpon had snapped the line.

It is fortunate that no tarpon struck my plug immediately because it could have cost me my tackle and maybe a finger. My reel had backlashed and I had to unravel the tangled line. A moment later, a giant tarpon inhaled the plug and in a split second discovered its mistake. It spent more time in the air than in the water before my line failed. At the same time a school of very large fish rolled so close by that they rocked our boat.

The rest of that morning brought more of the same. The tarpon struck most of the lures we threw at them, but also threw most right back.

Two-hundred-pound tarpon are extremely rare. This 208-pound specimen was taken in the Tibiti River, Surinam. (Florida News Bureau/Dept. of Commerce)

Tarpon are among the most exciting jumpers of all the saltwater game fishes.

We cast, hooked, and dueled with tarpon without a break until, by noon, my arms and shoulders were tied in knots from the constant pressure and whirling reel handles had barked skin from my knuckles.

Our score for the morning was nothing to brag about. Of twenty-two tarpon hooked at least until the first inevitable jump, only one was brought to boat and immediately released. The others absconded with eight lures and considerable line—and reduced the mechanical innards of one casting reel to so much junk. This was, however, the start of one of the greatest fishing adventures I've ever experienced.

Costa Rica, a Central American republic less than half the size of Ohio, has in fact been the site of our best fishing trips. My first visit to Costa Rica took place in January 1959, at which time we spent only a few days on the magical Parismina. For the remainder of that trip we concentrated on the country's Pacific coast, where we found the largest accumulation of game fish I had ever seen to date. For two days our offshore boat was surrounded by vast shoals of dolphin, sailfish, and rainbow runners.

The second trip came a decade later, when the first visitor accommodations were set up on the Parismina River—a modest rancho for anglers and birdwatchers. Even today there is no way to get there except by landing a light aircraft on the beach where the river empties into the Atlantic. I had always wanted to return to the Parismina. When my old friends Dick Kotis and Leon Martuch told me they wanted to test new equipment under the toughest possible conditions, I needed little persuading to accompany them. Our reward was that unforgettable encounter at Laguna California.

Probably the first tarpon ever captured on rod and reel was taken by a Samuel H. Jones of Philadelphia and his guide, John Gardiner, in 1884 at Florida's Indian River Inlet. Since then countless sports fishermen have pursued the species, which surely ranks among the greatest, most exciting game fish on earth, no matter whether taken on heavy or light tackle. Tarpon are extraordinary jumpers and only a fraction of the fish hooked are actually boated. Nonetheless, tarpon fishing has become a mania, a challenge, even an addiction for many anglers.

Just what is this fish that breaks rods and intimidates fishermen? Known scientifically as

Megalops atlanticus, the tarpon also goes by the names silverfish, silver king, *savanilla*, *grande écaille* (in Louisiana), *sábalo* (in Latin America, where it is most plentiful), and *show-a-wee* (in Seminole). No matter what it is called, the tarpon is a member of an international family that includes the herring oxeye, the bonefish, and the ladyfish.

Built like an enormous herring, the tarpon has a deep, compressed body that is a shining, silvery tone from the head to the tip of the tail. Some specimens have a slight pinkish tint on the sides, while others have a faint olive tone. Larger in girth than the males, females of the species are believed to be more agile and more lively in action, though most experienced guides can see no difference in the type of contest waged by either sex after being hooked. The truth is that both sexes are excellent, uninhibited, shoot-the-works battlers.

The body of a tarpon is entirely covered with large, almost circular scales that range in diameter from 1 to 3½ inches. Each scale is composed of thin transparent layers of a parchmentlike substance which, taken together, resemble armor plating.

Far too little is known about the life history of a tarpon. Virtually nothing is known of the species' spawning habits or spawning areas, but it's assumed—from scale studies—that at the end of one year a tarpon will be between 12 and 24 inches long. At the end of the second year it may be from 24 to 36 inches long, and after three years a tarpon should measure a formidable 4 to 5 feet. Of course, these figures are only approximate. In some regions, tarpon grow far faster than that; in other regions the growth may be much slower. Florida Gulf coast tarpon average larger than East coast or Keys tarpon.

Generally the smaller tarpon inhabit estuaries, creeks, canals, and similar places a few miles back from the coastline. Often these areas will be brackish, but occasionally freshwater-filled. Larger specimens up to 100 or more pounds are normally found in deep holes at entrance passes to oceanic and open Gulf of Mexico waters. Tidal channels are excellent places to find the larger fish, but again it must be emphasized that large tarpon may also be found in shallow inshore waters, as in the Parismina River, Costa Rica.

The tarpon grows to a length of more than 8

feet but few that size have ever been seen, dead or alive. The largest specimen ever recorded was taken with a net by commercial fishermen on August 6, 1912, near Hillsboro Inlet on the Florida east coast. It measured 8 feet 2 inches long and its estimated weight was 352 pounds. The world's record for hook and line was a 283-pounder taken in Venezuela in 1956. But only a few individuals over 200 pounds are taken in any one year's time. The largest I have ever seen was a 204-pound fish hooked on live bait in the Tibiti River, Surinam. But a tarpon just half that size is tough to handle on any tackle and it is something to brag about when you've used light casting gear. Tarpon taken by anglers will average 30 to 50 pounds, but 100-pounders are not at all rare.

Though this herringlike species occurs in tropical and subtropical habitats on both sides of the Atlantic, its existence in the coastal waters of Nigeria, Senegal, Dahomey, Ivory Coast, and elsewhere in West Africa is not well known. In the New World tarpon range from French Guiana and Surinam northward up the Atlantic coast and around the Gulf of Mexico to the Florida Keys. Stragglers have been caught as

Tackle manufacturer and expert plug-caster Dick Kotis with a Costa Rican tarpon.

Excellent tarpon fishing is found within sight of the overseas highway, U.S. 1, to Key West, Florida.

far north as Hatteras and Virginia. But the greatest concentrations occur from Panama northward to southern Mexico, especially during springtime when the species moves en masse to spawn in many Central American rivers. Tarpon avoid cold water and have an apparent tolerance of from 64 to 104 degrees Fahrenheit.

Basic tarpon fishing probably means drifting or still-fishing with natural bait: crabs, mullet, shrimp, catfish, or pinfish. Along the Florida Gulf coast, however, trolling is the more popular method. In fact, year after year the largest tarpon are taken by trolling, which is only natural since the heavier tackle involved is better suited to handling larger fish. But like plug-casting or spinning or fly-casting, catching tarpon successfully by trolling is largely a matter of knowing which waters to fish. Once that is determined the rest is relatively easy: simply toss a whole mullet, a strip of mullet, a needlefish, a balao, a large plug, or a large bucktail jig overboard and draw it behind the boat. Trolling is also a good way to explore and to probe new waters because the bait is working for you all the time.

Standard tackle on the charter tarpon boats is a 20- or 50-pound test outfit with a stainless-steel leader. Trolling plugs, feather jigs, and spoons weighing about 1½ ounces are normally used, though there is a trend toward lighter lures fished on lighter and lighter tackle.

Much of the sport of tarpon fishing comes simply from hooking the fish and hanging on for as many jumps as possible, rather than actually boating the fish. So instead of trolling or still-fishing tackle, many anglers now use heavy-duty saltwater-bait casting rods, spinning rods, or fly rods. A popular choice of pluggers is a 6-foot rod with a stiff tip and 200 or more yards of 15-pound test monofilament on a casting reel with smooth, reliable drag. A tarpon spinning rod should be a little longer, with a spinning reel full of 12-pound test line, capable of tossing ⅝-ounce lures. Both plug-casters and spinners use cable leaders or shock lines at the business ends of the regular casting line to survive rubbing against a tarpon's jaw and armor-plated body.

A number of sportsmen consider fly-fishing for tarpon to be the top thrill in all angling—and they just may be right. The standard tackle for this type of fishing is heavy, in order to handle large, powerful fish and also to cast a good distance into a sea wind. Tarpon demand a rod with backbone enough to drive a large hook into a seemingly impenetrable jaw, in other words a 9¼- to 10-footer in fiberglass.

Tarpon fly-casters use both streamer flies (feather minnows) and popping or darting bugs tied on 2/0 to 5/0 hooks. Between fly and 12- to 15-pound-leader tippet is a short (12″) section of 100-pound-test monofilament to resist abrasion where it will surely occur. Tarpon take best a slow retrieve, usually of a fan wing streamer

Fly-casting for tarpon provides first-rate sport, as this trio demonstrates at Boca Parismina along Costa Rica's east coast.

tied with long hackle feathers. The wings should "breathe" as the streamer is retrieved.

There are a good many places, especially around the Florida coastlines, where tarpon run small, say in the 10- to 20-pound class. In these instances, much lighter spinning and fly-casting tackle can be used. Although these "babies" are even more active and acrobatic than the bigger ones, they can also be very selective at times. Smaller streamers are necessary, and especially some which imitate fingerling mullet or shrimp. Small bass bugs have worked very well.

There are many productive spinning techniques, but perhaps the most common is to travel or cruise across shallow bays, in the mouths of rivers, among mangrove islands, until a school of tarpon is sighted. Quite often it is possible to find them as they roll and travel close to the surface, a maneuver visible from far away. The object then is to cast a lure ahead of them and to retrieve it with sharp jerks of the rod tip. Some days a fast retrieve is best; more often a slow to medium speed is most successful. If all goes off as intended, a tarpon will strike, and if the hook is solidly set, a wild battle is on.

Another most effective way to fish for tarpon, particularly when they are not in evidence on the surface, is to cast blindly in channels and in other similar areas washed by the tide. Generally it is best on a rising or falling tide, rather than a slack tide, but in either case the idea is to cast a jig or a strip of live bait, to allow it to settle to the bottom, and then to retrieve it in short, steady, sharp jerks back along the bottom. Some days the technique is absolutely deadly. On other days it's only good exercise. If it doesn't work, try slowing down to a very slow, creeping retrieve.

There are almost as many different opinions on a tarpon's favorite color as there are tarpon fishermen. Probably most experienced fishermen would favor either yellow or white, whether the lures be streamer flies or backtail jigs. Still others prefer brown and combinations of yellow and brown and yellow and red. Today, many of the casting plugs are designed in completely authentic mullet finishes and have proved very successful. So have the blue-tinted plugs. Especially good, too, are the nearly transparent, silvery surface plugs which seem to be pure murder on some days. Recently a natural needlefish finish has proved effective.

The best tarpon fishing of all takes place at night, for the simple reason that these jumbo herring are largely nocturnal. Thus your odds of tying into a record-book fish are greatly enhanced and the thrill of it is indescribable. Yet to date very few anglers venture out at night in pursuit of the mighty tarpon.

The greatest mistake an angler can make is to try to boat or unhook a tarpon that is still "green," i.e., not played out sufficiently. Sportsmen have been seriously injured, some even killed, while attempting to land a tarpon too soon. Near Carmen, Mexico, I once saw a large green *sábalo* nearly destroy the deck of a small boat; the boatman himself was lucky to escape with only a hook driven through the palm of his hand as the fish jumped back in the water.

When fishing in jungle rivers such as the Parismina, and especially in smaller ones, it is not uncommon for a tarpon to "climb aboard." What invariably follows can be compared to tossing live grenades onto the deck. The best thing for any angler to do is to hit the water and leave the boat to the tarpon.

Tarpon come and go, appear and disappear mysteriously. No one has ever been able to plot their travels and migrations with complete accuracy, but their natural range includes all the fringe waters of the Gulf of Mexico plus the coastal waters of such islands as Cuba and Puerto Rico.

Beginning at Key West or thereabouts, tarpon follow the U.S. East coast northward in springtime and early summer, going about as far as North Carolina, at which point they're often seen and caught from July to early September.

Also starting from Key West, they follow the west coast of Florida northward, probing into all the rivers and bays all the way to Panama City and Pensacola, where the fishing is best in August. It's also at this time that tarpon appear in diminishing numbers all along the Texas coast, especially from Corpus Christi to Brownsville.

Any list of outstanding tarpon waters would have to include the following places: the Panuco and Tampico rivers in Mexico, the area around Carmen and Campeche in Mexico, the San Juan River in Nicaragua, all the rivers that drain into the Atlantic Ocean in Costa Rica, the entire Gulf of Mexico coast of Panama, as well as the Canal Zone waters, which are extremely good. Maybe one of the best places of all to catch a record fish is Surinam, where such jungle rivers as the Coesiwijne and Tibiti contain very large specimens.

Luckily for both the species and for sport fishermen, the tarpon is not good to eat. Because the flesh is gray, coarse, and tasteless at best, nearly all tarpon caught on hook and line are released unhurt.

Tarpon guide Russ Gray prepares to gaff a tarpon hooked on a fly rod by internationally known angler Stu Apte in the Florida Keys.

LADYFISH

Any saltwater angler lucky enough to find a school of ladyfish actively feeding near the surface can keep busy for a long time—if he has proper light tackle. This is perhaps the most underrated game species swimming in warm seas. Pound for pound, a ladyfish is one of the liveliest fish around. These tiny cousins of the tarpon are superlative performers *anytime*, but when they're on a feeding spree, they're even wilder and faster than usual.

The minute a lady feels the hook, it goes into a series of unbelievably violent catapults into the air that continue sometimes until exhaustion. It's the only fish I know that can run while jumping and jump while running. For fast concentrated action, there's no fishing on earth exactly like ladyfishing.

Ladyfish (*Elops saurus*) are also called chiros and tenpounders (even though few ladyfish have ever reached 10 pounds). A 3- or 4-pounder is an extremely good one. But if ladies *did* grow as big as tarpon, it would be virtually impossible to land them on any tackle.

Throughout the years the ladyfish has been confused with the bonefish or banana fish (*Albula vulpes*), but except for the silver color and the fact that both belong to the same family as the herring, there is little resemblance between the two. The bonefish never jumps and the ladyfish never stops jumping. And rarely does a ladyfish venture out onto the shallow flats frequented by bonefish.

Ladies range as far north as Maine, but they're seldom caught far beyond Florida and only rarely as far north as the Carolinas. In Florida waters they might be found anywhere except in the open sea. They even move occasionally into brackish water and have been taken in the southeast corner of Florida in water almost completely fresh. They're most numerous in Gulf of Mexico waters from Tampa Bay southward.

I have seen tremendous concentrations of ladyfish in a number of areas and have enjoyed every encounter with them. In the area where the Rio Grande enters the Gulf of Mexico the going is particularly good. Acres and acres of water there are often in a constant boil as countless ladyfish gorge on schools of tiny baitfish.

We didn't have any trouble hooking these ladies on any bait at all. I started by using a light spinning outfit with a ⅛-ounce jig, but that was too easy. Soon I waded to shore and assembled a light, 7-foot freshwater panfish fly rod. With this tiny wand, and using small bluegill floating bugs, I had ladies climbing all over each other to get at the bugs. It was a wild and woolly session and it ended only because I was too tired to cast anymore.

Not many people fish deliberately for ladyfish, probably because they are so completely inedible. But on light spinning tackle or fly-casting tackle there is no more lively fish to be had. Some of the better lures are the yellow-and-white streamer flies or bucktail jigs in ⅛- and ¼-ounce sizes. Fly-rod poppers are also excellent because of the action they can stir up on the surface. Perhaps the most effective bait of all, however, is a tiny silver spoon or a silver spinner in ¼-ounce size. Ladyfish go crazy over these.

It is difficult not to catch ladyfish once you've found a school or a location where many are concentrated. There is just one important bit of advice to give and that is to retrieve the lure as rapidly as possible in short sharp jerks. Completely unwary, and never shy or temperamental, ladyfish can be taken by anybody who can cast well enough to hit the water once in a while. They like to feed in inlets and passes and along the beaches and bayous of the Gulf coast. They seem to move in these places on a strong incoming tide, but the truth is that they're busy nearly all the time and you can catch them in good numbers even on an ebb tide.

2

THE BILLFISHES:

Sailfish, Swordfish, Marlin

Cruising across the tropical ocean currents of the world is a magnificent family of fishes known as *Istiophoridae*. They are pelagic, which means they roam and live on the open seas. All are distinguished by spearlike noses or bills.

This clan of billfishes includes the sailfish (which is the smallest of the family); swordfish or broadbill swordfish; white, striped, black, and blue marlin. It's possible that the blue marlin is only a color phase of the black, or vice versa. At any rate, some marine biologists classify the two of them together.

But no matter what the classification, all are incomparable game fishes and, unlike most other fishes described in this book, special tackle, special techniques and boats, plus other considerations, are necessary to catch them.

SAILFISH

There are two sailfishes in American waters. The Atlantic or eastern sailfish ranges throughout the tropical Atlantic and occurs from Massachusetts to Brazil. The Pacific sailfish is found throughout the tropical Pacific and Indian oceans. In the American Pacific, it ranges from Baja California to northern Peru.

Today in Florida alone, sailfishing is a multimillion-dollar industry with hundreds of charter boats and private cruisers plying the blue Gulf Stream in search of these splendid fighters. The same is true elsewhere. In Mexico, such Pacific coast and Gulf of California cities as Acapulco, Mazatlán, and La Paz have grown many times their original size in recent years, in

An Atlantic sailfish clears the water in Florida's Gulf Stream. (Florida News Bureau)

Pacific sailfish caught in action off Mazatlán, Mexico.

A sailfish angler awaits a strike in the Gulf Stream off southern Florida. (Miami-Metro Department of Publicity and Tourism)

part because of the excellent sailfishing that occurs offshore.

Scientists call the Atlantic sailfish *Istiophorus americanus*, while the Pacific sailfish is known as *Istiophorus greyi*. The word *Istiophorus* means sail-bearer and refers to the fish's high dorsal fin, which folds into a groove along the back except when the fish surfaces or becomes extremely excited.

The back of the sailfish is a beautiful, metallic, dark blue, which blends into silvery sides and a white belly. The sail is exquisite—a mixture of purple and blue with vertical rows of small black dots.

But it isn't until a sailfish is startled, excited, or injured that its colors really become vivid; at such times, whole waves of color flash through the entire body of the sailfish. This phenomenon is especially evident when a fish is hooked near the boat.

The life histories of most saltwater game fishes are mysteries, but quite a bit more is known about the Atlantic or Florida sailfish than about any of the other billfishes. It's known to spawn, for example, in late spring and early summer in certain shallow waters along the Florida sands. At this particular period the females, heavy with roe, are sluggish fighters, and no wonder, because a single prolific female may carry as many as 4½ million eggs.

The number of sailfish in our oceans, or even in the Gulf Stream, would be fantastic if all these eggs hatched and the larvae survived. But since countless predators feed on the eggs and young, only a very small percentage ever reach maturity.

The baby sailfish, which bear no resemblance to their parents for quite a period after they hatch, gorge themselves on tiny shrimplike copepods. As they mature, they gradually turn from a diet of mollusks to one consisting primarily of small fish. Researchers once found a greedy young specimen no more than three quarters of an inch long—including the bill—which had a viperfish nearly as long as itself folded up inside its stomach.

As they grow in size and become more and more able to fend for themselves, sailfish sometimes move inshore in considerable numbers. Juveniles from 5 to 8 inches long have been found along the Carolina coast in summertime. But cold weather and northerly winds seem to drive them south. Within a year after birth they may have reached 5 or 6 feet in length, which is a suitable size to please most sport fishermen. Three or four years seems to be the normal lifespan for Florida sails.

Sailfish travel alone, occasionally in pairs or in small groups and infrequently in small "packs." It is always extremely exciting to see several at once. On one memorable occasion, while fishing out of Marathon, Florida, I was lucky enough to see between twenty and thirty of them in one group. They appeared to have a school of small fish, probably blue runners, all balled up in one spot.

Occasionally a sailfish would dash into the smaller fish, slashing at them with his bill, while the others circled and jumped wildly into the air in a strange and frenzied manner. It was a primeval spectacle and a good example of the law of the sea, whereby large fish eat small fish and small fish eat smaller fish in order to survive.

Some sailfish will strike a bait the instant they sight it, an event that is among fishing's most thrilling moments. They lash out with their bills, sometimes over and over again before actually grabbing the bait. Other sails will seize the bait in their mouths immediately. Still others will follow it for five minutes . . . or ten minutes . . . or even longer, stalking closely behind. Maybe they're merely curious, but when they act this way the mounting suspense is almost impossible to stand.

Unfortunately sailfish following bait will seldom strike, even when certain tactics are used to tantalize them into doing so, such as cutting the motor and permitting the trolled bait to sink slowly. Occasionally, but only occasionally, the fish will grab it at once. Then the action begins.

Most sailfish are taken by two techniques: on live bait and/or by trolling. According to many anglers, the best live baits are blue runners from 8 to 10 inches in length, small enough, in other words, for a sail to swallow easily. Others consider live mullet as more effective, in fact, the best bait of all. But more often than not they settle for sand perch or grunts because these are easier to obtain than mullet. It's only a simple matter to troll a small spoon or jig across a reef to catch enough grunts or sand perch for a whole day's fishing.

Live bait is normally fished from outriggers far out on each side of the fishing boat. The

Stu Apte duels with a Pacific sailfish in Panamanian waters.

baits are allowed to swim along from 6 to 10 feet beneath the surface of the water. It's always possible to tell when a sailfish, or some other large game fish, approaches because the baitfish dash and dart frantically about, trying to escape. That's enough to start the adrenaline pumping and it's just another reason why billfishing is the popular and exciting sport it is.

Any fishermen can be worked into a fever pitch while a sailfish decides whether or not to strike a freely swimming baitfish. If he doesn't strike immediately, it's often a good idea to yank the clothespin from the outrigger, thereby freeing more line and allowing the baitfish to swim farther and more freely from the boat.

As popular for sailfishing as the use of live bait is trolling a whole fish—a mullet or a balao—behind the boat. So that they appear as lively and as natural as possible, the entire backbone of the baitfish is removed so that it becomes limp and can give a genuine, live performance as it bounces across the surface of the sea. A skipping-type motion is achieved by speeding up the boat until the bait skips along the surface, leaping from wave to wave.

There are many different opinions on this, but most experienced sailfishermen would agree that 5 or 6 miles an hour is the best trolling speed, no matter what bait is used. Usually the outrigger baits are trolled from 40 to 60 feet behind the boat. In addition, one or two teaser or fooler baits are sometimes trolled much closer to the boat.

Anyone, with or without skill at fishing, can catch a sailfish if he can afford a charter. The captain of almost any charter boat, no matter whether he is in Florida or in Acapulco, will take care of the job. In Florida, for example, you

A typical small outboard-motor craft used for sailfish trolling close to coastlines.

can charter a boat from Palm Beach, Miami, Stuart, Marathon, or any of the other communities near the Gulf Stream. The boat captain will hurry you out to the Gulf Stream, checking by radio to learn where the fish are hitting on that particular day. Meanwhile, the first mate will rig up the tackle, prepare the bait, place it on the hook, and all you have to do is sit back in your deck chair, holding the rod if you like or simply soaking up sunshine and marveling at the extraordinary blue of the water.

If you stay at this business of trolling long enough, a sail will eventually rap at your skipping bait. Ordinarily this is the signal to throw off the free-spool lever of the reel, count ten as the bait falls back, throw the free-spool lever in gear again, and strike as hard as you can. This is the orthodox procedure and it normally works.

However, more and more sails are being taken on lighter tackle and for the most part this is all for the better. When given a chance (i.e., when taken on light tackle), a sailfish is a spectacular battler. He leaps and greyhounds across the ocean's surface time and again. But if you do choose to take sailfish on the lightest possible tackle, it is best to carry your own gear wherever you go. In too many cases the charter boat will supply you with "regulation" gear designed to handle marlin or tuna and it's just a bit too heavy for the most fun with sailfish.

The best rod for sailfish has a light 6-ounce tip, a 6/0 reel and a hook size appropriate to the test of line used. Recently, especially with the lighter glass rods, fishermen have been using 4- and 5-ounce tips. A 4/0 hook is matched to 12-pound lines; 5/0 hook to a 20-pound line, 6/0 hook to 30-pound line, and a 7/0 hook to a 50-pound line.

But the larger the hook the heavier is the barb and the hardest part of the sail's mouth to hold is the upper beak. A smaller barb does a better job of hooking, but if it is used on lighter line, the strike must be lighter in order not to break the line.

Today the consensus among charter-boat skippers in the Florida Keys is that any line under 20-pound test is too light for sailfishing if the angler is not experienced. They figure that with a 20-pound test line an average sail—say from 35 to 40 pounds—can be landed in twenty to thirty minutes, after which the fish, when released, will still have enough energy left to fend for itself among its natural enemies.

Since sailfish have no commercial value and are not especially tasty on the table, nearly all except trophy fish should be released. In this case trophy fish are often the smallest rather than the largest fish. A 2- or 3- or 4- or even a 5-pound sailfish, for example, makes a handsome mount.

The average size of sailfish caught in the Atlantic is 35 or 40 pounds. Anything smaller than 25 pounds is a rarity. Anything larger than 60 pounds is an extremely fine, bragging-size fish. The largest sail reported from the Atlantic by the International Game Fish Association measured 8 feet 5 inches and weighed 141 pounds, 1 ounce. It was caught in 1961 off the Ivory Coast, Africa. The largest Pacific sailfish, by contrast, measured 10 feet 9 inches long and weighed 221 pounds. This catch was made by C. W. Stewart in the Galápagos Islands. It isn't unlikely that a 300-pounder will be caught some day, possibly in the same Galápagos archipelago or near Cocos Island off Costa Rica.

In recent years traditional trolling tackle for sailfishing has given way to light tackle—to spinning, plug-casting, and fly-casting tackle. Sailfish, particularly Pacific sails, have been conquered by casting and on very light lines. These catches, common today among serious saltwater fishermen, would have been considered impossible a decade or so ago.

Casting with any light tackle for sailfish involves the following procedure: A teaser or bait is trolled behind the boat in the traditional manner but the bait does not contain a hook. When a sailfish appears, stalking in the wake of the bait, it is retrieved slowly toward the boat, tempting the stalker to come closer. Then the caster, standing in the stern, casts a fly, plug, or spoon to the sailfish. If the lure is retrieved in an enticing manner, the sail strikes and a battle begins. Fortunately sailfish will willingly strike a variety of lures, including surface plugs, and the strike is a dramatic thing to see.

An important point should be inserted here. In order for a fisherman to qualify for an IGFA record on light tackle, any lure or fly cast to an ocean game fish must be retrieved by the fisherman from a stationary boat and *not* trolled. This requirement applies as well to other ocean fishes

The first mate on a charter boat shows off the large sail of a sailfish caught by trolling in the Gulf Stream. (Florida News Bureau)

A red silk kite with its own oversize reel is often used to present bait to billfish some distance from the fishing boat.

such as wahoo, tuna, dolphin, and even marlin.

Another newly popular method of fishing for billfish (and other ocean species) is kite fishing, which works as follows: In a good ocean breeze, a colorful kite is flown downwind (behind) the boat. Through clothespins attached to the kite line, baited lines are paid out as through outriggers. Depending on wind velocity and size of the kite, baits can be delivered and fished farther away from the boat than with outriggers. In fact, live baits can be allowed to swim naturally on or near the surface in this manner. Although a little more difficult, kite fishing is also possible—and effective—from shorelines, bridges, breakwaters, and jetties. Kites are also used when trolling with rigged or live baits.

Sailfishing does strange things to otherwise normal people, as the experience of Horace Witherspoon of Corona del Mar, California, proves. Witherspoon was fishing in an annual tournament off Acapulco with Frank Givens of Los Angeles and William Kortenhaus from Newark, New Jersey, when suddenly all hell broke loose.

Givens had a strike while trolling which gave him control of the boat. Accordingly the other anglers started to reel in their lines, but that's when a sailfish suddenly inhaled Witherspoon's bait and was hooked. Right away the sail started circling the boat as Witherspoon stood on the bow to keep the two lines from becoming tangled. Then Witherspoon fell overboard, lost his glasses and hat, but held on to his rod and reel!

Givens and Kortenhaus wanted to take over his rod and reel while he climbed back into the boat, but Witherspoon refused because under tournament rules a catch is disqualified if anyone else touches an angler's tackle.

Witherspoon managed to pull himself up enough to plant the rod in a porthole, loosening the reel drag so that his line wouldn't break. Then he climbed aboard, grabbed his gear and boated the fish twenty minutes later—unaided. Here is a serious sailfisherman, no matter how you view him.

Anglers from all over the western United States have been experiencing this fast and frantic fishing in the Pacific for many years now. There is good airline service daily between such major cities as Los Angeles, San Diego, Dallas, and Houston, with the various busy sport-fishing centers along the Gulf of California, along the Pacific coast of Baja California, mainland Mexico, Panama, and Costa Rica.

The excellent fishing for Pacific sailfish doesn't end at the Mexican border. Almost the year round, sails of unusual size and in great numbers exist all the way down the coast, past Costa Rica to Panama and even to northern Peru.

SWORDFISH

More than a generation ago, in his *Tales of Swordfish and Tuna*, Zane Grey wrote that "swordfishing takes more time, patience, endurance, study, skill, nerve and strength, not to mention money, than any game known to me through experience or reading." That is still true today. Fishing for swordfish is one sport that clearly establishes the difference between the serious, dedicated fisherman and the casual angler.

Catching a broadbill swordfish is an outstanding angling feat that comparatively few sportsmen have been able to do. Zane Grey, for example, caught just six swordfish in a lifetime devoted to fishing which ended in 1939. Once Grey spent ninety days fishing off Santa Catalina. All together he sighted no less than 87 broadbills. The bait was presented to 75 and an even dozen were hooked and fought. But only one swordfish of 418 pounds was landed during that three-month period! Of course he had very

A heavy swordfish taken at night off Miami is swung ashore. (Miami-Metro Department of Publicity and Tourism)

crude tackle compared to the equipment available today.

It isn't that broadbills are scarce. They exist in fair numbers off our North Atlantic coast and in temperate waters elsewhere around the world. Many are harpooned or caught on handlines by commercial fishermen. But the real trick to catching a swordfish is finding one that will take a trolled bait on the surface—much as a brown trout inhales a dry fly.

Even though a fisherman might spot as many as five or six fish on the surface in a day's exploration, it is rare when one can be teased into striking. Broadbills feed in deep water and when seen on the surface they probably are only resting and not interested in feeding. Most swords taken on the surface are found to have full stomachs, so the real problem is to excite their interest in a trolled bait without driving them down into deep water again.

Many methods to lure broadbills on the surface have been tested. But probably the best is to skip a bait—a bonito, a flying fish, a mackerel, or a herring—from an outrigger so that it will pass directly before the fish, maybe even touching its sword if the fish seems to be asleep. Sometimes this presentation arouses the fish enough to slash blindly, impulsively, at the bait in a fit of temper. Frequently this sudden slashing will cause the fish to foul-hook itself in the sword or the gill covers.

When a broadbill seems to be moving on the surface, rather than resting motionless, the most frequent tactic is to circle ahead and draw the bait just in front of the fish, crossing its line of travel until it either slashes at the bait or vanishes into deeper water.

When a swordfish taps the bait, the same procedure is followed as with all other billfish. The drag on the reel is released so that the bait falls back, allowing the fish to take it. Some experienced guides advise counting to ten before throwing in the drag lever once more. Others may allow as much as 100 yards of line to drift out from behind the boat, without regard to time. In any event, it's wise to allow the fish to get a good firm bite on the bait.

There isn't any way to predict accurately what a broadbill will do after he is (miraculously) hooked. More often than not it will sound deep on a first, strong, headlong rush. After that it is likely to return to the surface and, at least for a short period, fight furiously on the top. In this case it will be exhausted much sooner than if it decides to wage a deep fight.

The deep fight is far more bewildering and painful to the fisherman because it is necessary to pump the fish to the surface only a few inches at a time. Also, a contest like this can last for a long, long time. Many ten- to twelve-hour struggles with broadbills have been recorded. One 450-pounder required nineteen hours and fifty minutes to gaff. And even then, at the last minute, a broadbill is likely to escape.

In spite of these staggering statistics, a fisherman who desperately wants a broadbill for his trophy room can do so at quite a number of widely scattered places. On the East coast there are a number of charter-boat captains who understand swordfish and swordfishing in the Long Island and Martha's Vineyard areas. Of course, weeks may pass when nothing is seen. But invariably there are those times when swordfish will be spotted after the first hour out on the water. A swordfisherman must have something of Captain Ahab in his character because the swordfish is the Moby Dick of big game fishes. To engage it in combat, it's necessary to spend long days and long hours on a bright sea, searching with tired and burning red eyes for two dark symbols—a matched dorsal fin and tail—before a swordfish becomes a reality. Often it's a disheartening and exhausting business and the only reward is hours and hours of punishing battle in the fighting chair.

Although the swordfish is about 60 million years old and although it lives in temperate waters almost completely around the earth, its spawning grounds, habits, and migrations remain a personal secret. Only one spawning area in the New World has been located and it exists on the north coast of Cuba. There, during late spring, a female swordfish may swim close enough to shore where the water is pale green and broadcast its eggs at random. When this is finished, it swims away.

Each egg is no larger than the head of a pin. The eggs simply drift with wind and tide and, of course, most of them are destroyed or eaten by other aquatic creatures. Enough survive, however, and eventually hatch into larval swordfish. Each one is less than 1/8 inch long. A few of these manage to reach maturity.

Only a few really small broadbills have ever been located, and those are certainly far from the handsome, streamlined adults that anglers are proud to catch. The skin is blotchy and covered with strange glassy scales. The dorsal fin flops along the back like a ribbon. Instead of a stout sword, the young fish has a thin, syringe-like beak that bristles with teeth. But it is voracious, strong, fast, and probably has a ravenous appetite. When it reaches about a yard in length, or a little more, it begins to change. Soon the young broadbill becomes the near-perfect example of an extraordinary saltwater game fish.

Suddenly the scales are gone, the skin becomes blue black with silvery flanks, the dorsal fin has grown high and stiff, and the lower jaw has receded. All the teeth have vanished from the upper jaw, which has sprouted outward into a flat stubby sword—flat rather than round, as are the bills of sailfish and marlin.

The full-grown broadbill is a most efficient marine mechanism. It's probably among the fastest fish in the world, though judging this is not an easy thing. How can anyone accurately compare its top speed with such other will-of-the-wisp fishes as the wahoo and false albacore. The swordfish's backbone is short and strong. Its sword and skull are neatly fitted together and there is a porous ethmoid bone in the forepart of the skull that acts as a shock absorber when the broadbill is using its sword. It's evident from its structure and also from commercial fishing catches that a broadbill can withstand the pressures of great depth. Its abnormally large eyes can gather in the faintest rays of light. All of these traits make it a formidable creature and it's no wonder that blood-chilling newspaper stories appear from time to time of swordfish attacking small boats and generally causing havoc in the sea.

Even though swordfish are widely distributed, as we pointed out before, and even though they are really quite plentiful, broadbills are never commonplace—and perhaps never will be—on the weighing scaffolds around marinas and sport-fishing docks. Perhaps the best reason is that sport-fishing methods have been too inflexible and too unimaginative for too long.

During the past few years, the catch of swordfish by sport fishermen has accelerated, thanks to a few pioneering individuals. Such expert anglers as Bob Stearns of Miami have been fishing at night off Florida's southeast coast and have been hooking swordfish. It has also been discovered that swords will strike well after dark off Mexico's Cozumel Island. Much more experimentation must be done, but in time swordfish could be much more frequently taken than in the past.

MARLIN

Many fishermen consider marlin the most spectacular big-game fish in the world, and with good reason. Marlin have all the qualities of a great game species. They're strong, they're fast, and they leap repeatedly when hooked, sometimes tail-walking in the manner of sailfish. And they can cross almost 100 feet of ocean surface in one wild tail-walking spree.

Marlin, sailfish, and swordfish are often confused and a common mistake is to call all of them marlin swordfish. Of course, this is a misnomer since the round bill or spear of a marlin bears little resemblance to the flat, bladelike weapon of the swordfish.

Three general species of marlin inhabit the deep blue waters and ocean currents of the world. These are the white, the black, and the striped marlin. The blue marlin, which is common in Atlantic waters from Venezuela northward, may be a subspecies of the black marlin, or vice versa. In addition, there are many other local names for unusually colored marlin found in tropical waters—the so-called silver marlin is an example—but these are only color phases of the black and/or blue marlin. At least that's the current thinking of ichthyologists.

Many outstanding new marlin waters have been discovered in recent decades, and the development of better tackle has made it possible to catch the fish in difficult waters. The newest promised land for these biggest of billfish is off the Pacific coast of Panama where light-tackle-record black marlin are lurking.

Fishing for all the gladiators, marlin as well as sailfish and swordfish, is pretty much the same. The common method is to troll, using outriggers so that the bait can be skipped across the surface. The most popular marlin baits are about the same as those used for broadbills—mackerel, bonito, herring, flying fish, or whatever similar fish are most abundant locally.

But marlin, especially the larger ones, have an unusual and disconcerting habit of their own. Frequently a huge, dark form will be spotted following the skipping bait for a quarter mile or more before the marlin decides to charge the bait, *if* it decides to charge the bait at all. Unlike sailfish and smaller marlin, the jumbos seldom grab the bait on their first rush. Instead, they may rap it savagely several times with their bills.

There are two ways to handle a reluctant marlin. One method is the drop-back routine in which the reel is flipped onto free spool and the bait is allowed to drift freely far behind in the wake of the boat. The other way is to keep skipping the bait and perhaps even to gather in more line to make it bounce more lightly across the surface of the water. What occasionally results in this case is a wild, chilling strike at a half-flying bait that is truly spectacular to see.

Any fish with the great physical potential of a marlin can give a fisherman all the action he can handle. Occasionally it goes even further than that. Dr. Harry Minton of the Canal Zone was fishing in the Pearl Islands just off Panama early one morning when he happened to hook a good fish on 36-thread line. By one o'clock he was still engaged with the fish. Somehow he was able to

A white marlin is swung aboard a sailing yacht off the Cuban coast.

fight it down to a belly-up position right along-side the boat.

One of Minton's companions grabbed a gaff, reached over the side and sent the gaff home. That was like splashing turpentine on a tiger, be-cause at that instant the marlin came to life and jumped on board the ship. In a blinding display of gymnastics the marlin smashed just about ev-erything on board, slashed out at the gaffer, and jumped back into the sea.

Two hours and forty minutes later, Minton was finally able to bring the marlin to gaff a sec-ond time. Quite a performance for a fish that weighed only 240 pounds!

The white marlin, *Makaira albida*, which is the smallest of the marlins, ranges in the Atlantic Ocean from Venezuela northward through the West Indies to Massachusetts. The rod-and-reel record for white marlin is a 161-pounder taken in the Gulf Stream off Miami Beach in 1938. Other good white marlin waters would include Ocean City, Maryland; Rehoboth, Delaware; the Cape Hatteras region, North Carolina; off Montauk, Long Island; and about 35 miles off Virginia Beach, Virginia. All of these are especially good as the whites migrate up and down the coast

each summer, appearing in numbers at first one place and then another in order.

Earlier in the spring, Walker Cay and the Biminis in the Bahamas are hotspots. Another outstanding white marlin fishing hole—from March through October—is off the north Vene-zuelan coast. Vast schools of marlin gather here to feed on concentrations of baitfish that con-gregate in these waters.

Striped marlin, *Tetrapturus audax*, named for the conspicuous stripes that appear along the sides of their bodies after death (a feature not typical of the other marlins), are found only in the Pacific, from the Chilean coast northward to Baja California and southern California state, and around Hawaii, Fiji, Korea, Japan, the Philip-pines, New Zealand, Formosa, Tahiti, and sev-eral other Pacific localities. The world's record striped marlin is a 692-pounder taken off Balboa, California, thirty years ago, though some experts insist this was a black rather than a striped marlin, since the latter rarely exceed 400 pounds.

Striped marlin eggs have never been recog-nized, and to date very young striped marlin have not been positively identified. Adult stripers in spawning condition have been en-countered only in the South China Sea and in the central Pacific Ocean. Most spawning in these waters apparently takes place during April, May, and June. Once they have hatched, marlin probably grow quite rapidly; it is believed that they can attain a weight of 100 pounds in about three years. The food of the striped marlin is predominantly fish and, to a lesser extent, squid, crabs, and shrimp.

Of all the marlin, the striper is the one most inclined to make repeated, spectacular leaps out of the water (whereas the white marlin or-dinarily jumps the least). The best fishing local-ity for striped marlin in southern California is that belt ranging from the east end of Santa Catalina Island to around San Clemente Island, and south in the direction of Los Coronados to the Mexican border. Off Baja California, they are best caught in the summer and fall months.

The Pacific black marlin, *Makaira indica*, the largest of the billfish clan, is pretty much confined to the coasts of Chile, Peru, and Ecua-dor. The most fabulous black marlin fishing spot of all used to be Cabo Blanco, Peru, thanks to the confluence there of two great and fetile

Dick Kotis with one morning's double-header: a large Pacific sailfish and a black marlin.

ocean currents. But the fish have for some reason vanished from the area. The largest black marlin are now being caught off Australia's north Queensland coast.

Although, as mentioned before, it may be a subspecies of the black marlin the blue marlin (or Atlantic blue marlin or Cuban marlin), *Makaira nigricans ampla,* ranges throughout the West Indies and the Bahamas and appears in numbers along the East coast of the United States as far north as New Jersey. The largest game fish in Gulf Stream waters, it has never been encountered on the Florida west coast. It has, however, been taken off Texas—near Port Isabel—and around Cuba and Puerto Rico. Blue marlin fishing reaches a peak around Havana in July and many big ones have been landed just outside the city's harbor. That's also true at San Juan, Puerto Rico. Good concentrations of blue marlin occur off Bimini, Bahamas, where the first individual was caught in 1933. Although they are present throughout the year, there is a pronounced run of the fish late each June. The peak concentration occurs from early July to about the first of August.

While the blue marlin is known to feed deep it also feeds near the surface on occasion. Gulf Stream blues average out between 200 and 300 pounds, but there is an actual record of a 1,200-pound blue marlin taken by nonsporting means.

Besides being the dazzling jumper that all marlin are, the blue of the Atlantic is also an extremely dogged battler. Fishermen have hung on to big ones in excess of 15 hours and the longer the battle continues, the greater the odds are stacked in favor of the fish. It's extremely good advice, therefore, for the prospective marlin fisherman—or swordfisherman or tuna angler— to get into good physical shape before he tackles these big gladiators.

It's extremely wise to exercise arm and shoulder muscles and even to develop one's wind. Handball and swimming are especially good training, but the best idea is to see a professional trainer or a doctor who specializes in muscles and muscle development. Either of these men can prescribe a set of training rules and a series of exercises that will not only strengthen the muscles but also make fishing for any of the billfishes a more pleasant and productive experience.

3

SNOOK AND BARRACUDA

It is often said that snook are big for their size and that's a most fitting description for a great game fish. There really is something about a snook, especially a big one, that causes even veteran fishermen to forget all they know about fishing. They may freeze on the reel and apply too much pressure, or they may forget to apply any pressure at all.

A snook is a relatively slender and handsome fish shaped somewhat like a freshwater walleye. Its head is certainly pikelike, long and flattened with the lower jaw protruding. Its color is silvery with, occasionally, a lemon-yellow tint, depending on the color of the water from which it comes. The lateral line is always a solid black.

Somehow the game fishes of America always manage to have quite a number of popular local names and the snook is no exception. In Florida, snook is pronounced snuke. Elsewhere it's called robalo, snooker, sergeant fish, sea pike, brochet de mer, and ravallia. Scientifically, it's a member of the genus *Centropomus*.

There are three kinds of snook in Florida waters, another in the West Indies, and others in the Pacific off the Central American coast. Of the three Florida snooks, one is a small critter that rarely grows more than a foot long. It's quite uncommon and of little interest to fishermen.

A second Florida snook is fairly common on the lower east coast, but it too is fairly small, weighing at most about 3 pounds. But the snook that is of most value to fishermen is *Centropomus undecimalis*, which averages from 3 to 5 pounds, but has been known to reach 60 pounds. In Florida, 10-pounders are fairly common and every year a number of snook are taken over 30 pounds.

The snook ranges from Venezuela northward along the Gulf coast of Central America to Texas and then eastward to Florida, including the entire Florida coastline except the northern half of the east coast. It also occurs around some of the Caribbean islands, such as Puerto Rico, but it is unaccountably absent around many others where there is extremely good snook environment. The snook can be classified as an inshore tropical and subtropical species because it never ventures very far into the sea; at least, it's never caught far from land. It concentrates along beaches and in channels and tidal rivers, which comprise much of our southern coastline.

A snook hooked on spinning tackle in a southern Florida mangrove channel makes a wild jump. (Florida News Bureau)

According to Dr. Luis R. Rivas of the University of Miami's Marine Laboratory, and one of the world's top authorities on snook, any snook will spend as much as half of its lifetime in freshwater. He points out that snook frequently ascend creeks and rivers into freshwater and once there display many of the tendencies of freshwater fishes.

Snook are very much like largemouth bass in certain of their characteristics. When the food supply is good enough, some snook probably never leave the freshwater creeks or canals in which they are born. Others travel widely and move to saltwater. There is much room for biological research here. Intensive tagging studies would reveal much about the habits and migrations of snook.

Snook have been taken in the Caloosahatchee River and the St. Lucie Canal, which combine with Lake Okeechobee to form the cross-Florida waterway. Perhaps they even use this waterway to travel from the Atlantic Ocean to the Gulf of Mexico. While fishing for bass, I have seen snook in the Moonshine Bay area of Lake Okeechobee, though I have never been able to hook one there.

In many ways the snook is a plug-caster's dream come true, because on occasion it can be ridiculously easy to fool. Other days it is a little more difficult, but generally speaking it's just hard enough to catch to be interesting. This is also a fish that doesn't require any digging of live bait. It's a good bet that more snook are taken on jigs and plugs than any other saltwater fish.

Either feather, bucktail, or nylon jigs are especially effective in inlets and passes, in the surf, and in any water deeper than, say, 5 or 6 feet. These jigs are especially deadly when snook seem to be lying on the bottom. Then it's best to cast the jig up into the tide and to retrieve it in short sharp jerks right along the bottom, kicking up clouds of mud or sand as it is retrieved.

There are times when a wooden or plastic plug will do as well or perhaps better than a jig, and this is particularly so when snook are in shallow water or lying up tight under the mangroves.

A surface plug is perhaps the most exciting lure of all to use on snook, since they will often try to chew it to pieces. Any angler who has had experience casting surface plugs for bass will have great success with snook because the fishing is almost exactly the same. The main difference is that the surface plug must be retrieved in faster, sharper jerks and it must be given more action.

An important word about using plugs: On the surface, the best plugs are those that have no built-in action and which the angler must manipulate with the clever use of his rod tip; but snook will take some of the plugs with built-in action when they are fished just under water. The best color in artificial lures is a highly debatable matter, but a majority of the best snook fishermen prefer yellow, with red or red-and-white, or orange following closely.

It's hard to match the fly rod and fly-casting tackle for getting the most action out of snook. Both streamer flies and large-size, sturdy, bass popping bugs are murder on snook of small to medium size. But there is one drawback to fly-fishing: snook are terribly tough on the tackle. If you are fishing in fairly open water, such as a bay or lagoon, where there is enough room for a fish to run and cavort freely, fly-casting will suit you quite well. But if you're fishing in mangrove country, you'll be snagged and hung up a good

A large streamer fly of the type commonly used by saltwater fly-casters for snook, tarpon, and barracuda.

part of the time. If you don't mind that, stick to the fly-fishing and have the time of your life, but remember that it's expensive.

Fly-casting is especially deadly in most of the canals of southern Florida, especially those close to the Tamiami Trail, which are heavily fished by natives and tourists. A surface plug will often spook some of the more gun-shy snook. It's in these waters that streamers and bass popping bugs will catch as many as five to ten times as many snook as casting lures. The best-size streamer or bucktail fly is about 3 inches long tied in size 2 to 1/0. As in plugs and jigs, yellow seems to be the most popular color.

No angler should go forth for snook without using a wire leader between his line and lure. Snook have razor-sharp, saw-toothed spurs on their gill covers and with these they can neatly cut any fishing lines. But a light, braided, stainless steel leader from 12 to 18 inches long will take care of that.

In recent years most of the biggest snook have been taken in estuaries and tidal portions of rivers along Costa Rica's Atlantic coast. Certain fishable areas of the Panama Canal also are red-hot. Odds are that record-breaking snook are still waiting to be hooked.

ATLANTIC OR GREAT BARRACUDA

Nearly every angler has preconceived ideas about barracuda long before he ever catches one. According to popular lore, they are bloodthirsty killers, the pack-traveling wolves of the sea.

They're not game fish, is one conclusion, and they're not good to eat. They're simply dangerous and warm saltwaters everywhere would be better off without them. These are commonly held notions which, nonetheless, couldn't be further from actual fact.

The truth is that the barracuda is among the finest game fishes in the world. Of course it's a killer, but so is every other fish that swims; a barracuda is only more efficient. What's more, it rarely hunts in packs. With bridgework as sharp and deadly as a hundred scalpels, it can neatly cut a fish almost its own size in half, but that doesn't keep it from being a thrilling jumper and a strong, durable fighter. But best of all, it's an abundant fish, widely distributed in warm saltwaters everywhere. No special, expensive gear is necessary to catch it. It's any man's game fish and can be taken from rowboats or from bridges as well as from expensive charter boats. You can find cuda in mangrove channels or on open weedy flats, cruising over coral reefs or on the edge of ocean currents. This fish surely gets around.

There are many ways to catch barracuda, but day in and day out the trolled or skipped mullet fillet is the best bait of all. It's wise to remember one important point, though. Small cuda, up to about 30 inches, are the most willing of strikers anytime you find them. The bait can be alive or artificial, floating or sinking; they'll usually wallop it as soon as they see it. But once a barracuda becomes an adult, it's a different story. It looks mighty carefully at artificials and then seldom likes what it sees. Most trophy specimens are taken on live or cut bait.

The fierce-looking barracuda is a wide-ranging denizen of warm saltwaters, both inshore and far out in deep ocean currents.

For small cuda, the best baits are ¼-ounce, white or yellow bucktail jigs, fished on a light spinning outfit. The only departures from standard bass or trout fishing techniques are a faster retrieve and a braided-wire leader. The latter is essential, no matter what type of tackle is used. A freshwater fisherman seeking barracuda for the first time should be certain his reel will not be damaged by use in the salt.

A common method is to anchor on the edge of a reef or a tidal current and then to fish the bottom leisurely with cut bait. Usually it's a simple matter to catch a whole live box full of yellowtails, grunts, gag groupers, or mutton snappers. Often enough a big red grouper or a jewfish is hooked to make it interesting. Anyway, the yellowtails and snappers can be used whole and alive as bait. They're hooked through the dorsal fin, rigged several feet below a large cork float, and then allowed to drift about 100 feet down-tide of the boat. If all goes well, barracuda will spot them quickly and a fisherman will have his hands full.

If action doesn't develop soon, the grunts (which are numerous enough to pave the bottom in places) are cut up and used as chum. Chumming, incidentally, is another technique often used to attract barracuda to any given spot.

We were anchored off Tarponbelly Key one morning when a school of cero mackerel suddenly appeared around us. We caught several on white bucktails, including a fine 12-pounder, when another cero hit close to the boat. In almost the same instant, a tremendous barracuda boiled up from behind and . . . then neatly clipped off the rear two thirds of the mackerel. I reeled in the head and noticed that the barracuda followed it in. Without removing the hook, I simply tossed the head back in again and the cuda grabbed it.

I let the fish run off with 30 feet of line, waited while it paused, and in the next instant set the hook hard into immediate, lightning resistance. I was using only 6-pound line on a reel that held about 200 yards of it—and I had visions of some sort of light-tackle record when that fish exploded out of the water. Maybe I didn't have a chance, but for twenty minutes or more I was still in the game. I just held on and nothing more. The fish peeled off too much line, though, and after making a wide circle around the boat, a knot failed. But so it goes.

The barracuda is a formidable-looking, elongated, silvery fish with a weird grin. But perhaps its most important characteristic, at least to fishermen, is its unusual curiosity. Skin divers have long known (and worried about) the cuda's habit of swimming close to them and of staying close by—watching everything that goes on. I don't recommend to my friends that they push this curiosity too far. There's no need to get reckless with such natural mayhem equipment as a barracuda's jaws.

But experienced anglers in the Florida Keys use this curiosity to considerable advantage. The motor of a boat seems to attract cuda as surely as chumming. Invariably they'll investigate the wake of a passing boat and sometimes follow it for a considerable distance. Divers have often seen them do this. The lesson here is to troll or to cast close in the wake of a moving boat rather than ahead of it or off to the sides.

Almost any sort of tackle is suitable for this

trolling if you can afford to replace any broken items. Of course, extra-heavy tackle can take much of the wallop from the sport, but very light tackle is just as bad. There isn't much fun in the long and drawn-out kind of contest that can follow with too-light tackle. A good outfit is a saltwater spinning or casting outfit with 12- or 15-pound line. For the big cuda around outer reefs, which run 40 pounds or better, a 6/9 outfit is fine. That means a 6-ounce rod tip and 9-thread (27-pound test) line.

Ordinarily the fly rod doesn't have a large place in barracuda fishing, but I remember one time when it did. We were fishing a mangrove bay in the West Bay section of Grand Cayman, a lonely tropical island with better than ordinary fishing, about 300 miles southeast of Havana. Though we had tarpon and snook in mind, we found instead the area alive with 2- to 3-foot cuda. They would hit nearly anything we tossed at them, but just for the novelty I rigged a fly rod and tied a large bass popping bug to the finest wire leader I could find. No bass ever hit the bug as hard or as often as these miniature cuda.

There are monster cuda roaming our American coasts, but none is likely to exceed the existing world record, a 103¼-pounder caught in the Bahamas thirty years ago. It's conceivable, though, that the record for 12-pound line could be broken. This was a 42-pounder taken in 1951 off the coast of Nigeria—where many over 50 pounds are taken on heavier gear. The 20-pound-line record is a 59½-pounder from the vicinity of Key Largo.

An important characteristic of barracuda is that they can be found in many different kinds of waters. We've mentioned how they congregate around bonefish flats and occasionally it's possible to take them there on regular bonefish tackle and bonefish lures. In many ways a barracuda is a much more exciting fish to catch in such shallow water because it will jump repeatedly, something a bonefish will not do.

It has also been mentioned that cuda thrive over coral reefs and like to cruise offshore. But I've also found that extremely large ones prefer to linger around mangrove channels and small mangrove islands. An especially likely place is where a narrow channel widens into or joins a deep hole or depression. Such places are numerous from Florida to Panama.

A great barracuda is boated in a shallow bay of the lower Florida Keys.

In British Honduras, for example, wherever we found a pocket or deep hole in the mangroves, we would surely find barracuda lurking there. Usually it was a single big cuda rather than several small ones. Sometimes they would strike and sometimes they wouldn't, but their presence was always exciting.

The great barracuda is an extraordinary mechanism. Besides its formidable bridgework, it has other physical characteristics that set it apart. Even in the clear water it's often difficult to spot a barracuda because of a camouflage that enables it to blend into coral heads, grasses, the shadows of mangroves and wharves and especially the skeletons of old shipwrecks.

Out of the water a cuda is a shiny silver in color, but its dark-green or bluish back and the darker bars and blotches on the sides tend to make it inconspicuous no matter where it happens to be. And the colors on a cuda's back and flanks become dimmer or darker according to the surroundings.

Some of the best waters for the great or Atlantic barracuda are around the Bahama Islands and off the more remote Florida Keys from Marathon to the Dry Tortugas. A good outfit for a fisherman who is particularly interested in barracuda is a fairly stiff action, two-handed spinning rod about 7 feet long. But regardless of the tackle or the line, no bait should be presented without at least an 18- to 20-inch length of wire leader. Number 2 wire is suitable.

CALIFORNIA BARRACUDA

The California barracuda, *Sphyraena argentea*, is the only member of its family known to inhabit the Pacific coastal waters of the United States. Three smaller species are found in temperate and tropical waters south of California and about twenty-two kinds of barracuda have been identified from all the oceans of the world.

Even though the California cuda is the largest of four species found along the Pacific coasts of North and South America, it never approaches in size some of the giant barracuda of the tropical Atlantic or those taken far out in mid-Pacific.

Atlantic barracuda have attained weights in excess of 100 pounds whereas the largest California record seems to be a 17½-pound fish caught in 1958. Females grow bigger than males and almost all barracuda larger than 10 pounds taken off California are females.

California barracuda have been caught at various times all the way from near Wrangell, Alaska, south to Magdalena Bay, Baja California. But recently they have seldom been taken or even observed very far north of Point Conception or San Francisco. Perhaps more than any of their cousins they are a schooling species and appear to prefer staying close to offshore islands and to the mainland.

A number of biological studies have been made on California cuda. These revealed, for example, that a six-year-old female weighing under 7 pounds contained 484,000 mature eggs. About 75 percent of all California barracuda will spawn when they are two years old, and the spawning season usually extends from April through September, with the greatest activity in May or June. It's possible that a single cuda spawns more than once each season, and the young ones up to 6 inches in length are quite often found in shallow waters close to shore. The small editions, from 6 inches to a foot in length, are excellent baitfish for other species.

The fact that barracuda are extremely voracious and that they feed on a large variety of small pelagic fishes is an added boon to fishermen. Perhaps the greatest number are taken on live bait presented near the surface. Almost an equal number are taken on trolled artificial lures, some of the most effective of which are bone jigs, silver jigs, spoons, and red and white feathers. Of course, strips of cut bait or whole fish can also be trolled.

Since the California barracuda are most often taken accidentally—on heavy tackle meant for other fishes—they do not give the impression of being extremely game. But taking them on spinning tackle or very light trolling tackle is an entirely different matter. A wise fisherman will always carry a light outfit on board in the event that he runs into a whole school of California barracuda.

4

BONEFISH AND PERMIT

Bonefish are neither the strongest game fish nor the fastest, but they rate high on both counts. Wary, mildly unpredictable, non-jumping but splendid long-distance runners once they're hooked, bonefish are widely available in many warm saltwaters of the Americas.

Here is one fish you see before, during, and after the strike. If you happen to be a serious trout fisherman somehow transplanted to the salt, the odds are good that the bonefish will become your favorite fish. I've known completely addicted trout fishermen who never again raised a rod for trout after dueling with their first bonefish. The thrill is contagious.

Bones belong to a vast breed of herringlike fishes, which means that the ladyfish and tarpon are among their first cousins. But except for slight similarities in appearance and structure, they're different from their more acrobatic relatives in everything from general behavior to feeding habits.

It has been said and written that bones are strictly shallow-water feeders, but I don't believe it. Anglers often catch them in numbers in deep channels among mangrove "islands" while casting both jigs and live bait for other species of fish. Most bonefish of the Hawaiian Islands are also taken in deep water. But I'll admit that they spend long periods in shallow waters, on alcohol-clear flats, and during these periods they usually seem to be feeding or cruising in search of food. Since this is the only time that fishermen really see them, it's easy to assume that they feed exclusively in such a shallow habitat.

But the fact remains that, for all practical purposes, the best and only place to fish for bones is in completely transparent water from a few inches to no more than 2 or 3 feet deep. In such an environment, any fish is bound to be skittish and timid. Obviously an angler must use a careful, cautious approach to hook them.

In heavily fished areas, bonefish do become sophisticated and therefore extra caution is necessary to score. Perhaps this accounts for the widely circulated idea that bonefish are only for experts—that they're hard to fool, hard to hook, and hard to land once hooked. But little of this is true.

On the flats, a bonefish generally cruises against or angles into the tide, digging and grub-

The bonefish, also called, appropriately, gray ghost or gray fox, is a hard target to see cruising across shallow flats.

bing in the mud bottom for crabs, shellfish, mollusks, or whatever. Sometimes an individual seems to pick up every object he finds, mouthing it before he either swallows or spits it out again. Maybe it's this habit of sampling everything that makes him grab an artificial lure that has none of the "odor" or "feel" of a live critter.

Still another widely held misconception is that bonefish feed only on a rising tide. It *is* likely that they prefer to feed on a rising tide on a certain flat, or maybe on a whole chain of flats, but elsewhere they prefer falling tides or even slack tides. Just as there are certain flats where fishing is most productive at high tide, so are others most "alive" during a retreating tide, and still others are best during half tide.

No matter what the tide, however, fishing for bones, which is as much hunting as fishing, is a fascinating game of wits and testing one's eyesight. Except for a rare incident or two, I've never caught a bonefish I didn't spot beforehand. Sometimes it is only a gray or dark shadow that an angler sees. Just as often it's the tip of a tail, or maybe even the whole tail breaking the surface as a bone moves about with his snout poking into the mud. In either case, there's a definite knack to spotting the movement. It's tricky at first, but all at once an angler with average eyesight catches on; from that day, he can spot most of the bones within his range. The more spotting experience, the better.

Except on the dullest days, both beginners and veterans of the flats find that glasses which reduce glare are absolutely invaluable to reduce eyestrain as well as to reveal fish "camouflaged"

underwater. I'd say such glasses are almost as important as a reel in bonefishing.

Bonefish can be taken in good weather or bad (with a sudden cold spell having the worst effect), but the ideal time to see them, as well as to catch them, is in early morning or late evening when the surface is slick and calm. Then their antics are more readily visible for longer distances. And if you happen to have the low sun at your back, there's an added advantage, because the same sun is in the eye of the bone. That seems to make it less selective when following your lure.

These gray ghosts or white foxes—as implied by the scientific name, *Albula vulpes*—are sometimes as curious as fish can be. Often they follow lures they have no intention of striking and this can grow gray hairs on any angler. On days when this happens frequently, the pressure and the suspense become so great you can hardly stand it. But the characteristic curiosity goes even further. When poling across a flat, I've flushed bones, only to see them run, make a wide circle, and come up behind the skiff to see what chased them in the first place. Occasionally a follower can be caught.

No bonefish or macabi (Spanish) or banana fish (from the tapered snout?) or boneyhead (as on Grand Cayman Island) or sanducha (as the Cubans call it) is as impressive in appearance as it is game. In fact, it's rather odd-looking. The color is white chromium, shading to pale olive on the back. Most distinctive is the armor-plated, abrasion-resistant head with a pointed, almost piglike snout. Inside the head is a matched set of grinders stout enough to convert the toughest crab shell into digestible vitamins. This mechanism can also, in time, reduce a fishhook to basic metal.

Even the most garrulous guides of the Florida Keys speak softly when roving across bonefish flats. This might be an indication of a bone's keen hearing, but most ichthyologists doubt it's *that* keen. Still, bones will react to the slightest scuffling or vibration from a boat. Their eyesight is extremely sharp, too. And from the manner a hungry bone can locate live bait from far, far away, it's obvious that it has a most acute sense of smell. Which brings us to baits and how to use them.

There's a near-foolproof technique with which anybody can catch a bonefish, granted, of course, he can first locate the fish. It is far from the most exciting way, but it *is* deadly. Simply bait up with a fresh shrimp, alive or dead, and toss it ahead of, and up-tide of, a feeding fish. Then just sit back and wait for the bone to find it, which he will surely do. It may be tiresome and nerve-racking, but if your purpose is to catch a bonefish by any means, this is your best bet.

Sometimes a few shrimp are scattered about a flat to attract them and to start them feeding. Then all at once a bone picks up a shrimp that happens to have a hook embedded in it. The fisherman raises his rod sharply and the reel sings.

Still another baiting technique is to take a live conch and crush the shell, leaving the meat inside. Eventually bones will find it and, frustrated at being unable to eat the contents, will become aroused and search frantically about for something they *can* swallow. What they finally settle for may just be a bait or a bucktail jig.

Light spinning tackle is the best bet for the average angler, no matter whether he's using live bait or counterfeits. If it's bait, he just casts it ahead of his fish as described before and waits patiently. If it's an artificial, he casts and tries to retrieve it in a rather slow, enticing manner beyond the bonefish's snout. Bones have been hooked on a variety of lures, but only a few are consistently effective; the jig, from ⅛ to ¼ ounce in size, is far ahead of all the rest.

Of course, all jigs in those sizes are not suitable. A productive flat may contain everything from ribbon grass and oyster beds to coral tips and fans, so a lure must be designed to wiggle through these obstacles as well as to run shallow rather than deep when retrieved in a slow, erratic manner. In other words, the metal head of the jig must be flattened horizontally, rather than be round or bullet-shaped, for the best performance.

The first of these flat-bodied jigs I ever tried was a homemade model with orange bucktail and peacock herl tail. It was designed by Captain Bill Smith of Islamorada, Florida, and it was deadly. Now there's a similar lure on the market called "Wiggle Jig." Many anglers have been able to take bones on the same type of pickled pork frog used by freshwater bass fishermen, and some moderate success has attended the use of soft plastic lures also meant for freshwater species. It might be that more experimentation with the plastics would be worthwhile.

Fly-fishing for bonefish differs from spinning

Spinning for bonefish in a shallow bay punctuated with mangroves.

only in the basic tackle used. The approach, the presentation of the lure, and the retrieve are virtually the same. You simply substitute a fly for a jig or chunk of bait. And the best fly almost wherever it's used is a Pink Shrimp, also made by Phillips. This fly was inspired by late author-angler Joe Brooks, who during his angling career took more bones on flies than perhaps any other angler before him.

Other effective fly patterns are the hackle or bucktail streamers in size 1 or 1/0, preferably in all white or all yellow, with or without plastic "heads" and eyes. In areas where bones seem especially spooky, a streamer dropped gently in the water will cause much less alarm than any heavier spinning lures.

Contrary to popular opinion, catching a bonefish on a fly isn't a feat beyond the ability of an average fisherman. An angler *does* need somewhat different equipment for fly-casting the salt, but with that equipment and the ability to use it, he can catch as many bonefish as a spin-caster.

The critical item of either spinning or fly-casting tackle is the reel. (*But bear in mind that is equally true for nearly every type of saltwater game fishing.*) It must be well built and sturdy enough to take a terrible beating. It must have a smooth, entirely dependable drag and a sufficiently large line capacity. For bonefish particularly, you need a spinning-reel spool that can hold 200 yards of 6-pound line. It doesn't hurt to have even more, because instead of a bonefish you could conceivably hook a permit that might run even farther and faster. A good trick is to tie a short length of 8-pound or 10-pound nylon between the lure and the regular 6-pound line with a blood knot. This arrangement will stand more wear and tear when a bonefish is hooked.

The fly-fisherman will want a big, single-action reel, such as one of the larger Medalists, to hold 200 yards of 18-pound to 20-pound back line as well as the casting line.

You do not need a guide to catch bonefish, but if you can afford it, why not engage one? An experienced guide can save plenty of valuable fishing time you would otherwise spend searching for fish. He will also eliminate much uncertainty by knowing which flats are best at which times of day. And of course a guide can eliminate much of the drudgery of the sport,

such as poling a skiff across the flats, obtaining bait, etc. But, even so, a guide isn't necessary, particularly if you are an adventuresome sort of angler.

If you're fishing alone, you have two choices. Stand in your boat and drift with the wind across the flats—or put on a pair of sneakers and go wading. In either case, observe the water all around you, trying to look *through* the water rather than studying the surface. Here again Polaroid glasses are invaluable. When you spot anything, even a shadow or an unidentifiable movement, make a cast just in case. You'll make mistakes and cast at ghosts, but they're worth the occasions when a shadow suddenly reacts like a genuine, live bonefish.

With only a few exceptions, the various great game fish we've discussed are hard, vicious strikers. Sometimes every fish in a school (as I've seen among dolphin, jacks, mackerel, tarpon) will race for the bait. I've seen schools of bonefish do it too, but only rarely. Nine days in ten they're dainty rather than savage strikers, a good point to remember, because it's so easy to strike too swiftly when you can see the whole show. With most other fishes, it's more common not to strike swiftly enough.

Playing and landing a hooked bonefish isn't too difficult and sometimes it's not even too exciting. There's nothing to do but hold the rod high overhead. The structure and texture of a bone's mouth is such that a hook seldom pulls out, so if you allow your fish to make its first long run with only a light drag, half the battle is won. Other runs will follow, but they're progressively shorter and weaker and you can progressively tighten the drag.

The gray ghost is an internationalist who has been caught in such widely separated latitudes as South Africa, Japan, Cape Hatteras, and the Red Sea. However, it's in the warm shallows of tropical America that the species is most abundant, or at least most available to fishermen.

Bones grow big and ultrasophisticated around Bermuda, where they're seen most often along white beaches. Live bait is the proper medicine here. They're not so big, though far more numerous in the Bahamas. The flats encircling Grand Bahama Island, especially at West End, are great, as are most of those around huge, lonely Andros Island to the south. Not so well known are Crab Creek on Munjack and the mossy flats of Angel Fish Creek on Little Abaco Island.

Add also these hotspots in the Bahamas: Green Turtle Cay and Sandy Point on Great Abaco Island, Cat Cays; the Biminis; Harbour Island, Spanish Wells, and Rock Sound on Eleuthera; Pot Cay and the area near Andros Town on Andros Island. No doubt there are others still to be "discovered."

I've caught bones off Grand Cayman and at Cuba's wonderful Isle of Pines. Elsewhere around mainland Cuba there is extraordinary bonefishing, with many suitable waters on the south and east coasts of the island all but unexplored. Some fishing also exists around Puerto Rico (around the island's southwest quadrant, mostly), the Virgin and Windward islands, and along the Mexican coast, at Yucatán and Cozumel.

But even though the modern bonefisherman is a widely ranging species, the Florida Keys region—from Key Largo southward to the Dry Tortugas—remains the Mecca of the most serious and devoted. Fishing may be better elsewhere, but this is where it all began and this is where nearly all return someday.

In 1909 the Matecumbe Club was built at a spot on Upper Matecumbe Key (now known as Islamorada) by a dozen anglers interested in bonefish and nothing else. Irvin S. Cobb was an early guest there. At the same place exactly forty years later, Joe Brooks began to demonstrate for writers, photographers, guides, and fisherman alike that Keys bones were great light-tackle and fly-rod fish. His demonstrations attracted at first a trickle and then hordes of fishermen, and established a tradition that persists to this day.

But no matter what the locale, every bonefisherman eventually finds that the sport is far more than just finding and catching the elusive gray ghosts. It's feeling the warm water wash your feet as you stroll across a strange aquatic pasture. It's stopping to watch sea urchins in the ribbon grass or a guitar-shaped ray making a jet stream in its frantic dash to escape. It might be the sight of roseate spoonbills flying to roost in a sunset or the more formidable spectacle of a sawfish meandering across your path.

Bonefishing is all these things—and more.

Stu Apte holds a very large bonefish taken with saltwater spinning tackle.

PERMIT

Not too many years ago the permit, *Trachinotus goodei*, which is the largest member of the pompano family, was scarcely known to fishermen. But in recent seasons the growing number of bonefishermen who spin- and fly-cast the vast flats around the Florida Keys have found it a frequent resident of many of the finest bonefish waters. It's encountered on many flats between Government Cut at Miami Beach and the Dry Tortugas. Elsewhere it's found on flats encircling Cuba and along the Central American coast from Yucatán southward to Nicaragua.

The permit likes its flats a little deeper than does a bonefish. It also likes them to be closer to deep water. But it can be caught on these flats in the same manner as a bonefish, which means with crabs, crawfish, conch, or hermit crabs for bait.

A permit is incredibly shy, easily spooked, and completely unpredictable. Unlike the more accommodating bone, it does not appear to frequent the same flats day in and day out. Although permits will, on occasion, take such artificial lures as bonefish jigs and streamer flies,

Dick Kotis holds a large Florida permit, considered by many anglers to be among the top game species.

With his boat anchored nearby, a spin fisherman wades in lukewarm shallows in search of bonefish or permits . . .

only a relatively few of them have been taken in this manner.

When a permit is hooked, there is no tougher, faster fish anywhere in the lukewarm shallows. The first run is followed by several equally long runs until a fisherman believes he has hooked a fish several times its size. The average size of a permit is between 10 and 15 pounds, though 30- and 40-pounders are not unheard of. And if anybody cares to tackle anything more formidable, there are some 60-pounders out there.

Although a permit caught on shallow flats offers the most excitement, a fisherman's best bet is to look for it elsewhere. The channels or passes, and deep waterholes of bays along both Florida coasts, are the best types of water in which to conduct your search. On the east coast, permits range northward as far as Fort Pierce. On the west coast, where the species is popularly known as the Mexican pompano, it ranges northward past Panama City, Apalachicola, and Pensacola, and maybe completely across the Gulf coast to Brownsville, Texas.

The result: a good, hard-running permit. (Miami-Metro Department of Publicity and Tourism)

SPOTTING FISH ON THE FLATS

It is necessary to see fish in the water, in many saltwater situations, in order to catch them. Even in mid-ocean, you watch for the telltale signs of feeding fish near or on the surface. But spotting is most important for such species as bonefish, permit, and tarpon found on shallow saltwater flats. To be successful an angler simply must be able to see fish. Fortunately there are a number of aids available.

Consider proper headgear first. You need a cap, preferably a baseball-type cap with a long bill to shade the eyes even when the sun is low. The underside of the bill should be black or very dark. For added insurance, try darkening your nose and cheekbones with nonreflective cosmetics sold to camouflage the faces of deer and duck hunters.

Sunglasses are even more important than a cap, although you should wear both always. Though there are a bewildering variety of sun-glasses available, you want only one kind, i.e., glasses with polarizing lenses. The ideal glasses will also have blinders or side shields to keep sunlight from bouncing off water into the backs and sides of your lenses. Blinds somewhat hinder peripheral vision, but they eliminate enough glare and eyestrain to more than make up for it. To my mind, ideal sunglasses should also be yellow-tinted because of the greater contrast afforded. However, a good many offshore anglers and boat skippers prefer gray or smoke-tinted glasses.

Best visibility underwater comes from keeping the sun at your back, as opposed to looking (and fishing) into the sun. Also, the higher above the surface you are, the better you can see, which is the reason many flats fishermen build (or have installed) rear platforms above the decks of their boats. Because it is easier to peer into the water when the surface is calm than when riffled by wind, mornings and evenings may prove to be better times to go fishing. It is also more comfortable at these periods.

5

FISH OF THE OPEN OCEANS:

Dolphin, Wahoo, King Mackerel, Spanish Mackerel, Cero Mackerel, Common Bonito, Oceanic Bonito, Cobia

DOLPHIN

In the Hawaiian Islands it's called mahi-mahi, in Latin America, dorado, and in Japan, shiira. But whatever its name, the dolphin—sometimes even dolphinfish—ranks high among the ocean's most spectacular and most attractive game fishes. Every year in late spring or early summer a multitude of sportsmen along Florida's southeastern coast eagerly await the arrival of large schools of dolphin. When the dolphin do appear, the azure Gulf Stream is crisscrossed by hundreds of watercraft, from modest outboard boats to expensive, outriggered charters searching for the golden schools. But this is no isolated example. Saltwater anglers pursue dolphin with great en-

thusiasm whenever and wherever in the world they appear.

Although dolphin are present all year in the Florida Gulf Stream, spring and summer are when thousands of small "school" dolphin are available. These small (1- to 5-pound) fish are extremely voracious, striking readily at almost any lure or bait. Often entire schools of a hundred or more are caught by clever anglers, who merely stop their boats after locating a school, chum the dolphin alongside with bits of fish, and haul them in one after the other. This is one reason why they are such favorites with small-boaters, who can load up the boat with any equipment.

Larger dolphin usually travel in pairs or alone,

Small-school dolphin such as these keep anglers busy in the Gulf of Mexico near Panama City, Florida. (Panama City News Bureau)

but their appetites never diminish. I have known them to gobble up two or even three trolled baits in a single lightninglike pass before the startled angler has time to react. They may even be spotted from a distance as they "greyhound" across the water in pursuit of a trolled lure.

Among the most exquisite of all ocean game fish, dolphin are renowned for their brilliant coloration (mostly blues, greens, and yellows) as well as for their fighting ability on the end of a line. They are caught by possibly more fishermen and in greater numbers than any other ocean game fish off the southeast Florida coast. Dolphin are extremely desirable as trophies and taxidermy firms everywhere mount thousands of them each year.

Worldwide wanderers of warm seas, dolphin are valuable commercial fish in Japan, China, and Hawaii and are widely used as a food source throughout the islands of the Pacific Ocean and Caribbean Sea. There are two species of dolphin, although for the untrained observer they are difficult to distinguish. The common dolphin, *Coryphaena hippurus,* is more abundant and grows to a much larger size than its smaller relative, the pompano dolphin, *Coryphaena equisetis.* The pompano rarely reaches 2 feet in length, while the common dolphin grows to 4, sometimes even 5, feet. Pompano dolphin are seldom caught by sport fishermen, although they mix freely in common dolphin schools. It may

be, therefore, more a matter of misidentification than true scarcity.

The main difference in appearance is that the common dolphin is relatively long and slender, while the pompano dolphin is fairly deep-bodied, hence the name "pompano." Also, the pompano dolphin lacks the brilliant colors of the common dolphin and tends to be more of a uniform silvery color, especially after death.

Not nearly enough is known about the dolphin's movements and life history. Its colors, which blend into blue or green or gold, seem to change with the mood of the fish. The color of an excited or injured fish can change while you watch. But gaff the fish and swing it aboard a boat, and the vivid shades soon fade to a dull and lifeless brown.

With just one quick glance it's possible to tell the difference between a male and a female dolphin. The male has a blunt, high head, while the female is more streamlined. The female's forehead is fashioned in a graceful curve from the mouth to the front of the blue or purple dorsal fin.

The dolphin has an extremely rapid growth rate, coupled with a very high mortality rate. Those school dolphin taken off southern Florida in spring and summer are probably only two or three months old, while the trophy-sized 50- or 60-pounder may be only a three-year-old. In a dolphin biology study of 1963 and 1964, scales obtained from over 500 dolphin were examined for age marks. Only 121 one-year-olds were found, nine two-year-olds, and one three-year-old. The oldest dolphin examined was four years old and weighed over 76 pounds. At the time, it was a new all-tackle world record. The present world record is an 85-pounder caught in the Bahamas.

Dolphin have been kept with some success in large aquaria, and nowhere is their rapid growth rate more striking than in captivity. Undoubtedly this is due to an abundant and easily obtained food supply. In 1963, three 1-pound dolphin were placed in the reef tank at the Miami Seaquarium. Two died very soon, but the third, a male, lived for almost seven months before he jumped out of the tank and was killed. He weighed slightly over 35 pounds, for a growth rate of almost 5 pounds per month. Two dolphin at Florida Marineland grew from about 1½ pounds to almost 35 pounds in less than eight months.

Dolphin spawn off southern Florida from about November through July, although most activity occurs from January to March. Each female dolphin may spawn two or three times in a season, releasing from 200,000 to over a million eggs each time. Eggs and sperm are cast free in the ocean and fertilization is by chance, as with many other open-ocean game species. The eggs hatch in two to three days, at which time the tiny dolphin are about 4 millimeters long.

Young dolphin mature and first spawn when only about 18 inches long, well before they reach one year old. In fact, dolphin hatched in December or January may mature and spawn the following spring and summer.

There is something primitive and strangely beautiful about finding a school of dolphin far out on the open ocean. First you spot a piece of driftwood or a palm log, perhaps with a pair of albatrosses perched upon it. Then when you drift closer you spot a fluid, darting shadow just beneath. If you troll or cast a lure, almost any lure, close enough to the shadow . . . lightning strikes at once. And you can feel the sudden shock of it from the tip of your rod to the tips of your toes.

Among the strangest, most exciting aspects of dolphin behavior which fishermen have exploited is the dolphin's habit of associating with floating objects. Anglers have always known that windrows of sargassum weed, floating planks, logs, or any other drifting objects are likely to have dolphin underneath or in the near vicinity. Japanese commercial fishermen build bamboo rafts, called *tsuke*, which they anchor in the ocean. Periodically they inspect a raft, and if dolphin are present in sufficient quantities they either set a net around it and capture the dolphin underneath or lure the dolphin away from the raft and then encircle them with the seine.

Scientists and fishermen have long puzzled over this association with floating objects. It has been suggested that the fish are seeking shade from sun or using the objects to scratch and rid themselves of parasites, but research leads elsewhere. Perhaps open-ocean fishes such as dolphin use floating objects as "schooling companions" or, as one ichthyologist suggested, "as visual stimuli in an optical void."

There is little doubt that dolphin feed on small organisms attracted to the flotsam. Drifting sargassum serves as shelter and a temporary home for a variety of juvenile and adult fishes, as well as many small crustaceans. Food habit studies of the dolphin show that these organisms make up a large portion of the dolphin's diet. Pieces of sargassum itself have been found in dolphin stomachs, although probably the fragments were ingested by accident while the dolphin was feeding on small fishes or crustaceans off the sargassum.

Dolphin serve as prey for a variety of ocean predators. Blue marlin seem to relish dolphin, and several instances have been recorded of blue marlin chasing dolphin and even impaling them on their bills. Dolphin are also notorious cannibals and feed heavily on smaller members of their own kind.

In North American waters, dolphin range northward along the Atlantic coast as far as Virginia, and occasionally are caught still farther north. They are most numerous in the Gulf Stream along the Florida coast. In the Pacific, dolphin range from San Diego south to Panama and beyond, and are perhaps even more numerous in the Pacific than in the Atlantic.

Generally speaking, the smaller the size, the more dolphin will be together in one school. Some years, schools of small dolphin that weigh only a pound or less suddenly appear in such great numbers that they cover areas several miles in extent. And a few large dolphin stay in the

Many dolphin are taken by billfishermen on tackle too heavy for the species.

and maneuverability. They seldom go very deep to sulk for long periods of time, as do some other ocean fishes, and ordinarily they do not run great distances in one direction. Rather, they feint and spar, jump and go greyhounding across the ocean, sometimes in leaps from 10 to 20 feet which display their beautiful iridescent colors in the tropical sun. Few fish can approach them in jumping ability, in straightaway speed, or in sudden change of pace.

Some confusion has arisen over the dolphin's name. In ancient times the Greeks used dolphin to identify a mammal of the porpoise family, and porpoises of the Mediterranean are still called dolphin, as they are occasionally in waters along the Florida Keys. But to sport fishermen in North America, dolphin always means the great game fish of the ocean currents.

shade beneath them as below sargassum weed.

The average size of a dolphin taken on the Florida east coast is about 7 or 8 pounds. Most are caught by trolling with strip baits, block-tin squid, spoons, jigs, or feathers. A large percentage of them are hooked when a charter boat is fishing for larger fish and therefore with tackle too heavy for the dolphin to give its best fight. Ordinarily, 20-pound line is highly satisfactory and is enough to catch the largest dolphin in the Gulf Stream.

Once one of a school of dolphin is hooked, the balance of the school can be held within reach by tying the first one close to the stern of the boat as a decoy, after it is landed. The other dolphin will continue to strike as long as the fishermen are interested in such steady action. When found in schools, dolphin will strike at almost anything—surface or deep-running plugs, streamer flies, live bait, spoons, spinners. They're the most obliging of fishes.

Enough cannot be said about the game qualities of this rainbow-colored fish, especially on light tackle or spinning tackle. Although they are extremely strong swimmers, they do not fight with the sheer force of tuna and amberjacks, but rely instead on their blinding speed

WAHOO

Another of the exciting and mysterious wanderers of the open sea is the jagged-tooth wahoo, *Acanthocybium solandri*. Some anglers maintain that the wahoo looks very much like an assassin, though actually it is a sleek, slim, handsome fish. Its dark-green or steel-blue sides with yellowish bars have a burnished silver finish which rubs off on a fisherman's fingers. The long low dorsal fin has around twenty-five spines and is followed by a series of finlets. It also has large irregular teeth and a beaklike upper jaw. It is only because this species is occasionally confused with the kingfish that these physical characteristics are given in detail here. Any other resemblance to the kingfish or a king mackerel is superficial.

Check any wahoo closely and you discover a few similarities to marlin and swordfish. The wahoo's upper jaw looks suspiciously like the vestigial remnant of a bill or a beak. Ichthyologists long argued about the wahoo's relation to billfish and finally placed it in a class by itself: *Acanthocybiidae* (a term with obvious links to the class of billfish).

Anglers have not been able to agree on the wahoo, either. For decades the fish had only local names. It was called *ono* off Hawaii, *ocean barracuda* or *kingfish* in continental U.S. waters, *queen fish* in the Caribbean, *springer* off Brazil, *peto* off Cuba, and in the waters of Bermuda, *the pride of Bermuda*. The story goes that one day an excitable angler hooked into one and watched 300 yards of line evaporate from his reel in seconds. "*Wahoo!*" the fisherman shouted, and the name survived. However, the wahoo has a close relative in the Fiji Islands. It is a heavier fish called walu. Some say that "wahoo" is merely a corruption of "walu," but the first story is much more appealing.

Except possibly for the dolphin, no fish rushes so swiftly, so surely toward a bait. And few fish can match a wahoo's bite once it strikes. Its teeth are triangular, close-set, joined around the base to form a sort of semicircular saw blade. This explains why no other fish breaks off so easily, so often, and why a lot of expensive big-game fishing rigs are rusting in the ocean depths.

The wahoo has its share of tricks and escape mechanisms. Its opening run is unexcelled, pound for pound, by any other fish in the ocean. A fisherman is absolutely powerless to stop it without snapping the line. It is normal for wahoos to race 250 yards after striking a bait, and it is not unknown for them to go twice that far to strip a reel bare. More than one angler has gone to the beer cooler and returned seconds later to find his reel empty. The opening run can be so fast that it mesmerizes even experts.

According to one charter skipper: "I've seen them get a strike and not grab the rod out of the holder. They sit there stunned, watching, listening to the reel scream. You have to holler three or four times before they'll pick up the rod. Then they forget what they know. They tighten down on the drag and that's a guarantee the wahoo will break off. Or they thumb the reel instinctively and then you can smell burnt flesh."

In North American waters the wahoo roams farther at sea than most fishermen ever penetrate, which is unfortunate. It is caught as far north as Cape Hatteras and southward to South America. It also exists in numbers in the Pacific (but only far out of sight of the Pacific coast) and in the Indian Ocean. The Pacific off Panama is productive. Some of the best wahoo fishing occurs around islands far from major coastlines. Bermuda, for instance, is excellent, and many large specimens are taken there. Another good example is the Cayman group in the Caribbean. Around both Bermuda and the Cayman Islands, the fish sometimes come in close enough to shore to be caught occasionally over the outer reefs. They seem to be most abundant, or at least the most willing to strike, in winter and early spring.

Except in areas where they are known in great abundance, not too much fishing is done specifically for wahoos. Mostly they are taken by anglers trolling for other larger fishes. They will strike spoons, feather jigs, large plugs, or strip baits, with the last probably the best of all.

Since the average weight of a wahoo is between 20 and 40 pounds, medium tackle is heavy

A charter-boat mate sinks a gaff into a wahoo, among the fastest game fishes in the sea. (Miami-Metro Department of Publicity and Tourism)

enough for the best of them. The current record is a 139-pounder taken off Marathon, Florida.

In my book, the wahoo is one of the most underrated game fishes in the sea. The black marlin is the species most often credited as the fastest of all ocean fishes, but this is something not easily measured. Tackle weight and ocean currents would also be factors. In any competition the blinding, bewildering speed of a wahoo would have to rate that fish very close to the top.

The best way to handle a wahoo, once securely hooked, is to allow it to run freely (but with no slack line) for the length of a couple of football fields. Then after tightening up, allow the fish to run again, in which case it may turn directly toward the boat, allowing line to be retrieved onto the reel. Some wahoos run so far so fast that they are dead on arrival. But live ones should be released immediately, because they are not the finest of table fishes.

KING MACKEREL

More often called kingfish or king in Florida waters, the king mackerel follows a migratory pattern that makes it unavailable to sport fisher-

men for long periods of time. Schools of kings follow a seasonal migratory route that takes them south in the fall and north in the spring. The runs on Florida's east and west coasts coincide both in times and in numbers. And both follow the same cycle, ranging from years of great abundance to other years when the fish are quite scarce.

Though vast schools of kings winter in southern Florida waters from Fort Pierce or Stuart southward to the Dry Tortugas, they are not always available to fishermen, since they spend a good part of this time in extremely deep water. It's interesting to note that the larger fish are sometimes found in the green waters closer inshore than the smaller kingfish caught on the edge of the Gulf Stream. Of course, this situation isn't always true.

The strike of a kingfish is sudden and shocking. Although it doesn't compare with a dolphin as an aerialist, occasionally it will make a remarkable jump above the surface of the water. One charter-boat captain told me that he had a kingfish jump completely over his boat and that meant it had to jump at least 6 feet out of the water for a lateral distance of more than 12 feet.

The average weight of a Florida kingfish is

A good catch of kingfish taken from a surf boat off South Africa's Indian Ocean coast.

about 8 pounds, but quite a number are caught each year in the 40- to 50-pound range. The record is a 76½-pounder taken in 1952 by Bob Maytag in Minimi, Bahama. Kingfish have been known to grow 6 feet in length.

King mackerel are among those species of saltwater fish that can be chummed to the surface with live shrimp, which is also an effective bait for them. But no matter what the bait, an average kingfish is a mighty sporty proposition when the tackle is on the light side. The 6/9 tackle is ample for trolling with block-tin squid, spoons, large feathers, balao and mullet strips. It's best to troll rather slowly and to get the bait down very deep, which can be accomplished by using a wire line or by running the boat in tight circles or figure eights. Leaders should be as long as 20 or 30 feet when the fish are very deep.

SPANISH MACKEREL

Members of the mackerel family are found all over the world in tropical and temperate oceans and in many seas which adjoin them. They are extremely prolific. Although they are prey to many other fishes, and furnish an important part of the diet for some of these, they still remain abundant and supply a vast percentage of the world's fish markets. Of course, they are widely caught and held in high esteem by sport fishermen.

In Florida waters, where the species follows a migratory pattern almost identical to that of the king mackerel, the Spanish mackerel is the second most important fish commercially. Only the mullet has greater value to Florida commercial fishermen.

If you are fishing offshore in Florida and see an excited cloud of gulls and terns, the odds are good it will be a school of Spanish mackerel—or maybe cero mackerel—leaping from the surface as they work their way through a ball of baitfish. These mackerel seem to have an endless appetite for mullet, menhaden, silversides, or any small fish found in numbers in their vicinity.

Often called the spotted mackerel because of the bronze or golden spots on its blue-green sides, the Spanish mackerel is quite a handsome fish with an iridescent silver belly and black and yellow pectoral fins. Although they may wander as far north as Cape Ann, Massachusetts, they are extremely rare north of New Jersey and exist there only in midsummer. They are most abundant around the Florida Keys.

The Spanish mackerel often wanders offshore in large schools, appearing a little closer inshore during midsummer, when it seems to be spawning. It feeds mainly near the surface on small fish and occasionally on squid. It reaches a length of 6 feet and a weight of 20 pounds, though the average Spanish mackerel would run only about 2 pounds. There is one record of a 25-pounder taken in commercial nets.

A wide variety of fishing techniques can be used to catch Spanish mackerel, but trolling and spinning with bucktails are the most common fishing methods. Many mackerel are taken by fishermen trolling for larger fishes. Feather jigs, small metal squid, and spoons will always account for plenty of action when they are passed near a school of feeding fish. A mackerel strike is swift and its sizzling first run is really spectacular for the size of the fish.

Casting toward the edge of a school of feeding mackerel will provide a spin-caster or fly-caster with all the excitement he can handle. These light-tackle methods are becoming increasingly popular along the Texas coast where Spanish mackerel gather each spring.

It's very important to use a fast retrieve or a fairly rapid trolling speed when after Spanish mackerel. Even feeding fish will often ignore a bait that is not retrieved fast enough. A 3-foot wire leader and plenty of backing line for a long run are always necessary. All mackerel, especially the Spanish, are delicious eating. But the fish must be cooled immediately to preserve its fine, delicate flavor.

CERO MACKEREL

The cero, third member of the mackerel family found in North American Atlantic waters, is frequently confused with both the Spanish and king mackerel. In size, it ranges somewhere between them. Its average weight is about 4 pounds, but it has been known to attain a length of nearly 5 feet and more than 25 pounds. It tends to live in tropical waters and is less migratory than the other mackerels.

Seldom found north of Miami Beach, and most abundant in the Florida Keys, it is caught

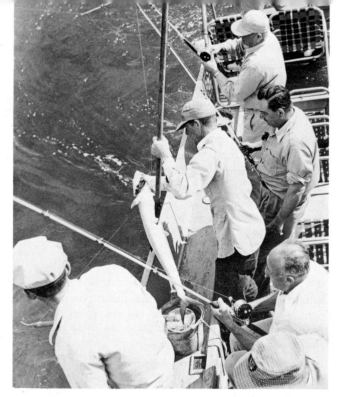

Kingfish and mackerel are taken seasonally in large numbers by anglers on Florida party boats.

throughout the summer, usually by anglers fishing for other species. The tackle, bait, and lures that are effective on Spanish mackerel are also effective on cero. Less oily than its cousins, the cero is perhaps the most delicious of mackerels.

COMMON BONITO

Its name notwithstanding, the common bonito is a unique fish because of its speed and extraordinary fighting qualities. As streamlined as any fish in the sea, it is faster than any of the ocean fishes except for the dolphin, wahoo, and swordfish.

Bonitos occur from Cape Cod southward to Florida and into the Gulf of Mexico. They usually roam the offshore waters along the edge of the Gulf Stream in large, compact schools and stay fairly deep most of the time. An encounter with a school of menhaden, alewives, or similar small fishes will lure bonitos to the surface to feed. Occasionally schools of 1- to 2-pound bonitos (the average range for the species) are encountered in inshore waters.

A 4/6 outfit is sufficient for any bonito fish-

ing, but of course there are areas where a fisherman might also run into other larger fish and therefore it's wise to be rigged for heavier game. A wire leader is a necessity because of the bonito's small but extremely sharp teeth. Spoons, squid, and feather jigs are the most common artificial lures used. But small baitfish, crabs, clams, or a strip bait behind a spinner are extremely effective when bonitos are busily feeding.

Since the bonito itself is an extremely fine bait for larger fish, charter skippers often troll weighted lines close behind the boat, using block-tin squids on feather lures for bait. On these short lines, bonitos often provide quite a bit of action. Of course many bonitos are caught on lures and on heavy tackle trolled for other species, such as sailfish, marlin, and tuna.

But when hooked on light tackle, large bonitos are extremely difficult to stop. The strike is hard and the first run is deep, fast, and boring. They never seem to give up and even a 5-pounder is enough to make a fisherman feel that he has done a full day's work.

He's a wise fly-caster or spin-fisherman who takes the opportunity, when he finds bonitos feeding on the surface, to make a few casts into the center of the school. Ordinarily he'll need only one cast because, no matter what the lure, a bonito will take it and from that point on it's a long hard tug-of-war which the fisherman will always remember.

Although the average common bonito, *Sarda sarda*, weighs only about 2 pounds, it does attain a maximum weight of 20 pounds and a length of 30 inches.

OCEANIC BONITO

The oceanic bonito or skipjack tuna, *Katsuwonus pelamis*, sometimes mistakenly called arctic bonito, is really a fish of tropical waters and is actually a closer relative of the tuna than of the bonito. In some regions it's called albacore and false albacore.

This sleek and heavy-bodied wanderer of the open ocean will average about 3 or 4 pounds but can attain a weight of 20 pounds. In 1952 the record specimen weighing 39 pounds 15 ounces was taken off Walker Cay, Bahamas.

The appearance of the oceanic bonito off the

United States coast is very erratic. It rarely shows up in appreciable numbers, but when it does, it's generally in spring or summer. Often the species is found mixed up in schools of the common bonito, and of course the same type tackle will take either of them.

I've encountered some schools of oceanic bonitos feeding on the surface offshore from Bermuda. The approach of a school was always a most thrilling experience because they would strike readily at our spinning jigs and then make long powerful runs across the surface of the ocean. No matter whether we were trolling for wahoos in deep blue water or anchored over a reef far from land, someone on board would always keep a wary eye for feeding bonitos. That's a grand recommendation.

COBIA

In many, many years of saltwater fishing, I've only caught one cobia of respectable size, but I've had my share of experiences with them.

While fishing Key West waters with Captain Lefty Reagan, I hooked three cobias on three casts right underneath the lighthouse on Smith Shoal. Any one of these three cobias would have been worth a first prize in the Annual Metropolitan Miami Fishing Tournament, but all three of them wrapped my line around the barnacle-encrusted legs of the lighthouse and that was the end of that. One of these cobias, I should add, jumped repeatedly like a tarpon and this, Reagan assured me, isn't something that happens every day.

The cobia or ling, lemonfish, crabeater, or, scientifically, *Rachycentron canadus*, is a cocoa-brown fish with a single longitudinal stripe. From some angles it resembles a freshwater channel catfish, without the whiskers, or a saltwater shark. The cobia's natural habitat is around floating logs, buoys, light towers, offshore wrecks, oil rigs, or in the center of riptides. Most of its food consists of such bottom forms as flounder and crabs. And although the fish gives the impression of power and deliberate movement, it is swift enough to put on a sudden burst of speed which has surprised many a smaller baitfish as well as many an angler. In a number of ways, the old crabeater is as rakish in action as in appearance.

Ordinarily the cobia travels alone or in small groups of two or three. Not particularly abundant along our south Atlantic seaboard, this species is seldom found north of Chesapeake Bay, though it does become more common in the Florida Keys and along our Gulf coast from Florida to Mexico.

Spring, especially from mid-March to mid-May, is by far the best time to fish for lemonfish along the Gulf coast. Usually they're caught by trolling with a spoon or by still-fishing with shrimp, croakers, or similar live baits. Heavy tackle is advisable when fishing around oil rigs or sunken wrecks because the minute a cobia feels the hook it will dive beneath the nearest underwater obstruction in an effort to slice the line.

One common technique developed recently is to troll very close to any kind of offshore structures with heavy metal line. In this way the fish can be horsed to safety immediately after it strikes. Mostly a good fast troll of from 5 to 6 miles an hour is most effective.

Even though the cobia will average as much as 20 pounds, and 6-foot-long 100-pounders are not unheard of, I always think of the species as a medium- or light-tackle fish. I never pass a buoy, lighthouse, or channel marker without making several casts nearby, and it doesn't make too much difference which lures are cast because a cobia will take strip baits, eel skins, deep-running plugs, and almost any artificial with a darting-type action. Its strike is heavy and its runs are quick and unpredictable. A cobia is just as apt to run toward the boat as away from it. But no matter which way it moves, it is extremely powerful and its fight is dogged and jarring. For trolling, 6/9 tackle is usually adequate.

One of the greatest concentrations of cobias occurs late each spring along the northwest Florida coast. There it's possible for a fisherman to catch quite a number of large specimens in a single day. Around Panama City the cobia is often found traveling in company with large mantas. Many fishermen deliberately search for these mantas and then troll and cast all around them. Perhaps the reason for this strange association is that the mantas uncover many items of food that a cobia would ordinarily miss.

6

THE TUNAS:

Bluefin, Yellowfin, Blackfin

Men have pursued tuna ever since they first ventured out on open seas. Pliny, in the first century A.D., relates that the school of tuna that met the fleet of Alexander the Great on one occasion was so vast that only by advancing in battle formation, as if against an enemy, were the ships able to cut their way through the school. Evidently exaggeration about fish is not an invention of modern writers.

But even before Pliny, the regular appearance of vast schools of tuna was a known phenomenon throughout the Mediterranean. In ancient Rome the first tuna of the season signaled the beginning of a great festival called Thunnaeum, a pageant during which a fish was sacrificed to Neptune, God of the Sea. Today fishermen still search for tuna not only in the Mediterranean, but also in the New World. They still celebrate the first catch. But in two thousand years of fishing, anglers have learned little more about tuna than those first Roman fishermen knew.

BLUEFIN

There are a number of different species of tuna around the world, all of them pelagic, which means they travel endlessly on the open seas. But the largest and most impressive of all is the bluefin, *Thunnus thynnus,* or horse mackerel, as Yankee boat captains call it, which probably reaches its greatest size in the waters on the North American side of the Atlantic Ocean. The largest bluefin, taken off Nova Scotia in 1979 by Ken Fraser, measured about 13 feet long and weighed 1,496 pounds.

The bluefin is almost worldwide in distribution, since it is found on both sides of the Atlantic and in the Pacific as well. In Europe it ranges from Norway southward to the Mediterranean Sea (Danish waters are particularly good during mid-August). It also occurs off the African coast southward from Gibraltar to the Cape of Good Hope. On the Atlantic coast of

After a grueling fight, a large bluefin tuna is gaffed in warm waters off Bimini, Bahamas.

America its general range is from the central Caribbean northward to Newfoundland. In 1958 a bluefin weighing 30 pounds was tagged at Guadalupe Island, Mexico. Five years later, and 6,000 miles away, it turned up in Japan weighing over 240 pounds.

All of the tuna are efficient, relentless beasts of prey, with enormous food requirements. Since the bluefin is by far the largest of the tuna, it is also the most voracious eating machine of all.

A schooling fish that feeds principally on smaller schooling fish, the tuna is one of the chief enemies of its own relative, the mackerel, as well as of menhaden and herring. Tuna will even attack dogfish sharks; in fact, whole dogfish weighing as much as 8 pounds have been found in the stomachs of bluefins. In addition to almost any kind of schooling fish smaller than itself, the tuna consumes vast quantities of squid as well. There is no doubt that its appearance in any local waters and its movements across the ocean are governed by the abundance or absence of fish on which it depends.

But as terrible as tuna surely seem to smaller fish, even the largest bluefins are preyed upon by killer whales. The killers are known to seize them by the back, near the head, thereby cutting the spinal cord for an instant kill. At other times, bluefins have been found stranded in shallow water from which they could not escape. Apparently they reach this predicament by pursuing smaller fishes or perhaps while fleeing from killer whales.

Although fishermen have hunted tuna for food for at least twenty centuries, it was only in the past fifty years that anglers sought tuna for sport. The records are most obscure on the first angler to catch a bluefin on hook and line, but one of the first was a Wedgeport schoolmaster named Thomas Pattilo, who ventured out into Liverpool Bay, Nova Scotia, in 1871.

This pioneer had only 32 fathoms of ordinary cod line wound on a swivel reel of unreliable design. He used a steel hook ⅜ inch thick, 8 inches long, and with a 3-inch shank. Then with a single companion to do the rowing he went fishing.

Pattilo quickly hooked a monster tuna, which towed his boat across the harbor much faster than his friend could row in the other direction —until it hurtled head on into a fleet of herring netters. One netter was swamped and the rest were scattered in confusion. One of the angry herring fishermen finally cut Pattilo's line, thus enabling his first tuna to escape.

But on the next attempt there were no herring fishermen nearby, and at the cost of blistered hands and an aching back Pattilo achieved complete success. Somehow, in spite of his crude tackle, he boated a tuna weighing over 600 pounds.

For reasons which bluefin fishermen know better than anyone else, tuna fishing can become a pure addiction, though it usually is more hard work than it is a lively sport. Because of their streamlined body proportions and ample dimensions, bluefins have been aptly called the torpedoes of the sea. Among the speediest of fish, bluefins have been observed keeping pace with a ship logging 8 knots.

Their bullet-shaped heads and oblong bodies seem to cut through the water with a minimum of drag. Their dorsal and pelvic fins fit into grooves as the fish propel themselves forward with a quick motion of powerful, crescent-shaped tails. A taut, mucus-covered skin with minute scales slides easily through the water.

One indication of the bluefin's extraordinary speed is its manner of pursuing the unique and graceful flying fish, a staple of its diet. When chasing a flying fish, a tuna seems to estimate its trajectory and then captures it when it reenters the sea. That means that a tuna would have to be moving far faster than the 8 knots mentioned before.

The bluefin's weakness for flying fish inspired a curious method of angling dubbed the tuna-lane or the kite-fishing technique, first devised by Captain George Farnsworth of Avalon, California, and it since has been adapted to fishing elsewhere.

Just after World War II, Harlan Major, a fishing writer, learned about the kite-fishing technique and introduced it to the East. He passed the method on to Tommy Gifford, a game fish guide from Montauk, New York, who, before long, had boated the first white marlin, the first tuna, and the first broadbill swordfish ever taken on kites along the Atlantic coast. Since then he has flown his kite successfully for sailfish as well as these other species in almost all eastern United States waters, as well as those of Nova Scotia, Bimini, Cat Cay, Cuba, Puerto Rico, and Jamaica.

As you can guess, the angler's line is fastened by a clothespin to the kite string and the bait skips over the surface of the water in a manner tantalizing to many of the big game fish. The technique can be used when trolling or—if there is a wind—when still-fishing.

An average angler's best chance to catch a big bluefin is to intercept one of its annual migrations at one of the regular fishing ports along our coast. On chartered boats, the method most universally used to catch bluefins is to chum for them. Menhaden, herring, or mackerel are ground up into an oily "liquor" and slowly spilled over the transom of the boat into the sea. As this chum dissolves into the tide, it lures the big tuna close to the stern of the boat where a bait is waiting for them.

Baits are usually 6 to 10 1-pound herring (usually with their backbones removed), spaced about a foot apart and tied to a piece of tarred cord. The cord is attached to a light string about 15 feet long which in turn is tied to a 15-foot bamboo pole. The angler's hook, buried inside one of the herring near the end of the string, can be any size from 6/0 to 12/0.

A deckhand or first mate stands in the stern of the boat, alternately raising and lowering the long pole, thereby causing the herring to skip along the tops of the waves as the tuna come near. This is to simulate an actual school of herring in flight.

If all goes well, a striking tuna will swirl up behind the teaser and grab it. He may gulp only one of the herring or he may take all of them. If the angler is lucky, the gulp will include the herring which has his hook embedded in it.

When the tuna makes the first run, it usually sounds, breaking the light cord which attaches the string of herring to the bamboo pole. That is the moment when an angler sets his hook. It's an exciting moment which he had better enjoy to the fullest because from that point on it is nothing but pure, back-breaking drudgery.

When a giant bluefin is solidly hooked, it will make one terrific run after another trying to free itself. It'll shake and shudder and frequently tow even a heavy boat for many miles. And if not handled skillfully, it can snap an angler's rod and line with apparent ease.

Charter-boat captains resort to another technique that is very effective at slack tide with the boat completely adrift. A 1-pound herring is hooked through the back and dropped astern. Just above the wire leader a toy balloon is attached with a light piece of string and small safety-pin swivel. Occasionally the balloon can be moved up or down on the line to change the depth of the bait. If and when the tuna strikes, the balloon simply disintegrates and the long hard fight is on.

The proper line size for bluefin is 39-thread (or even 79), but since other fish (white marlin, sailfish, wahoo) are often taken in the same water, a boat captain may recommend that his more experienced customers use 24-thread line.

In 1935, Michael Lerner, a big game fishing pioneer with experience around the globe, went to Nova Scotia for a whirl at the fabled swordfishing. On his way back to Yarmouth to catch the Boston ferryboat, he stopped for gas near Wedgeport. He happened to have his big game fishing gear in the car and that led to fishing talk with the gas station attendant and a group of cronies gathered there.

Lerner's ears almost popped when he heard about the 1,000-pound bluefin tuna that the natives said were regularly harpooned at the mouth of the Tusket River and at Soldier's Rip, a tidal channel so named because a troop transport once foundered there off Wedgeport.

Without further conversation, Mike canceled his reservation on the Boston boat, rigged a crude fighting chair in the stern of a lobster boat, and went tuna fishing.

That first day out he caught two tuna. Two days later he caught another bluefin, but business called him back to New York. The business transacted, he was back in Wedgeport a week later and in eight days of fishing boated 21 large tuna weighing a total of 3,677 pounds! As a result of this effort, Lerner convinced several commercial fishermen and lobstermen to rig their boats for sport-fishing. And a number of years later the International Tuna Cup match was organized in the tiny lobster town of Wedgeport.

Like moths to flame, big game anglers came from all four corners of the globe to match their skills and muscles with giant bluefin tuna every September. And the action was definitely worth the trip. Even though the matches do not exist anymore (because in recent years the bluefins wouldn't cooperate and wouldn't guarantee to arrive at Soldier's Rip at the same time as the fishermen who traveled from as far away as Havana, Cape Town, and Lisbon), they were among the most colorful events in saltwater fishing history and no chapter on tuna fishing would be complete without mentioning them.

The giant bluefin is found at various times of the year all along the Atlantic coast of North America, from the Bahamas and Cuba northward to Newfoundland. They cruise in a roughly circular migration that begins in their spawning grounds somewhere in the Straits of Florida, that vast, deep blue "meadow" area between Key West and Havana. Traveling northward from there the 500-pound bluefin tuna usually pass Cat Cay and Bimini in the Bahamas in May and June. They reach Montauk Point, Long Island, and Rhode Island in late June and early July. Of all tuna summering grounds (including Cape Cod Bay), Wedgeport, Nova Scotia, has always had the biggest concentration of tuna from August through September. Occasionally, large concentrations are found as far north as Newfoundland. As the winter months arrive, the bluefins begin their southward migration, which carries them past Bermuda and on to the Lesser Antilles.

The winter migration continues in a westerly direction off the Venezuelan coast and by February the fish are running past Jamaica. A possible spawning ground may be in the Windward Passage between Cuba and Haiti. Scientists believe that some tuna head north through the passage and also up the Old Bahama Channel and Mona Passage, between the Dominican Republic and Puerto Rico, northward toward Cat Cay and Bimini.

Besides the bluefin, there are several other species of tuna which anglers agree are among the world's great saltwater game fishes. Scientists, on the other hand, are not in such complete agreement as to their classification. For example, some marine biologists believe that the yellowfin and the Pacific yellowfin are identical fish. Others do not. Still other marine biologists believe that the Allison tuna and the yellowfin are one and the same. Since specific scientific identifications, however, are seldom of great interest to anglers, we'll consider the yellowfin, the Pacific yellowfin, and the Allison indistinguishable for the purposes of this book.

YELLOWFIN

Compared to its larger cousin, the bluefin, the yellowfin is a mystery as far as its habits and migratory patterns are concerned. A few are taken off our Florida coast from the area around the sea buoys of Government Cut, off Miami Beach, northward about as far as Fort Pierce. The first fish appear in midwinter, usually remain through May, and seem to prefer the green water just inside the Gulf Stream. The average weight in this area is less than 100 pounds, but the yellowfin quite possibly grows to 400 pounds. Like all tuna, yellowfins strike hard on strip bait and feathers. Once hooked, they prefer to fight a deep fight.

Fifteen- or 24-thread line is generally accepted as adequate, although more experienced anglers take them on 9-thread line. And like all the tuna, this one feeds on smaller fish and is itself a good fish to eat.

When fresh out of the sea and still alive, the yellowfin is brilliantly iridescent, with a golden or bright yellow stripe along the flank. It has yellow fins, a bluish black back, and whitish or pearl bellies, but soon after death the bright colors fade and the yellow colors disappear completely.

The apparently international yellowfin (or its kin) is found in tropical parts of all oceans—in waters from 60 to 85 degrees. It probably will not tolerate either colder or warmer waters than these and it seems to gather where there is a meeting of one or more different ocean currents.

The record yellowfin recognized by the International Game Fish Association weighed 388½ pounds and was caught in 1977 off San Benedicto Island, Mexico.

BLACKFIN

The blackfin tuna, also called long-finned albacore, albacore, black tunny and little tunny, is among the most beautiful of the tunas and one of the handsomest fishes in the sea. Its distinquishing characteristics are long pectoral fins extending to the back of the front dorsal. A broad, bright, yellow band around the middle exists on most but not all individuals, and on some is an extremely brilliant color.

Blackfins swim in small compact schools. They approach shore erratically at times, but in large numbers. During some years they hardly appear at all. The average size is less than 15 pounds, but 3-feet-long specimens weighing up to 42 pounds have been caught in American waters.

The strike of a blackfin is hard and sudden and its first run is always a long one. It fights strongly and deep. Since it is generally caught by anglers in pursuit of other fishes, the tackle is most often too heavy or too light. Ordinarily, 6/9 tackle is ample.

The deep-swimming blackfin is caught in greatest numbers on weighted line with strip bait, spoons, or block-tin squids. Once a school has been located, it is possible to catch quite a number of fish on casting tackle with deep-running lures. Just as many other ocean fish do, blackfins will often follow a hooked fish.

In recent years all of the world's tunas—and other big game species as well—have suffered a decline in numbers because of commercial fishing, especially a kind of fishing called long-lining.

Though relations between sport fishermen and their commercial cousins have never been exactly cordial, in recent years they have been strained to the breaking point. No longer satisfied with harvesting the traditional "meat" fish, commercial fishermen from Japan, Scandinavia, and Russia have invaded the world's best sport-fishing areas with superefficient methods that devastate the populations of game fish.

The commercials' methods are as brutal as they are efficient. Instead of nets, which are useless against big game fish, the fishermen string out "long lines"—ropes or metal cables anywhere from 2 to 60 miles in length with baited hooks attached every 12 to 25 feet. The long

An angler plays a blackfin tuna hooked near the lighthouse off Key West.

Blackfin tuna is a superb game fish when taken on a light plug-casting outfit and surface lure.

lines are left in the water for twenty-four hours or more, supported by buoys and equipped with radar beacons to spot their location for the boat. Fish hooked on the long lines fight hopelessly against the miles-long cable until they drown or are mutilated by sharks. Off Baja California enraged Mexican sport fishermen counted more than 300 sailfish on the 2,000 hooks of a single long line. The line was only one of five laid by a Japanese boat that fished the area for fourteen days. Total estimated catch: 21,000 sailfish.

The Japanese can think of nothing better to do with the coarse oily sailfish than grind it up into fish sausage. But marlin is considered a delicacy in meat-short Japan, where it is served fried or raw—garnished with soy sauce and horseradish to make a dish called *sashimi*.

Sport fishermen around the world have been bombarding government agencies with complaints about the commercial long-liners. Now, tired of waiting, some protesters are taking matters into their own hands.

In Jamaica, sport fishermen blasted away at a long-liner's glass floats with rifles. In Acapulco, only the timely arrival of a Mexican coast-guard boat averted a shooting match between charter-boat vigilantes and a Japanese long-liner armed with a machine gun. These instances of violence will never solve the problem, but they do illustrate the depth of it.

7

THE JACKS

The jack crevalle, *Caranx hippos,* is the most abundant member of a large family of fishes. It's also one of the most dogged, rugged, untiring game fishes an angler is ever likely to meet. It frequents the green waters between the Gulf Stream and the Atlantic shoreline and seems to thrive across the entire Gulf of Mexico and down the Central American coast. The crevalle likes tidal bays or channels and has a special preference for hard sand bottoms where inlet currents scour out small crustaceans or harbor schools of smaller fishes. The crevalle also ranges along southern beaches just beyond the breakers in schools varying from 5 or 6 to 30 or 40 individuals.

Whether small or large, the jack is always a school fish, with all individuals in a school of very nearly the same size or age group. A 15-pounder is considered an extremely good jack, though in rare cases, jack crevalle reach 40 or 45 pounds. More than any other fish, jacks have proved a terrible disappointment to fishermen in southern saltwaters. For a moment or two the fisherman thinks he has hooked a record-size snook or channel bass or maybe even an extra-large trout, but then eventually he feels the steady throbbing or pulsating on his line and he realizes he has hooked a jack. After a fight worthy of a 15-pound trout, the angler reels in a jack of only 3 or 4 pounds. Still, every fisherman should catch several large-size jack crevalles simply for the education involved. It's good conversation material and a good muscle builder.

There's little doubt that for strength and endurance no fish in shallow inshore water can measure up to the jack crevalle. Although it's certainly of light-tackle size, it can be strong enough to take much of the sport out of light-tackle fishing. It's just too strong for its own good. And if you should hook a big one on light tackle you have a day-long job on your hands. Or you can cut your own line.

A jack is as obliging as it is tough. It will strike a wide variety of baits, either trolled or cast, furiously and with the suddenness of a sledgehammer blow. It takes surface plugs and deep-running lures equally well and seems to have a preference for yellow. It will take cut baits and live shrimp fished either on or close to the bottom around bridges and pilings. Quite a number of large jacks are hooked, but only a small percentage of them are landed by bridge fishermen.

The best lures of all for jacks, however, are the yellow feather jigs and bucktails in ¼-ounce spinning size, or yellow streamer flies. In either case, it's best to use a fast, whippy retrieve.

Ordinarily it isn't very hard to find jacks. In fact, they'll find you. If you cruise very long in Florida shallow waters, you're almost certain to find a school of them feeding in frenzied, violent fashion on the surface. If you can somehow keep up with them and manage a cast or two into the school, you're almost certain to have a strike no matter which lure you're using, though there are a few exceptions.

Occasionally, jacks will gather for long periods of time in areas where mullet or small menhaden are extremely plentiful. In such a situation, jacks can become selective and pass up many of the natural or artificial baits which are otherwise effective. The best way to tempt such temperamental jacks is to try a small darting or wounded minnow type of surface plug. It should be hurried and skipped across the surface as rapidly and erratically as possible.

The jack family is distributed in warm and temperate waters around the world. Some of the jacks, such as scads and bumpers, are only small forage-size fish while others, like the Pacific yellowtail and the Hawaiian ulua, reach big game proportions. Some jacks travel in deep water while others live on the surface. Some of them are hardly fit to eat—and the crevalle would probably fit in this category—while others, such as the pompano, are among the finest food fishes of all. But no matter how varied their habits and qualities, one characteristic is certainly common to all of them: they belong to the toughest and most powerful clan in or out of the ocean. And the biggest and toughest of them all is the amberjack, *Seriola dumerili*.

The world's record amberjack is a 149-pounder taken in 1964 off Bermuda. But it's possible that amberjacks of more than twice that size exist in the waters of the world. From time to time many offshore fishermen in the Gulf of Mexico hook but are unable to stop or to turn large fish before they vanish with all the line from a reel. In nearly all cases these appear to be amberjacks.

At times bay and inshore fishermen along the Florida coast and the Louisiana coast around Grand Isle encounter schools of baby amberjacks averaging about 18 inches, or slightly more, in length. Finding and catching these fish is pretty much like finding and catching jack crevalle of the same size.

Ordinarily the larger amberjacks stay close to the outer reefs along our shores and in water from 30 to about 140 feet deep. They prefer the larger, more precipitous reefs punctuated with coral caves. Wherever you can find such environment you can usually also find amberjacks. Occasionally charter boats encounter amberjacks around patches of floating weeds in the Gulf Stream while fishing for sailfish.

It isn't a difficult matter to tie into a big amberjack. There are a number of charter boats that specialize in amberjack fishing, especially out of Panama City, Miami, or Key West, cities near good amberjack water.

Two important methods are used to catch the big amberfish. One is to troll parallel to the reefs, with live fish, cut bait, or large feather jigs. Perhaps a better and more productive method, especially if the day is reasonably calm, is to drift-fish along the outer reef while using live grunts or yellowtails for bait. An angler is almost certain to hook several amberjack in a day's time by fishing in this manner. His only problem is to land them.

Suitable tackle should be heavy with at least 20-pound test line because the amberjack's fight is a deep-down, relentless, boring effort. Once a jack gets into a cave or a hole in the reef, there is nothing to do but break the line.

Amberjacks seem to be more plentiful on the offshore reefs during winter and spring and it's thought that they move to deeper waters during late summer and fall.

Although amberjack fishing always verges more toward hard labor than it does to fast, exhilarating sport, it has a great fascination for many fishermen because the species grows to such unusual size. And every time an angler wets a line in amberjack water, he has as good a chance as anyone to hook a new world's record fish.

The amberjack is not a bad food fish, and is extremely delicious when smoked. Oddly enough, its flesh is considered poisonous in Cuba, where it is against the law to buy or sell amberjacks. In the Bahamas, on the other hand, it is very highly regarded as food.

Occasionally taken in Florida waters, the horse-eye jack, *Caranx latus*, is most common in the Bahamas. Its distinguishing characteristic is a large yellow eye and prominent scutes along the lateral line. Unlike the crevalle jack and another cousin, the blue runner, it prefers reefs and offshore waters almost exclusively.

Like the other jacks the horse-eye is a school fish that actively feeds upon small fishes, shrimp, and crustaceans. Its average size is about 2 pounds, but it can attain a length of 3 feet and a weight of more than 25 pounds. A 10- or 15-pounder, however, is a large horse-eye indeed and will give any angler's tackle a good workout. Horse-eyes will take either dead or live bait fished on the bottom and will strike either trolled or cast strip baits, feather jigs, and spoons.

Because of its appearance, the blue runner has often been called a cross between a bluefish and a crevalle jack, but of course there is no foundation for this belief. Actually, the blue runner, *Caranx crysos*, is thinner and more streamlined than most of its cousins.

The blue runner ranges along our east coast northward as far as North Carolina, but it is most abundant along the west coast of Florida northward to Biloxi and Mobile Bay. It's present along the beaches, usually on a flood tide when it comes in close to feed on smaller fishes, shrimp, and other aquatic life both on the surface and on the bottom. At this time it's also within easy reach of the skiff and bridge fisherman.

A school fish, the blue runner strikes hard on small block-tin squid, on shiny spoons, feather jigs, and strip bait. It's a hard fighter for its size, and casting, fly, or spinning tackle is perfect for this species. A blue runner will average about a pound or pound and a half in weight, but on rare occasions it reaches a length of 24 inches and a weight of 6 pounds.

Besides its appeal to light-tackle fishermen as a game fish, the blue runner is also an excellent bait for many of the larger offshore fishes.

Another member of the jack family and one that is often confused with the blue runner is the common runner *Caranx ruber*. It ranges throughout the West Indies, occasionally straying as far north as North Carolina. Unlike the

An amberjack comes aboard a party boat fishing in the Miami, Florida, area.

blue runner, it is a restless, wide-ranging fish of the open waters. Runners are found in great numbers around the Dry Tortugas, where it is taken by trolling with small strips of cut bait, with spoons or feather jigs. They rarely exceed 15 or 16 inches in length, but on light tackle they are extremely strong and active fish.

Although most jacks are completely unsophisticated in their feeding habits, there is one member of the family—the pompano—which is extremely shy and wary. At times it is almost impossible to approach within casting range of a pompano, let alone tempt it to take a lure.

The pompano, *Trachinotus carolinus*, is taken in good numbers along both coasts of Florida, but its exact range elsewhere hasn't been too clearly defined. A number of them are taken around Cuba and some of the other Caribbean islands, but beyond that nothing much is known.

Most Florida pompano are taken in the region from Miami northward to Jacksonville by surf-casting anglers using a unique cross-bait-trials technique. The bait is usually a small, inch-long crustacean called a sand flea. The surf-caster can easily find and dig a supply of these flea-shaped baits as they are left behind in the surf by each receding wave. The only problem is catching them before they burrow into the wet sand. If sand fleas are unavailable, shrimp or chunks of clam will do almost as well.

Any of the standard kinds of surf tackle or spinning surf tackle are used, plus a pyramid sinker and a No. 1 hook with a nylon leader.

The object of this cross-bait-trials technique is to make one cast at an angle to the beach and then retrieve the bait slowly so that the sinker leaves a trail across the sandy bottom. That completed, the fisherman walks farther down the beach and makes another cast designed to cross the trail made by his first retrieve. He then retrieves slowly to make another sinker trail which intersects and crosses the first one.

The final step is to cast the bait to the junction of the two sinker trails, and then wait for the pompano to act. The theory is that once a pompano, with its keen sense of smell, discovers one of the sinker trails it will follow it right to the sand flea bait. Though it does sound a bit ridiculous, I understand that it works very well. At least Florida's east coast fishermen catch plenty of pompano this way.

Another pompano technique used by both bridge and boat fishermen is jigging. Bridge fishermen simply lower a small ⅛-ounce, white or yellow feather jig to the bottom and then jiggle it up and down regularly. No retrieve is made unless an angler intends to move to another spot.

Using spinning gear, which is the most effective of all for pompano, boat fishermen depend on a slightly different technique. The idea is to make a cast, allow the jig to reach the bottom,

and then retrieve it ever so slowly, by raising the rod tip and reeling fast enough to retrieve slack as the rod tip is lowered again.

Pompano are known to be year-round residents of southern Florida waters but they are easiest to catch during migrations north along the coast. The migration along the east coast usually begins in February or March. Along the west coast it takes place a little later. Pompano arrive in Louisiana and Texas waters in April or May or sometimes as late as June.

These splendid food fishes are seldom taken in water more than 10 feet deep and when they are actively feeding they are seldom farther than 100 yards from shore. During calm weather they tend to remain in deeper waters—or at least not too many of them are taken at that time. But when the surf is fairly heavy, pompano often move right in among the breakers to catch sand fleas and coquinas. Also look for pompano just inside inlets and passes on an incoming tide and just outside the same areas on an outgoing tide.

A 2-pound pompano is a good one, though occasionally they reach 4 or 5 pounds and a length of 20 inches. Best known as a table fish, a pompano, once hooked, is nonetheless extremely game. The meat is rich and oily, with an incomparable flavor when fresh.

In certain isolated gullies and depressions in the reefs along Florida's east coast, fishermen frequently find another extremely game member of the jack family. It's the African pompano, *Hynnis cubensis*. For the fisherman or charterboat captain lucky enough to find one of these depressions, there is much excellent fishing in

Jacks make up a good part of the catch of most fishing fleets operating in Florida waters.

store because these Africans run in small schools and they will strike with abandon, one after another.

The African is a typical tough member of the jack family. It strikes the same kinds of baits and fights the same kind of dogged, throbbing battle. Fairly stout tackle should be used when fishing over a pompano hole because these fish attain a length of almost 36 inches and a weight of about 40 pounds, though the average is between 10 and 15 pounds.

The first signs of the dorsal and anal fins on the smaller Africans evolve into delicate filaments that stream out behind them. These filaments are almost always lacking in the larger fish, perhaps because eventually they are worn off against rocks and coral. The African pompano is edible, but the flavor of its flesh isn't nearly as delicious as that of the common pompano.

Perhaps the most beautiful member of the jack family is the rainbow runner, *Elagatis bipinnulatus*, also called the Spanish jack or Pacific jack. An elongated fish marked with bright blue and yellow stripes that fade quickly after the fish is landed, the rainbow runner is most frequently taken in the open-ocean currents or on the extreme outside edges of reefs by fishermen trolling for other species. Its average size is only a few pounds, but it does reach a length of 36 inches and a weight of more than 10 pounds.

I've caught many rainbow runners weighing up to 12 or 13 pounds on the open Pacific off Quepos, Costa Rica. They were terrific fighters and a few of them made exciting jumps. These fish were taken on everything from yellow feather jigs to streamer flies and bass popping bugs. Elsewhere they've been known to strike extremely large cut strips of bait or large metal spoons. Very little is known about the life history or migratory wanderings of the rainbow runner, despite its potential as a game fish.

8

THE DEEP FISH:

Snappers and Groupers

SNAPPERS

The mangrove snapper is a fine fish, widely distributed along both Florida coasts, on many offshore reefs, and inside waters around mangrove shores throughout the Caribbean. The mangrove is probably the gamest member of the large global family of snappers. It's almost as strong as any jack of equal size and is a wary fish besides. Ichthyologists assure us that fish behave or react by instinct or by impulse alone. But many snappers seem to have the ability to reason, especially in heavily fished waters.

Fish for snappers in wilderness waters such as the numerous tidal rivers of Andros Island, Bahamas, or at night, and the snappers may actually strike with abandon. But try them around the docks which they frequent in great numbers in busy Florida fishing areas and all but the smallest specimens ignore everything, live or artificial, containing a hook.

Mangrove snappers seem to thrive in numerous environments, over deep and shallow reefs, in the surf, in bays and lagoons, in creeks and rivers, and occasionally they will even ascend into fairly fresh water. Any mangrove snapper prefers cover and, as the name suggests, will often be found under mangrove roots along deep mangrove shorelines. Channel markers, bridges, piers, and docks are also favorite hiding places.

The average mangrove snapper taken on hook and line in Florida waters will weigh only a pound or less, but the species becomes more wary and more wise with each ounce of weight it gains. A 5-pound snapper is an extremely good one and 10-pounders are quite rare in Florida. Twenty-five to 30 pounds is about the maximum for the species.

Where fishing pressure is fairly light, the mangrove will strike a variety of surface plugs as well as deep-running plugs, trolled feathers,

M/Sgt George M. Shade of Eglin Air Force Base, Florida, poses with a 34-pound red snapper taken near Destin.

and strips of natural bait. It will also take a yellow or red streamer fly when it is cast in close to mangrove banks.

One particularly effective streamer-fly pattern has a heavy lead-wrapped body that permits it to sink quickly before being retrieved. Mangroves will also take almost anything in the line of natural bait, but they seem to prefer shrimp above all other items.

Although mangroves remain meticulously close to cover or to shade during daylight hours, they do begin to cruise out into the open as soon as night falls. During the day an angler should keep his cast close to any of the likely places mentioned before, casting beyond a reef and drawing his lure or bait over the top of it. An angler fishing mangrove shorelines should deliver the lure or bait as far back underneath the overhanging branches as possible.

The mangrove snappers found around piers and docks are very wise. They will feed upon anything thrown overboard, except a morsel with a hook in it. Many a first-time visitor to Florida has had the experience of dropping bits of fish to the snappers, including one that has a

completely hidden hook. Invariably the snappers will eat all but that one morsel.

Although the mangrove is quite game, no special tackle is needed to catch it. Ordinary casting, spinning, or fly-casting tackle are quite adequate for the task. When fishing especially for snappers, I use 8- or 10-pound line and a wire leader about 15 inches long. No matter whether the bait is natural or artificial, it's necessary to strike immediately and try to horse the fish away from protective cover. A substantial percentage of large snappers hooked escape by dodging back into a coral formation or into the mangrove roots. Then there is nothing left to do but break the line.

Except around piers and docks, chumming for mangrove snappers can be extremely effective. The idea is to toss bits of mullet, whole hog-mouthed fry, or shrimp chum into the water, a small amount at a time, until the snappers arrive to eat the free handout.

Ordinarily, snapper waters are clear enough so that you can see the fish approach and begin to feed. As more and more fish appear, increase the amount of chum until they begin to compete recklessly among themselves for the food. Then without interrupting the chumming, toss in one piece with a hook attached.

It's a good idea to use monofilament line with a small hook and without a sinker. Make the snapper forget his natural caution by making the bait look as much like the free-floating pieces of chum as possible.

Like amberjacks and a few other species, mangrove snappers have what is called a "feeding line." When not aroused, a snapper may seem completely pale in color. But a black or dark diagonal line running across the face and through the eyes begins to develop as soon as the mangrove snapper starts to feed. And the more actively it feeds (as on chum tossed overboard), the longer and darker the feeding line becomes.

Chumming can be a nuisance, however, and often it requires large amounts of bait. Fortunately, there's another method that is sometimes quite effective in taking large snappers. This also requires a good supply of either dead or live mullet.

Using a hook as large as 4/0, cast out a mullet and let it settle into likely snapper water. Ordinarily you will feel the inevitable biting and nibbling of small snappers. But ignore these. Do not strike. If the nibbles stop, reel in your line and put on a fresh bait. Then cast it again. Eventually a larger snapper than the nibblers will come along, chase the small snappers away, and take your bait. The theory here is that a large snapper can't stand by indefinitely while smaller fish enjoy a free meal.

Snappers will take feather and bucktail jigs on occasion, especially at night. But it has been said that any snapper, once it reaches a foot in length, can tell every artificial lure by its trade name, catalog number, size, and retail price. Perhaps that's the reason they seem to prefer the most bedraggled, chewed-up jigs imaginable.

Besides the mangrove, fishermen frequently meet four other members of the snapper family; the red, mutton, schoolmaster, and lane snappers. The mutton snapper is caught along both Florida coasts, but it is much more numerous along the east side. It's an extremely beautiful fish that undergoes chameleonlike changes of color, ranging from pale pink to lemon yellow and olive green. It's caught offshore, most often on hard or rocky bottoms where it mingles with groupers and other common bottom fish.

The average mutton snapper may only weigh 2 pounds, but occasionally it runs as long as 2 feet and as heavy as 25 pounds. Like all the other snappers, its flesh is white, firm, and among the best available in the sea. Excellent when cooked in almost any fashion, it is especially good in chowder.

Occasionally the schoolmaster snapper is caught inshore around the Florida Keys, but more often is around the Keys' outer reefs. It reaches its greatest abundance in the Bahamas.

Toothed like the mangrove snapper and even more wary about striking, it will sometimes take streamer flies, though it much prefers live shrimp or cut bait. Grayish in color with lemon fins, it strikes hard and fights stubbornly in the manner of its cousin. The schoolmaster will only average a pound or so in weight. Ordinarily those found on the reef will run larger than those found inshore around bridges and piers. The top recorded weight in Florida waters is 8 pounds.

The brilliantly colored lane snapper is seldom found farther north than Big Pine Key in Florida waters. It's quite numerous in the Dry Tortugas and reaches its greatest abundance in Cuban waters and along the Yucatán coast of the Gulf of Mexico. The lane is a school fish with a preference for sandy bottoms where tidal currents are fairly strong. It also loiters in deep cuts or channels close to mangroves.

In the Marquesas Keys—west of Key West—and in the Dry Tortugas, large schools of small lanes are known to cruise about in sheltered waters. These cruisers usually average less than a pound. A 2-pounder is a large lane snapper and probably the maximum weight is about 4 pounds.

Lanes will strike a number of different artificial lures, including surface plugs, bass bugs, and small, deep-running spoons. They will strike streamer flies and seem unable to resist either a live or a dead shrimp. Light fly tackle is perfect for these fish because of their small size and their willingness to take small lures. Many fishermen consider it the most delicious of all table fishes.

Red snappers are probably the most abundant of all snappers. They're also among the most stupid, and nothing more than a stout handline and a supply of meat is necessary to catch them, once a school or a bank of red snappers has been located. These snapper concentrations or banks are scattered all through the Gulf of Mexico and snapper smacks with large crews aboard fish for them almost the year round in extremely deep offshore waters. In an average year they land about 4 million pounds of this delicious fish. The average size will be about 5 pounds, but reds have been known to reach 40 and 45 pounds.

Along the east coast of Florida from Fort Pierce northward to the St. Marys River, red snappers are also found on offshore banks, but farther south along the Florida east coast the species is replaced on the reef by mutton snappers. Although a handline is the most handy and effective way to catch snappers, it is possible to use fairly heavy boat tackle, with a heavy sinker to reach the bottom quickly. Red snappers will strike at cut bait, shrimp, fish entrails, or almost anything of this sort.

The flesh of the red snapper is white, firm, delicate, and world-famous. It can be cooked in any manner, but it is best when poached or baked and served with a tart cream sauce.

Bottom fishermen in the Caribbean and the extreme southern Florida Keys encounter still another snapper, the dog snapper, which may weigh more than 100 pounds. It's found in company with groupers in deep water along outer reefs.

GROUPERS

Groupers of one species or another are found from North Carolina and California southward to South America. They provide an incalculable amount of sport and high quality food for bottom fishermen. Some groupers such as the Warsaw run to prodigious size, reaching several hundred pounds, while others are quite small. But the most common in South Atlantic and Caribbean waters is the red grouper.

Brown or brownish rather than red in body color, this heavy-bodied grouper is named for the bright orange-red coloration of the inside of its mouth. It's plentiful around most Florida inshore and offshore reefs and sometimes on hard or rocky bottoms in between. Although it will only average about a pound in sheltered water, it may average 5 pounds or more around offshore reefs. The maximum weight of a red grouper is about 40 or 45 pounds, at which weight it will be about 3 feet long.

Reef fishermen can hardly help but catch groupers since this pliant fish will take cut bait thumped along the bottom and will strike at feathers or other lures trolled over rock patches or coral heads. Red groupers feed on small fishes, shrimp, crayfish, crabs, in fact on anything. The species isn't exactly notable for its lively fighting qualities, but it is extremely strong and on light or medium tackle becomes quite a sturdy opponent.

I have taken red groupers, including some good ones up to 12 and 15 pounds, while casting with jigs along mangrove shorelines. It is possible to land only a small percentage of the big reds hooked in this manner because they immediately dive back into the protective cover of the mangrove roots.

Red groupers are extremely tasty, and should be skinned and filleted before cooking. The meat is excellent for chowder.

The Nassau grouper is most common in southern Florida waters, particularly in the Keys. It's taken only infrequently north of Tampa and Fort Pierce, and in those areas, only on the deepest offshore reefs, where it is found

A grouper taken spinning along the steep shoreline of southern Baja California, Mexico.

schooling up with red and mutton snappers. As in all groupers, the mouth is extremely large and contains several sharp caninelike teeth. The Nassau contains small scales set tightly in a tough skin. In deep offshore waters it will average about 5 or 10 pounds, though it can attain a maximum length of about 3 feet and weight of about 40 pounds.

In deep places, the Nassau can easily be chummed up close to the boat and held there with pieces of chopped chum. Although strictly a bottom fish, it will occasionally rise and become hooked on trolled spoons or large jigs. Most Nassau groupers are caught on trolled whole fish or on chunks of cut bait.

The black grouper is found all around Florida, at many points along both coasts. On the west coast it is the most abundant fish, except perhaps for the mullet. Though averaging less than 5 pounds in weight, black groupers in the 10- to 50-pound range are fairly common and 60-pounders are not unheard of.

Along Florida's west coast, the black grouper never ventures very far from reefs, hard bottoms, or rocky bank areas. Here the best bait is a live shiner, a live yellowtail, or a live grunt. It's wise to use stiff rods and fairly heavy tackle because the black grouper has a nasty habit of boring deep into underwater caves as soon as it is hooked.

On the east coast and particularly along the Keys, the black grouper is caught by trolling with strip baits, spoons, or feather jigs. After a very hard, sudden strike, it immediately bores straight down to find protection in a reef or rock pile. Trolling tackle should include at least 30-pound test line and maybe more, because once the black gets into a hole it's difficult to pry it loose. Sometimes drift fishing with small live fish, crabs, crayfish, or shrimp is effective, but extremely heavy tackle must be used to horse the fish upward immediately after the strike.

The yellow grouper is one of the smallest and most beautiful members of the family. It exists in an almost endless number of color phases which makes it extremely difficult to distinguish from other groupers, from rock hind, and even from other rockfish. The yellow grouper seldom wanders far from offshore reefs and is most abundant in the Bahamas, where it is caught by still-fishing or by trolling.

Another offshore reef resident frequently caught by bottom fishermen is the multicolored and spotted rock hind. Its distinctive red spots never change, even though the rest of the body frequently changes from gray to green or olive and brown. The average size of the rock hind is less than 2 pounds, and it is doubtful that the fish ever exceeds 8 pounds in weight. It's most abundant in the Florida Keys.

From the standpoint of size, one of the most impressive fishes in our warm saltwaters and the Gulf of Mexico is the spotted jewfish. A resident of rocky offshore reefs, tideways, and deep holes, the jewfish also likes the shelter of pilings, bridge abutments, underwater caves, and offshore drilling rigs. Occasionally it is found under the roots of mangroves in tidal channels in the Florida Keys area and in many places along the Florida, Alabama, Mississippi, and Louisiana Gulf coast. Other hotspots are the Florida Ten Thousand Island and Panama City areas.

Though jewfish average from 15 to about 25 pounds, 700-pound specimens have been taken on cut bait and shrimp fished right on the bottom. Although the jewfish would seem to be slow and sluggish, it strikes readily at feather jigs and strip baits trolled near the surface, over either inshore or offshore reefs. The strike of a large jewfish is sudden, and it feels as if the bait has become hung on the bottom.

Among the best live baits for jewfish are grunts, yellowtails, catfish, and crayfish. It goes without saying that extremely heavy tackle is necessary to raise these giants from the bottom. Fishermen who make jewfishing a specialty use ¼-inch manila rope with a heavy chain leader and hand-forged hooks. A good spot to tie into a jewfish is on the outer east end of a rocky pier or jetty.

There are a number of other fishes which might be included in the deep and delicious category. Some of the more common species are: the grunts, of which there are fourteen species in Florida waters; the southern and grass porgies, the margate fish, which is sometimes called pompom; the gaff-topsail catfish, the porkfish, hogfish, and squirrelfish. All of these are extremely good to eat and on light tackle are great fun to catch.

9

STRIPED BASS

The striped bass is an abundant species which hooks anglers in more ways than one. Striper fishermen trudge miles and miles along sandy shorelines to reach a bit of booming surf, just on mere rumor that striped bass have gathered there. It also causes them to creep and crawl over barnacle-encrusted rocks without regard for life or limb. Many will fish day and night until fatigue alone causes them to doze for an hour or so before returning to the beaches. It causes the faithful to mire and slide on muddy riverbanks or precarious jetties and to spend long hours on the slippery deck of a boat tossed by high seas.

It is easy to pinpoint the reasons for a striper's tremendous appeal to fishermen. There are other fish which grow bigger and still others which fight harder. A few are more handsome, and some are more difficult to catch. A very, very few are better on the table, but not many species rate so high in all these categories. A striped bass is a great game fish which has almost everything.

You can take stripers from the beach or by trolling for them offshore. You can catch them in protected tidal waters and inlets, and on all types of lures from tiny flies to thick hunks of crab. If the striper has one outstanding characteristic, it's the vast number of ways you can fish for it and the great variety of tackle you can use.

Say you're a heavy-tackle fisherman trolling offshore. Usually a big spoon or plug will tie you into a big fish. If you like light tackle—if you are a fly-caster or spinning fan—the inshore bays, channels, and estuaries of many coastal rivers will give you all the action you need. In addition, it's even possible to still-fish for stripers from an anchored boat, from a beach or pier, using anything for bait from shedder crabs, squid, and eels to sandworms, shrimp, or clams. The striper will eat anything it can swallow.

But no method of catching stripers packs all the high adventure and excitement of casting for them in the wild, wind-whipped surf. This can mean fishing with natural baits or with such counterfeits as metal squid, wobbling spoons, eel-skin jigs, or an assortment of plugs too numerous to list. It's true enough that surf-casting for stripers can be a heartbreaking proposition because it's so uncertain. The stripers have little regard for time and tides and a fisherman's convictions. Still, one of the greatest thrills which

*Dick Kotis manages a
36-pound striper, spinning
in the surf, with a Scudder
surface plug.*

*Jack and Frank Woolner
with a fine catch of striped
bass and beach buggies at
Cape Cod.*

saltwater angling has to offer is the hooking, playing, and landing of a large striped bass while chest-deep in surf.

As long ago as colonial times the striper was held in highest esteem. In 1634, William Wood set a rough pattern for modern outdoor scribes when he wrote: "The basse is one of the best fishes in the countrye and although men are soon wearied with other fish yet they are never with the basse. It is a delicate, fine, fat, fast fish having a bone in its head which contains a saucer full of marrow, sweet and good, pleasant to the pallat and wholesome to the stomach."

But it wasn't until after the Civil War that sport-fishing for stripers, or for any other species, became popular on our East coast. During the 1870s a number of now-famous fishing clubs were organized. Among these were the Cuttyhunk Club, the Squibnocket, Pasque Island, West Island, and Cohasset Narrows clubs. Only the Cuttyhunk clubhouse remains today, but for several generations the fisher-members and their guests lived high, practiced the fine art of chumming, and managed to catch many a fine striped bass on tackle far cruder than that used by striper fishermen today.

One peculiar but fascinating feature of these bass clubs was that most contained a large roost of pigeons, used not for shooting (a favorite sport of the time) but rather for communication with the mainland. In this way, club members, most of whom were New York businessmen, could conduct business while enjoying the fishing at the club.

But unaccountably, striped bass almost vanished from the New England coast during the early 1900s and these colorful old clubs gradually disintegrated. And of course the fishermen disappeared along with their clubhouses.

Even though striped bass or rockfish, *Roccus saxatilis*, have been taken since colonial times, very little is known about their habits and their life history. After the stripers reappeared in great numbers along the Atlantic coast in 1936, fisheries biologists at federal, state, and local levels were encouraged to find out something about them, but the task was far from easy. For one thing, the sea is a vast void in which a fish can hide, and establishing valid scientific data in such circumstances is complicated at best. Furthermore, government officials were reluctant to provide funds even for a matter so economically

and aesthetically important as the striped bass fishery on our East coast.

One of the most dramatic incidents in the history of American fish management involved the striped bass, and it occurred as long ago as 1879. Details are somewhat sketchy today, but it is known that a number of small striped bass were seined from the Navesink River in New Jersey and transported across the continent to San Francisco Bay. Only 435 fish survived the transcontinental trip. Twenty years later the Pacific commercial catch of stripers alone reached 1,234,000 pounds. In 1915, some 1,785,000 pounds were marketed from waters where stripers had never existed before!

Such an interocean transfer seems almost impossible to modern biologists, who now have the equipment to do such a thing easily. But in 1879 there were no aerated tank cars and so the fish were transported in anything available. Water in milk cans and makeshift aquariums had to be changed frequently and manually. It was also agitated by hand to keep the fish alive. And when the shipment passed the Mississippi, a few of the stripers were tossed in that river, according to an old account, "just for luck."

There isn't any way to estimate the number of stripers in Pacific coast waters today because commercial netting has been forbidden since 1935, and the striper has been considered a game species ever since. But the original planting has extended over a major part of the West coast from San Diego northward as far as the Columbia River in Washington. Today's stripers are even caught in fringe waters of the Gulf of Mexico, but here their activity seems to be confined entirely to fresh or brackish water.

Alabama sportsmen find them in good numbers in the Coosa and Tallapoosa rivers, sometimes 100 miles from the Gulf itself. This river population, and similar ones in Louisiana and Mississippi, are perhaps the result of numerous indiscriminate plantings of small stripers made during the late 1800s.

A striper's normal natural range is on the Atlantic seaboard from northern Florida northward to the Gulf of St. Lawrence. Between these two points, the fish can be found in many different environments, from the muddy waters of the Santee-Cooper drainages in South Carolina to the cold, noisy surf on some Maine beaches. Part of the population of striped bass in this normal range migrates over great distances; other stripers seem to migrate very little. And those that do migrate, do so in patterns which biologists still are unable to describe with any accuracy. Here are some examples of the striper's contrasting behavior. In the St. Johns River of Florida lives a population of sedentary stripers that doesn't seem to travel at all. In the St. Lawrence River the bass seem to make short journeys up- and downstream, but rarely leave the river. There are similar native schools in Nova Scotia and New Brunswick.

Recent studies have revealed that young fish spawned in the Hudson River rarely travel farther than Long Island Sound. In Chesapeake Bay, which is the largest hatching area for stripers, there are "groups" of fish which appear to remain or to circulate in the bay area throughout the year. But strangest of all the nonmigratory stripers are those which live in the Santee-Cooper drainage area of South Carolina. Stripers have always lived in these rivers, but until recently—after two giant dams were built to form Lakes Moultrie and Marion—they were able to return each year to saltwater. Now that the stripers are landlocked, they are spawning successfully and reproducing in vast numbers in an entirely freshwater environment.

The most mysterious and perhaps the biggest striped bass of all are those which migrate long distances up and down the coast. No one has been able accurately to predict their movements. What marine biologists suspect, though, is that schools swimming out from Chesapeake Bay, Delaware Bay, and from the Virginia Capes region join together with other passing, northbound schools. Probably they spend the summer in New England or even as far north as the Maritime Provinces only to return south again as autumn comes.

There are many excellent examples of the striper's unpredictability, but one of the best concerns the vast concentration that appeared during some years off Old Man's Rip near Nantucket Island, Massachusetts. Few of these fish were ever smaller than 20 pounds and most were quite a bit larger. These fish seemed to arrive in springtime and remained in the area until late November. But some years few if any stripers arrived at all and for no apparent reason.

Generally, it can be said that stripers follow the sun. They go northward as water temperatures increase and then they return south again as water temperatures fall. Most fishermen, however, do not care where stripers come from. They are far more interested in where to find them on the days they spend fishing.

Because stripers can be taken in so many varied situations, a fisherman must choose from a bewildering array of tackle. Of course everything depends upon the type of fishing he plans to do. For surf-fishing, a good rod should have a 30-inch butt and a 7-foot tip of from 10 to 16 ounces. The reel should be able to hold 200 yards of from 20- to 30-pound test line. It can be either a large, saltwater spinning reel or a casting reel with a star drag.

For boat fishing, use a regular boat rod with an 18-inch butt, or 5- to 6-foot tip of from 5 to 10 ounces, a reel which can hold 150 to 200 yards of 20- to 30-pound test line, 5/0 to 7/0 hooks on 24-inch wire or heavy nylon leaders. In addition, an angler should have a supply of 1- to 6-ounce sinkers, plus any of a wide variety of baits, including sandworms, bloodworms, softshell crabs, squid, menhaden, or plugs.

Since these fish seem to enjoy a turbulent environment—white water smashing against solid ground—a good spot to look for them is along rocky cliffs, breakwaters, or at any similar places where the wave action is violent. Here a light-tackle fan can have plenty of action spinning or fly-casting from shore. The ideal spinning outfit includes a rod from 6 to 8 feet long, a reel that can hold about 200 yards of 10- or 12-pound monofilament, and for artificial lures, a supply of small feathers, plugs, eel skins, and spinners. The spinners can be used with worms and other live bait. For live bait, a 2/0 to 6/0 hook is just about right. Of course, this same spinning tackle can also be used for trolling or casting from a boat.

It's fortunate for fishermen that striped bass will attack or eat anything that swims, creeps, or crawls in saltwater. While artificial lures can incite a bass into striking either through anger or through curiosity, the success of natural bait depends upon one thing—a striper's hunger. If the striper happens to be feeding, some natural live bait will probably work out best of all. If it is not actively feeding it's entirely possible that it will most often strike an artificial lure. Of course, there are times when it doesn't make any difference which is presented because everything from sooty terns to cigarette lighters have been found in their stomachs.

Sometimes successful striper fishing depends very much on an efficient intelligence system as well as knowing the habits of the fish and how to use your tackle. In such hard-fished areas as Montauk, Narragansett, Cape Cod, and elsewhere along the Atlantic seaboard, it's possible to keep track consistently of striped bass arrivals. Although many serious striper fishermen try to maintain strict secrecy when they find schooling fish or when they know a run has arrived, this information is bound to leak out. It's too hard to conceal the concentrations of fishermen and beach buggies along any popular area of coastline. It's also possible to keep track of striper movements and migrations by calling bait and tackle dealers on the spot or by carefully watching the outdoor columns in the local newspapers.

There aren't really any shortcuts to successful fishing, especially in the surf, except perhaps to imitate exactly the technique of an expert striper fisherman and/or to study the beach at an extreme low tide. At this time an ideal observation point is from the top of a car or beach buggy, or high on a sand dune. Then while the sea is at its lowest ebb and the ripping currents are still, it's possible to examine the conformation of the bottom in order to determine the probable haunts of feeding stripers. It's good to note any sudden drop-offs, holes, offshore bars, gullies, or cuts. It's also well to make a mental note (or even to draw a simple map) of eelgrass beds and mussel-studded bottoms. Also keep in mind any mud flats (where sea worms are likely to be plentiful) and all points where tide rips will develop as soon as the tide begins to flood again.

Striped bass are indeed partial to so-called "live" water. They are powerful, robust, and quite at home in swirling ocean currents or in a breaking surf. Perhaps it's because these turbulent areas hold masses of smaller fish in a kind of suspension. Although there are exceptions to the rule, the smaller stripers generally come closer inshore to forage. Either the larger bass wait until night falls, or they approach the shore via gullies or cuts, which an angler is fortunate to have located before the flood tide begins.

Pockets of white water or any obvious depressions in the surf line are apt to hold the largest bass of all. It's worth repeating that stripers do not like still water and it's a clever fisherman who looks for such turbulent areas as those scoured by strong currents, or choppy because of the most violent tide rips.

There are a number of unmistakable signs that striped bass are feeding in a given vicinity. Some old-time surf-casters insist that they can locate feeding bass by smelling them. Maybe they can. Anyway, it's believed that the fresh and pleasant scent that is given off when a striper is first landed is the same odor that can be distinguished simply by walking along a beach.

On other occasions, feeding bass are betrayed by telltale bulges on the surface and the sudden skittering of small baitfishes. The appearance of a slick in otherwise choppy waters is also worthy of investigation, and no fisherman ever fails to keep an eye on schools of menhaden as they drift along, even though apparently unmolested by larger fish.

The most dramatic evidence of feeding bass is the sudden gathering of such seabirds as terns and gulls. Occasionally, it's possible to find them circling and diving like interceptors locked in combat. And chances are that, underneath them, squid are squirting out of the water or mackerel are scattering nervously all about. Somewhere beneath all this activity is a school of striped bass.

Of course, birds gather when other fishes besides stripers are attacking the baitfish but few other species feed so noisily. Big bass splash and boil on the surface, sometimes swapping ends and slapping the water with strong, broad tails. Usually it's possible to see clearly the barred flanks of the feeding fish, but waste no time watching them. Get to the spot as quickly as you can and cast right into the center of the feeding. In such a situation, the odds are greatly in favor of the angler no matter what lure he casts.

There are about as many opinions on the best time of day or night to go striper fishing as there are striper fishermen, but the truth is that it's a twenty-four-hour proposition and the bass are likely to arrive on the scene at any time. At certain seasons, especially in spring and fall, daylight casting tends to be more productive than it is in midsummer. Along most of the Atlantic

Live-in beach buggies such as this one have four-wheel drive and convenient rod racks mounted on the outside.

seaboard it doesn't pay to spend much time fishing at midday during most of July and throughout August. Quite a number of veteran surf-casters regard a flood tide, no matter what the month, either very early in the morning or at dusk, as the ideal period.

Not too many striper fishermen will agree on which bait is consistently the best. Generally, block-tin squid, bullhead jigs, and small plugs work best for fish in the 2- to 10-pound class (at least according to a consensus of Cape Cod fishermen). But where the stripers are running larger than 10 pounds, much larger squid and the largest size in surf plugs or large rigged eels or eel skins are usually preferred.

When casting at night many anglers use large jointed plugs that operate just on or under the surface. Some prefer the noisy poppers, darters, and splashing-type plugs.

One of the greatest striped bass killers of all, for day or night along the Atlantic seaboard, is an aromatic but hard-to-cast combination of artificial and natural baits called the rigged eel or eel skin. There are all sorts of ways to prepare this bait, but the most common is to rig an eel skin onto a lead-head jig or some other casting weight. Either way, it should be retrieved slowly along the bottom. The best way to give an exciting and undulating motion to the eel skin is simply to raise and lower the rod tip during the retrieve. The rig actually should be made to bounce and crawl along the bottom.

One variation of the eel bait is simplicity itself: String a length of leader completely through the eel, attaching 2, 3, or 4 hooks at intervals, and then wrap a strip of lead around the eel's head to make it sink and to give it casting weight. An eel rigged in this way should be retrieved in the same manner as the eel skin and jig combination.

Landing a good striper in a heavy surf is not an easy or uncomplicated matter. Beginners too often make the mistake of trying to drag a fish through the inshore breakers. This usually results in a broken line, a snapped leader, or straightened hooks.

It's always important to let the surf work for you instead of against you. Pump the bass shoreward on each crest of a wave but allow it to slide back with the undertow. Then if your timing is correct you will find that it's possible to keep the fish coming on a wave that will eventually leave it high and dry on the beach. Now get there as fast as possible, grab the leader and pull the fish to a safe location far back from the water's edge. But never, absolutely never, try to remove the hook from a striper while it is still alive and kicking. Use a beer bottle, billy, or piece of driftwood to whack it on the head. Trying to remove a plug from a flopping striper too often results in surgery to remove the hooks from the fisherman's hand.

But surf-fishing involves dangers other than removing the hook from a big striper bass. If you have ever watched sandpipers, those tiny shorebirds that scamper lightly along the edges of every beach, you may have noticed that even these tiny birds occasionally are caught unawares by towering, incoming breakers. Since no surf-caster on earth is as agile as a sandpiper, it's evident that everyone who fishes from the surf is likely to get ducked someday. It's not always a pleasant experience.

No matter how practiced they are, surf-casters seem unable to resist the desire to wade in the surf and, once wading, they can't resist wading too deep. And no wonder, because often the best fishing lies near the outer extremity of the breaking surf. But great care must be taken not to be knocked down by the waves.

Never turn your back to an incoming wave and never let a wave catch you in the stomach. Keep a constant eye on incoming waves and meet them sideways with the legs braced to prevent being swept off your feet.

If you are knocked down by a wave, remember that the water tends to lift your feet and submerge your head. And this is true despite the fact that you may be wearing heavy waders, because the upper part of the body is heavier than the legs. But above all, in such an event, stay calm, paddle hard with your hands until you are able to regain your feet.

It isn't wise to wear hip boots because, no matter how cautious the angler, the waves will eventually reach over the tops and, except in the middle of the summer when the water is fairly warm, wet feet and legs in the Atlantic will soon make any fisherman uncomfortable. The best outfit for surf-fishing is a good pair of rubber waders and a waterproof jacket with a belt that will tighten about the waist and hold both waders and jacket snugly. Waders with felt soles are probably best for slippery rocks since the felt affords a better grip than rubber. But better even than felt is a pair of cleats, such as ice fishermen use, worn on the outside of the wader shoe.

Besides his terminal tackle, a surfer should always carry a sharp knife, pliers, headlight for fishing early or late in the day or at night, sunglasses, chapstick, creepers for movement over slippery rock, a gaff, a surf belt, a sand spike, and a billy. Sometimes a Coleman gasoline lantern is mighty valuable too.

Surf-casting is far more thrilling and a far more adventuresome method to catch striped bass than fishing from a boat. But still it probably isn't as effective in most places along the Atlantic seaboard. The boat fisherman, for instance, is not limited by how far he can cast. When a boat fisherman finds a school of fish, he can stay right with it casting into the school and following it as it moves along. When no striped bass are in evidence, he can keep exploring and probing by bottom-fishing, drifting, or trolling. And nowadays with the outboard motor so handy and so portable, trolling for striped bass in a variety of situations is a very easy matter.

Trolling is especially effective. An experienced charter-boat captain or guide needs only to troll across known gravel bars, past tide rips, and wherever the current clashes with underwater boulders, rocks, old wrecks, and piers. Shellfish beds are also extremely good striper grounds. In the Chesapeake Bay area, particularly, striper captains know all these locations as intimately as they know the backs of their hands. The best trolling lures are spoons, bullhead-type feathers,

A typical small boat rigged for fishing striped bass beyond the surf.

nylon and bucktail jigs perhaps with a strip of pork rind added. But no matter what tackle or what technique he decides to use, a trophy-hunting striper fisherman's best bet for a really big fish is in the vicinity of Cape Cod or such Massachusetts islands as Cuttyhunk, Martha's Vineyard, and Nantucket. The Narragansett, Charlestown, and Newport Beach sections of Rhode Island, Montauk Point area on Long Island, and the vicinity of Sandy Hook, New Jersey, are also good spots for stripers.

During midwinter a vast concentration of large bass, many over 50 pounds, always gather in the area of Cape Hatteras, North Carolina, but fishing conditions here are such that neither surf-casters nor trollers have had very much luck with them. There is always the ugly combination of rough seas, extremely cold, damp weather, a multitude of weeds in the water, and a disinclination of the fish to strike.

Here follows a state-by-state schedule of striped bass movements along the Atlantic seaboard:

In Massachusetts the high season usually lasts from early May to late November, sometimes later when weather conditions permit. The largest stripers, called "bulls" even though they invariably are female, arrive in the largest numbers about July 1 on the mainland coast and about June 1 off Cuttyhunk and Martha's Vineyard. The cream of Massachusetts fishing usually occurs from mid to late fall in the offshore tide rips and reefs near Cuttyhunk and Martha's Vineyard.

The season for casting and trolling for school fish around Cape Cod begins on May 1 and lasts until it is too cold or too uncomfortable to go out any longer. Ordinarily the first catches are made around Buzzards Bay and Falmouth. However, the best fishing doesn't begin until June or the first part of July and then it slacks off during midsummer only to improve again by mid-September.

Rhode Island has produced some of the greatest striper-fishing and some of the largest individual fish on the entire Atlantic coast. School stripers begin to arrive at such spots as Watch Hill, Weekapaug, Quonochontaug, and Point Judith about mid-April and remain until November. At Narragansett Bay, fishing begins about May 1 when the smaller school stripers arrive in great abundance. Later on, the trophy

fish show up in such celebrated locations as Beavertail, Brenton Point, Newport, and Sakonnet Point, all of which have produced many huge bass only a few pounds off the world's sport-fishing record. Block Island, though not as well explored by striper fishermen as the Massachusetts islands, nonetheless has great potential.

On the northwest shore of Long Island Sound, Connecticut does not catch some of the best runs of large bass. However, it does have extremely good fishing for school stripers. As early as March some of them appear in the Thames River near Norwich and New London. A little later, bass begin to run in the Niantic estuary. Other Connecticut hotspots where fishing begins from mid-April to early May are around Greenwich, Cos Cob, Norwalk, Darien, Southport, the mouth of the Housatonic and Connecticut rivers at Mystic, and at Stonington.

The Hudson River was shamefully polluted in the past, but massive efforts have resulted in vast improvement in water quality. It is now an important spawning ground for many of the school striped bass that are taken around Long Island and elsewhere along the New England coast. There is some light-tackle casting and trolling in the Hudson River itself as early as April 1. New York City anglers have much sport with school-size fish beginning at Flushing, Little Neck and Manhasset bays, and at Glencoe, near New Rochelle and Mamaroneck. Fishing off the south shore of Long Island at Jamaica Bay and at the Rockaways is good in May and in some years remains good until November.

Montauk Point at the extreme tip of Long Island is one of the greatest striped bass fishing areas in the world. Here it is possible to catch them by surf-casting or from one of the charter boats specially designed for use close to the wild and rocky surf. The biggest bull bass arrive here late in May and remain until mid-December.

Although Sandy Hook, New Jersey, ordinarily accounts for the largest striped bass taken in New Jersey coastal waters, there are a number of extremely good areas nearby. Fishing begins along the north shore of Delaware Bay about April 1. At the same time school stripers are available around Cape May and near Atlantic City, New Jersey. Barnegat Bay also has school stripers—sometimes throughout the summer and early fall months. The Manasquan River is a popular spot for night fishermen. Some ex-

A stringer of small-school stripers, which run around Rockport, Texas, in winter.

tremely fine bull bass are taken in this area early in the summer and late in September. Other New Jersey striper areas extend from Sea Girt to Long Branch around Sea Bright, off Monmouth Beach, and in the vicinity of the Raritan River mouth.

Striped bass fishing in Delaware waters isn't what it might be because of heavy pollution. Still, some fine bass are taken in Delaware Bay from (occasionally) as early as March 15 to late December. There is good fishing in Rehoboth Bay and Indian River Bay from April through December and in the Indian River inlet. This is the state's best-known striper area, and surf-casting for school fish gets under way on both sides of the inlet early in April. Here fishermen can continue to catch fish if they can stand the weather through January and February.

A list of the best bass fishing areas in Maryland and the District of Columbia would include Chesapeake Bay and all the rivers that drain into it, such as the Susquehanna, Elk, Sassafras, Back, and Patapsco. There are also excellent trolling grounds around such well-known places as Rock Hall, Bloody Point, Poplar Island, Herring Bay, Tilghman Island, Sharps Island, Solomons Is-

land, the Cedar Point area, and the Patuxent River.

In Virginia, where striper fishing begins in March, the Rappahannock and York river areas are good. So is the vicinity of Norfolk and the James River estuary.

From Virginia southward the striped bass becomes more and more a river fish, taken either in the streams themselves or in their mouths. Trolling is the most popular method, while surf-casting, the preferred method in the New England area, is not practiced here to any extent. Some scattered catches are made by surf-casters in spring and late fall, but it really isn't a developed technique.

Stripers are found in most of the Carolina rivers and in Pamlico and Albermarle sounds. The largest striper of which there is any record was a 125-pounder netted here in 1891 at the mouth of the Chowan River. The rod and reel record, incidentally, is a 73-pounder taken in Massachusetts in 1913. School stripers are taken regularly on fairly light tackle in the Pasquotank, Tar, Roanoke, Chowan, and Neuse rivers of North Carolina.

Limited fishing exists in the Piscataqua and

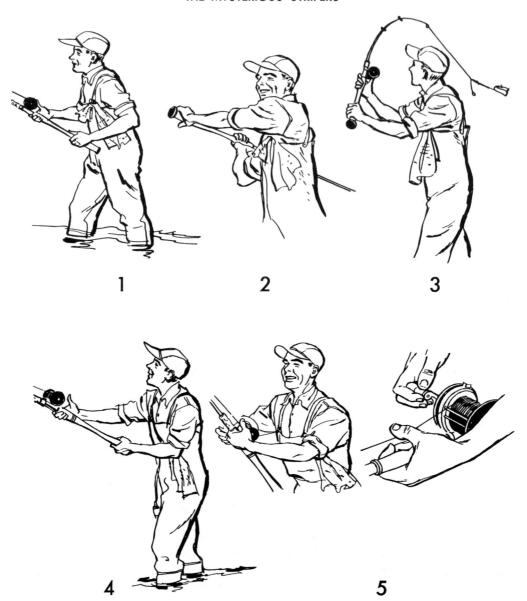

HOW TO SURF-CAST:

(1) *Put reel in free spool with drag adjusted for weight of lure. Left hand low on butt, and right hand just below reel with thumb holding spool. Lure should hang about 3 to 4 feet below rod tip.* (2) *Bring rod tip back by pushing left hand (on the butt) and pivoting rod on right hand. Overhand or sidearm swing can be used.* (3) *Cast forward as lure almost touches water behind you. Push with reel hand at same time pulling with hand holding butt.* (4) *Release spool so line flows freely. Timing will come only with experience. Thumbing reel is necessary to prevent backlashes.* (5) *When lure hits water take reel out of free spool. Shift rod butt to comfortable position between your legs or to rod holder, and move left hand up rod to just in front of reel. If squidding, start retrieve immediately. If bottom-fishing, strip out several feet of line so bait will settle to bottom. When retrieving, level-wind line with left thumb so line will play out freely on next cast.*

Hampton river systems of New Hampshire. In Maine there is a certain amount of fishing in Casco Bay, Penobscot Bay, and near Kennebunkport. Ordinarily the fishing does not begin here until mid-June and is all over by the tag end of September.

On the Pacific coast the best striper fishing is available in San Francisco Bay and in the San Joaquin delta area. There the fish are found during the summer months off sandy beaches and rocky shorelines, sometimes within casting distance of the shore. The beaches immediately adjacent to the Golden Gate are the best, year in and year out, but occasional large runs are encountered as far south as Monterey and as far north as Bodega Bay. Stripers along the Pacific coast do not strike as great a variety of live and artificial bait as they do in the Atlantic. Or so it seems to anglers who have sampled both oceans. Off California they seem to prefer shrimp and anchovies to all other live baits and on occasion will take a variety of jointed wooden plugs fished fairly near to the surface after dark.

Stripers up to 78 pounds have been netted off the California coast, but anything over 20 pounds is an extremely fine fish. Stripers occur in good numbers as far north as the Columbia River. Coos Bay, Oregon, is an extremely fine area, as is the famous Umpqua River.

10
CHANNEL BASS, BLUEFISH, WEAKFISH

CHANNEL BASS

One of the great thrills of saltwater fishing is to stand knee-deep in the pounding surf on North Carolina's Outer Banks when the channel bass are feeding close to shore. Mullet, on which they're feeding, spray up onto the beach as they try to elude the big bass. This doesn't happen every day, but it does happen often enough to be worth plenty of waiting.

One magic morning in November, after we had had two days of fruitless fishing, the big red channel bass appeared all at once. We spotted them just south of the Cape Hatteras lighthouse and for a long time they fed in an area too far out from shore.

But suddenly somebody shouted: "Bulls on the beach!" And sixteen fishermen were casting into them all at once.

When a big channel bass strikes a bait it's something like a blacksmith striking an anvil. Almost in the same instant a knot that I had neglected to check was broken and my fish was gone. But the fishermen on both sides of me connected immediately and one of the wildest melees I've ever watched ensued.

"Out of my way!" somebody hollered as he ran down the beach. "I've got a whale by the tail."

Before the morning was finished, reinforcements had arrived in beach buggies and many lines were tangled. Other anglers came in an airplane. But more than a hundred channel bass were landed and stacked like cordwood on the beach. Not one of the fish weighed less than 40 pounds and the largest ran about 59 pounds. It was a thrill that happens far too seldom.

This invasion of channel bass occurs several times a year in the vicinity of Cape Hatteras. Usually it happens in April and again in November, with the exact time depending on the weather. It isn't easy to be in the right spot at the right time and indeed it may seem impossible.

Channel bass, also called redfish, redhorses, red bass, red drums, drums, drumfish, or red choppers, rank among the finest game fishes in American waters. They range from Barnegat Light southward all along our coast to Mexico and beyond. Although they seldom venture farther north than the New Jersey coast, they're among the most important fish for surf-casters.

Peggy Bauer holds good channel bass—or redfish—taken along Texas Gulf coast.

They're also taken by trolling, by casting with light tackle in warmwater bays, and in South Florida waters they're even found on the same shallow flats that bonefish inhabit.

A surf-caster fishes for channel bass in the same manner that he would fish for stripers; the only difference results from the fact that redfish prefer calmer waters. They feed close to shore in a quiet environment, where they can search at leisure for crabs and other bottom food. Channel bass move so slowly and conspicuously while feeding that often they can be seen by a cautious fisherman. They give the impression of being sluggish until they feel the sting of a hook. Instantly they're off in a tremendous surge of power which can melt a hundred or more yards of line from a reel.

Surf-casting for the channel bass, which isn't a bass at all, but a croaker, can be done with either conventional gear or heavy spinning tackle. Since metal squid are very effective when casting to a feeding school, any bait-casting or wide-spool surf reel which can handle squid from 2½ to 4 ounces is suitable. Line testing 27 or 36 pounds is recommended, although an expert fisherman doesn't need it quite so heavy. When there is ample room to play a fish without fouling up anyone else, spinning tackle is excellent for this type of redfish squidding. Line of 10- to 12-pound test is stout enough, and lures from 2 to 2½ ounces are excellent.

Surfing for channel bass is mostly a matter of bottom-fishing, for which any angler needs a supply of patience. For this he'll also need the same gear as for casting squid—a wide-spool surf-casting reel or spinning tackle. On the wide-spool use 36-pound test line and a 4-ounce pyramid sinker to keep the bait from rolling and traveling in the surf. Use an 18-inch steel leader and several ounces of cut mullet, sand crabs, or shrimp.

The ideal spinning outfit includes a saltwater reel with 150 to 200 yards of 12- or 15-pound test line, a 2-ounce pyramid sinker and a wire leader. Size 6/0 or 8/0 O'Shaughnessy hooks are fine during the April and November seasons because the fish run larger during these periods. Too often, smaller hooks fail to hold in the fish's mouth and a trophy is lost. This happens most frequently when the point of the hook becomes buried inside the bait. The best surf rods for redfish should be from 8 to 10 feet long, for normal surf-casting and spinning.

It's wise to remember the channel bass habit of grubbing on the bottom, perhaps even of scavenging a meal that can be any kind of readily available fish, clams, crabs, or shrimp. Their jaws are made to crush shellfish easily, to eat the meat and spit out the shell. Many old-time surf-fishermen believe they can hear channel bass "drum" as they crunch shellfish close to the beach.

Channel bass fishing anywhere is a feast or famine proposition and it's possible that a fisherman can wind up skunked even after a whole week of hard effort. On the other hand, a man can strike it hot from the first cast and proceed to enjoy uninterrupted good fishing through an entire weekend holiday. But more often than not there will be a series of three or four very poor

A four-wheel-drive jeep is the only safe means to reach some remote surf-fishing beaches.

A channel bass fisherman scouts the beach from atop his van-buggy, which also serves as a seaside cottage when parked.

84

THE SALTWATER FISHERMAN'S BIBLE

days followed by a day or two of the fastest sport.

Year in and year out the best channel bass fishing occurs along North Carolina's sun-bleached Outer Banks. As actual real estate, the Outer Banks are about 200 miles of shining sand strip, rarely more than 3 miles wide, often a few hundred yards narrow, and interrupted only by an inlet or two along the way. To the east is the Gulf Stream of the Atlantic Ocean. To the west are Pamlico Sound, Currituck Sound, and a thousand pale-blue bays. Channel bass exist on both sides of this strip of sand.

Before the autumnal equinox, storms and hurricanes are spawned in this lonely world of water and wind. But in wild spring gales or in autumn calm, the waters all around contain channel bass as well as many other species of fish, some resident, some transient.

Not too many years ago the banks were inaccessible, but now two roads bring the entire area within easy driving distance of Norfolk or Raleigh, via a bridge from the mainland to Manteo (on Roanoke Island) and Nags Head. From Nags Head you can turn either north or south. Light planes can land on the beach, which is actually a 200-mile airstrip. Beach buggies can be rented at various places along the Outer Banks.

The channel bass fishing calendar in the Outer Banks area runs something like this: The bass begin to move at Oregon Inlet, Ocracoke, Hatteras, Drum Inlet, Topsail, and Morehead City in early April. By June the run has usually reached its peak. Later on, the hordes of bass move northward along the Atlantic coast and in early fall they return again—usually in October—on the southward migration. Both surf-casters and boat fishermen have two chances at them in this area.

Most of the channel bass taken when trolling from boats run extremely large, from 40 to 60 pounds during the spring and fall months. The Pflueger Record spoon, size 7, is an excellent one for trolling and has landed as many bass as any other artificial lure.

Farther south the Florida Bay area and the entire Ten Thousand Islands sector is one large channel bass nursery. Here the fish feed along the edges of banks and shell bars where small fishes, shrimp, and assorted crustaceans are very plentiful. But even where natural "baits" are abundant, the channel bass in Florida can be

taken in numbers on jigs, and nylon lures or trolled spoons. I have also taken them on small plugs cast and retrieved near the bottom.

Channel bass show up almost everywhere in Florida waters. I've taken them while bottom-jigging the vicinity of Punta Rassa, Sanibel Island, and Captiva Pass. Here the technique was simply to bounce a ¼-ounce yellow Upperman bucktail across the bottom of deeper portions of Punta Rassa Bay. Farther south in the Keys, near Islamorada, I found channel bass up to 8 pounds while searching the shallow, warmwater flats for bonefish. Although some jumbo reds are taken in the surf near Melbourne Beach, most of the Florida fishing is more tailored for the light-tackle enthusiast.

It's true that many channel bass are taken more or less accidentally while light-tackle fishing for other fish, but they can also be taken deliberately. One especially good technique is to cast the edges of oyster bars and mangrove islands. Although nine days in ten the best bait is a ¼-ounce bucktail jig, there are certain times when the channel bass will strike savagely at a small surface plug or at a popping bug cast on a fly rod. Since his mouth is on the underside of his head and not especially designed for surface feeding, the top-water strike of a channel bass is unusually noisy and clumsy, but extremely thrilling.

Generally speaking, saltwater fish require a faster retrieve of any artificial lure than does the average freshwater fish, but the channel bass is an exception. For this species a lure, whether it be a spoon, jig, plug, or fly, needs to be worked very slowly. Assuming that the fisherman is using jigs, he should retrieve the lures by turning the reel handle very slowly while twitching the rod tip ever so slightly to make the jig bounce naturally on the bottom. Surface fishing **must be especially slow and deliberate.** Occasionally a fisherman will notice a roll behind a surface bait, a good indication of the presence of channel bass. Even when the fish does roll, it's important not to speed up the retrieve because the channel bass just needs more time to take a top-water plug than the tarpon and the snook that share the same waters.

Except in the surf, no special tackle is needed for Florida channel bass, provided that all line guides, reels, and hardware are resistant to saltwater corrosion. A freshwater spinning outfit or

Leo Wadley with fine channel bass taken on plug-casting tackle.

casting outfit is ideal. The spinning outfit should include 8- or 10-pound line and the backing on the fly reel should have about 8- or 10-pound test. Such light gear is completely adequate. Although a wire leader is not absolutely essential for channel bass, it's wise to use one because snook frequently are encountered right along with channel bass.

There is extraordinary fishing for channel bass along the entire Gulf coast of Texas, probably with the best of it concentrated in the Galveston Bay area and in the Laguna Madre between Corpus Christi and Port Isabel. Here the fish are taken on artificial baits as well as on a variety of natural baits from shrimp to cut mullet.

In recent years, Texas Gulf coast fishermen have developed an interesting type of vehicle called a Water Scooter for fishing in the warm shallows of the Laguna Madre. Actually it's a shallow-draft skiff with a raised deck in the stern and a 10- to 18-hp outboard. An angler stands on the deck and steers the scooter from a standing position while he cruises about the bay in search of feeding channel bass. As soon as he finds them he cuts the motor and drifts as closely as possible to the school. Then he begins casting.

Since a Water Scooter can buzz along at up to 30 mph, a fisherman can cover plenty of water on a short fishing trip. And a small storage compartment on most of them permits carrying lunch, ice, spare tackle, and bait. It's possible that this curious craft could well be adapted to use elsewhere.

A few channel bass exceeding 100 pounds in weight have been taken in commercial nets. Based purely on statistics, here are several super hotspots for a trophy channel bass: the point at Buxton on Hatteras Island, the sloughs some ten miles north of the lighthouse at the Cape, the north shore of Hatteras Inlet, the north shore of Ocracoke Inlet. And the best time of the year to hit any of these places (and this has been true over a period of many years) is during mid-November.

BLUEFISH

In 1874, in a report of the United States Commission of Fish and Fisheries, one Spencer F. Baird submitted the following description of bluefish:

"There is no parallel in the point of destructiveness of the bluefish among the marine species on our coast, whatever may be the case among some of the carnivorous fish of South American waters. The bluefish has been well likened to an animated chopping machine, the business of which is to cut to pieces and otherwise destroy as many fish as possible in a given space of time. All writers are unanimous in regard to the destructiveness of the bluefish. Going in large schools in pursuit of fish not much inferior to themselves in size, they move along like a pack of hungry wolves destroying everything before them. Their trail is marked by fragments of fish and by the stain of blood in the sea. And where the fish is too large to be swallowed whole, the hinder will be bitten off and the anterior part allowed to float away or sink. It is even maintained with great earnestness that such is the gluttony of the fish that when the stomach becomes full, the contents are disgorged and then again filled."

Except for the professor's point about destructiveness of the bluefish, it would be hard to find a more colorful and more exact description of the species. The bluefish *is* destructive only in that it consumes an extraordinary number of other fishes. But this destruction is only a facet of nature's savage balance in the sea. Other species are equally "destructive," though their destructiveness is not so evident to fishermen.

Destructive or not, bluefish are surely among the most voracious fish in the world. It is not at all unusual to find a school of small bluefish chopping up and feeding on smaller baitfish while still another school of larger blues is systematically eating the small blues. They are, in fact, as cannibalistic as can be. This characteristic only serves to rate them among the finest fish that swim, from an angler's point of view. It isn't hard to find an angler who considers the Atlantic bluefish the greatest fighting fish for its size on the face of the earth.

Bluefish have even been accused (and perhaps with reason) of attacking man. During World War II, bluefish were said to attack fallen fliers along the coast of North Africa. While it is true that bluefish in the Mediterranean commonly reach a size of from 20 to 30 pounds, the reports have never been accredited. However, when you consider that a whole school of these blues could suddenly appear in water where a man is foundering, and perhaps bleeding, it's easy to see how such a story could develop.

The bluefish, *Pomatomus saltatrix,* is the only member of its family known to scientists. Its common names are almost too numerous to list, but some of those most frequently heard are skipjacks and snappers, both of which usually refer to small school fish of a pound or less. Years ago commercial fishermen called bluefish weighing more than a pound, tailors, and this name still persists in many areas, especially around Chesapeake Bay. Other old names include snapping mackerel, summer snappers, and greenfish.

Blues seem to range over the entire Atlantic Ocean and in most adjoining waters. What appears to be a midget strain—5 pounds maximum —lives off the coast of Brazil, while 45-pound giants have been taken off the North African coast. Any fish over 10 pounds, no matter where it's caught, is worth bragging about.

Much has been written and much more could be written about the strange cycles that govern the population of bluefish in Atlantic waters. Years of great scarcity follow summers of the greatest abundance. What causes these fluctuations isn't really known by anyone. Theories abound, but they are nothing more than that, and further mention of the cycling process here would be of no value to fishermen.

In the mid 1930s, the greatest bluefish run ever recorded by fishermen took place along the Carolina coast. At that time fishermen lucky enough to be on the scene saw as much as 15 miles of beach churned to a froth by vast schools of blues feeding on baby menhaden. Millions and millions of blues were so eager in their pursuit of the smaller fishes that every receding wave left windrows of them flopping on the sand. Perhaps this kind of run will never happen again, but everyone who has ever hooked a bluefish hopes that it does.

It's a good estimate that every bluefish will eat several times its own weight in food every day. A fisherman's main problem is where to find them. Great and far-reaching travelers, blues move with incredible speed from place to place along a coastline. Even when they are on a wild feeding rampage, they appear and disappear in flurries with a speed that makes it impossible for even the fastest fishing boat to keep pace. They are school fish of course, and they travel in groups ranging from as few as fifty fish to vast, incalculable hordes. And curiously enough, all the fish in a single school vary very little in weight; sometimes only an ounce or two separates the largest from the smallest among thousands.

Blues follow a fairly definite migratory pattern, going north in the spring and then south in winter much as do striped bass, who share some of the same waters. Though traveling blues are always on the prowl for mossbunkers or menhaden, their favorite foods, they will not pass up any species of smaller fish, including smaller bluefish, as we pointed out before. They're here today and gone tomorrow and whenever they are in a particular area, every serious fisherman thereabout hurries to get in on the great fishing that usually follows.

This is a debatable point, but the blue is directly responsible for the strange vehicle known as the beach buggy. As long ago as the era of Model Ts, fishermen were building custom conversions of these cars for use on sandy beaches. Today most of the vehicles have four-wheel drive and are equipped to carry fishermen and all their gear for a short holiday near the surf. Most contain a couple of crowded bunks and a compact galley.

Equipped with oversize, low-pressure tires, these beach buggies can be taken anywhere along a shoreline that is not too rough and rocky. Fishermen simply cruise the beaches in their buggies watching for fish feeding close to shore or for the wildly circling schools of gulls which somehow gather whenever a school of bluefish comes boiling to the surface. Almost as handy as the beach buggy are binoculars, which permit a fisherman to detect gulls much farther away and to scan a larger area of the water's surface while sitting in one place.

There are three major ways to take bluefish and all are deadly when the critters can be found in numbers. Trolling is the most effective of all because it is possible to fish four lines—two of them on outriggers—all at one time. And each of the four lines can drag a different bait: say an eel skin on one, a metal squid on another, a spoon on a third line, and a feather jig on the fourth. Of course all of these lures will take bluefish and the minute a school is located it's possible to have fish on all four of them at once. Unless the anglers are alert and on their toes, it will result in an impossible snarl-up of lines.

When a school of blues is located by trolling, it's best not to push right into the middle of them. Instead, troll quickly around the fringes of the feeding fish, picking up only those fish on the perimeter without alarming the whole school. Of course, it's fairly easy to locate the main body of the school by the inevitable surface disturbance and by the birds hovering overhead.

It's always a good idea to combine the casting of light lures with trolling. If a regular medium spinning outfit or even a saltwater fly-casting outfit is handy, one fisherman can start dropping streamer flies or block-tin squid or jigs around the edge of the school as the boat draws near. Nine times out of ten the caster will get a strike, and once hooked on this kind of light tackle, the bluefish is a performer almost without comparison.

Serious bluefishermen, almost no matter where you find them, are particularly adept in the traditional and fine art of chumming. Chumming has been mentioned elsewhere in this book, but it approaches its greatest effectiv bluefish. The idea is to anchor in a su. offshore and there start distributing big ground-up menhaden overboard. If all w cording to plan, the blues will scent the cl it drifts down-tide and they will follow "spoor" right up to the boat. As soon as ..ne school is within casting distance, the anglers begin to cast with block-tin squid or pieces of cut bait. As long as the chum holds out, it is possible to keep the school within close-enough range to hook a blue on virtually every cast.

Chumming is as fascinating a technique as it is effective. First there is the suspense involved in whether the fish will react to the chum or not. Then once they are in range, it's possible to use the lightest kind of tackle because the fish are near enough to see and are right on the surface. I've known fishermen who use extremely light fly rods with surface bass bugs which the blues chew to pieces in no time at all.

Quite a few bluefish spend the winter along the east coast of Florida from Biscayne Bay north to Cape Canaveral. There are also small schools of them wandering about the Florida Keys and north along the west coast as far as Tampa Bay. Usually they're concentrated around any inlet near the Gulf Stream and are noticeably absent from any muddy or silt-laden river mouths.

From Florida the bluefish seem to follow the Gulf Stream northward, which means that they are too far offshore while passing Georgia and South Carolina to be readily available to fishermen in those states. However, there are a few little-known but productive bluefishing spots in Georgia such as the Cumberland Island beaches, Jekyll Island, Sea Island, St. Simons Island, and the Sapelo Island region. Some blues are also caught off Beaufort, South Carolina.

Somewhere in the vicinity of Cape Fear, North Carolina, the large schools of bluefish seem to desert the Gulf Stream and to move closer to shore on a course which carries them as far north on occasion as Cape Cod. During April and May they're in numbers off the North Carolina coast and by June, usually, they reach the New Jersey coast around Barnegat Light. In every area, trollers usually catch the first fish and from them the word of the bluefish run is spread. Beginning in April or May and lasting throughout the summer, there's surf-fishing for blues from Cape Hatteras to Cape Charles, Virginia, and northward beyond Cape May, New Jersey. However, the best sport of all seems to begin during the main fall migration southward.

From September through November there is fast surf-fishing in the Montauk area and especially in the Cape May area.

But no matter when or where you find your bluefish and no matter how you're fishing for them, keep this one important rule in mind: Retrieve your lure swiftly, almost as fast as you can reel. If you happen to be in the center of a school of feeding blues, you'll have a strike almost as soon as your squid hits the water.

There's never any doubt about a bluefish strike. It hits like a rocket going full speed ahead and it will hook itself even before you can react and raise your rod tip. And once it's on the line, a blue will leap and cavort and perform like few other fishes in the sea.

Bluefishing may mean trolling for hours on end without a sign of a fish. Or it may mean driving along a beach that seems empty of any marine life. But when you do find your blues, it will be worth all the waiting and all the traveling and all the time you have invested.

WEAKFISH OR SEA TROUT

Weakfish, or sea trout as they are most often called, really belong to the croaker family. This means they are related to the drum, the croakers, the spots, the California white sea bass, and the totuaba, rather than to the freshwater trout family. One or more of three species of weaks are found all along our coast from Cape Cod to Brownsville, Texas. Dozens of towns along our south Atlantic and Gulf coast depend on weakfish for a good part of their economy. Weaks, in fact, are the most abundant and among the most popular game fishes in all of America's vast saltwaters.

The most important of the group, the spotted sea trout, *Cynoscion nebulosus*, is taken in abundance from North Carolina to around the tip of Florida and along the Gulf of Mexico.

The gray trout, *Cynoscion regalis*, is taken in greatest quantities in North Carolina waters, though its range extends northward to Rhode Island. It's especially abundant in Great Peconic

Bay, Long Island, and the Mullica River, New Jersey, where it's sometimes called the tide-runner. It is scarce in Florida waters and extremely rare in the Gulf.

The third and least important species is the white or sand trout, *Cynoscion arenarius*, which is found only on the west coast of Florida and in the Gulf of Mexico. It is a small fish, reaching a maximum of 16 or 17 inches in length.

The spotted weakfish is a handsome fish, extremely good to eat but otherwise not very impressive. Spotted weakfish do not belong in the same class with such game species as snook or bonefish or channel bass as far as being clever and hard to catch. Most of the time, in fact, they're extremely easy to catch. While many of the other well-known, southern game fish are durable, tough, and agile, the spotted weak is almost delicate, with fragile jaws. It never jumps and it's really not a very strong or exciting fighter.

But no matter whether they bore you or excite you, weaks are tremendously abundant and available, two qualities that more than make up for their lack of fight. Weaks are, in fact, the old standbys of thousands of southern saltwater anglers.

As we have seen, the range of the spotted sea trout includes Florida's entire east coast, with the biggest specimens found in lagoons from Palm Beach north to Melbourne. They are especially numerous in Florida Bay and all along the Gulf coast, particularly at such places as Cedar Key, Tampa Bay, Charlotte Harbor, and Pine Island Sound. Westward from Florida they are found in the vicinity of Mobile Bay, near Biloxi, at scattered points along the Louisiana coast, and they become very abundant in Galveston Bay and in the vast lukewarm Laguna Madre which extends from Corpus Christi to Port Isabel, Texas.

Almost no matter where they're found, spotted weaks are partial to grassy bottoms in bays, lagoons, sounds, on flats, and in almost any water from 2 to 6 or 7 feet deep. On a rising tide, they fan out across shallow grass flats to feed on shrimp and small fishes. Later they retreat again to deeper flats and holes as the tide recedes. At certain periods they feed along beaches of the Gulf coast, congregating around inlets and passes where the food supply is greatest. At these times schools of them are so dense that they seem to swim flank-to-flank in the water.

Spotted weaks are especially sensitive to abrupt changes in the weather. They may leave the shallow flats during very hot or very cold weather and spend longer periods in deeper water. But as soon as the weather levels out and a series of mild days begin to build up, they return again to the same flats where fishermen find them easiest to catch. If the weather remains warm they will roam the flats almost the year round.

Weakfish tackle should be extremely light. For one thing, there is no better way to lose a trout after he's hooked than to horse him, because his soft mouth rips very readily. And from a sporting point of view, only the lightest kind of gear gives the fish an opportunity to show what little it can do. Its most spectacular effort is a series of wallows on the surface, a tactic that sometimes permits the trout to spit out the hook.

It's a happy coincidence that the most sporting tackle for weakfish is also the most efficient. At times it seems freshwater spinning tackle was designed for this species, even more than for most of the freshwater fishes. You could travel around the world and not find a fish better suited to this kind of gear. Running a close second is a light fly-casting outfit.

Spinning tackle is so well adapted to trout fishing that the commercial anglers who work the Texas and Louisiana Gulf coast areas use the fixed-spool reel to account for almost half of their entire catch.

By far the largest percentage of weakfish are taken on such naturals as shrimp, minnows, or cut bait and, of these, shrimp has accounted for 90 percent of all fish taken. The simplest way to use shrimp is to impale a large one on a bare hook and cast it out with light spinning tackle. Retrieve it as slowly as possible in good weakfish waters. A good supply of shrimp is necessary because these critters are not tough enough to stay on the hook during rough use. (There are, however, a number of clever shrimp hook-harnesses on the market which make this tactic much easier.) More and more fishermen have discovered that buying and using live bait is absolutely unnecessary and just an extra expense. Small bucktails or small jigs are every bit as deadly and in most cases far more so than live bait. The best jig is a ⅛- or ¼-ounce size in yellow or white. There will be days when it is

Bait-fishing from a breakwater along the Texas coast produces flounder, redfish, sheepshead, and weakfish.

possible to use two jigs in tandem and therefore catch two trout at the same time. Still another extremely productive technique is to tie a streamer fly or a tiny, ¹⁄₁₆-ounce jig on a length of leader behind a heavier jig, which provides the necessary casting weight.

Jigs work equally well whether the trout are in deep or shallow water, over sandy or grassy bottoms. Many good weakfish waters in lagoons and flats are frequently cluttered with loose floating grass, at which times jigs are among the only lures that can be fished without continually fouling up. There are a number of jigs with piano-wire weed guides on the market and a supply of these should be in every trout fisherman's tackle box.

The best retrieve for weakfish is a medium speed that permits the jig to bounce lightly along a sandy or shell bottom. Or if the bottom is grassy, it's best to retrieve just a few inches above the tips of the grass. Sometimes it will be necessary to vary the retrieve, either to speed it up or to slow it down, but in most cases weakfish are not too particular.

Virtually every fish living in saltwater will at one time or another give an angler his money's worth, and there are occasions when even the sea trout puts on a decent performance. When feeding busily over the shallowest flats, more often at dusk or even after dark, the sea trout will strike top-water lures with considerable enthusiasm.

It doesn't make any difference whether the lures are plunkers, darters, injured minnows, or popping bugs, just so long as they're retrieved slowly and noisily. A weak will usually swirl or roll several times before striking, in which case a slight increase in speed on the retrieve usually makes the rolling fish take the plug. Some very large spotted weaks have been taken by casting with darter plugs around pilings and channel markers after dark.

Although only a few saltwater species will regularly strike freshwater lures with "built-in" actions, the spotted weakfish is, again, not very particular. Most of the standard wobbling plugs that are so well known to bass fishermen will take trout reasonably well at least some of the time.

A freshwater bass fisherman can also have the time of his life with weakfish by using a fly rod and small popping bugs, or wounded-minnow-type plugs on the surface. A size 1 or 1/0 bug of whatever color or shape is ideal, especially when worked slowly on the surface with loud pops and gurgles. Once while fishing in San Carlos Bay at night, we had action as long as my supply of bass bugs held out. But between the spotted trout and the ladyfish which attacked on almost every cast, we were able to get back to camp and to bed early.

The sand trout, which sometimes shares the same waters as the spotted trout, is a much harder fighter for his considerably smaller size. A 2-pound sand is an extremely good fish. Ordinarily the sand stays closer to the bottom in deeper water than his spotted cousin, and seldom ventures out onto the flats. It may be caught by casting small jigs across channels and then retrieving them along the bottom. Sand trout prefer the slowest retrieve as a rule and will even take a jig that is dragged rather than bumped across the bottom.

Although the goings-on around Cape Canaveral had a resounding effect around the world, it never affected the trout fishing around nearby Cocoa. This was and is still the best place for an angler with a trophy trout in mind. It's fertile and it's productive because the area is surrounded by many hundreds of square miles of flats that are protected from deep water. Close by, the trout have a choice of sand, mud, rock, seashell, or grass bottoms. Oyster beds, pilings, and broken-down docks—the favorite haunt of the biggest weaks—are everywhere.

There is also much evidence to prove that the best fishing occurs from a new moon to the full moon and from two hours before a high tide to one hour after it.

A good way to spot big trout in the Cocoa area—as it is elsewhere—is to watch the pelicans. As soon as the trout begin feeding across the flats, whole schools of mullet flush crazily ahead of them, sometimes jumping clear of the water. That's the signal for pelicans to stream out of the mangroves and dive onto the mullet, which are sandwiched between two perils. It's at this time that an angler must carefully watch his plug or he's likely to hook a pelican instead of a trout.

Weakfish are seldom more available than they are in the vicinity of Cocoa. In many places it's possible just to pull a car off the road along Sykes Creek, the Banana or Indian rivers and then wade out and begin casting. Though it's handy to have a guide and a boat, it really isn't necessary. Even the wind and the weather aren't a bad problem here because during a strong northern blow—common in winter—it's possible to fish in the Barge Canal, running east and west across Merritt Island. The canal is about 12 feet deep and when bad weather moves the trout into this canal, the concentration there is unbelievable.

As elsewhere, the regular fishermen at Cocoa are finding that the biggest weaks are most active after dark, at which time two different techniques are used. One is to drift and cast with a surface plug or a plug that resembles a needlefish. The second method is to drift while using jumbo shrimp, live needlefish, mullet, or balaos and to allow these baits to travel freely with the tide. A large float counterbalanced with an egg sinker is used to keep the bait about two feet below the surface.

When a trout strikes, the fisherman allows it to run without trying to set the hook until the

Many southern Florida bridges are hotspots for taking a great grab bag of fishes.

fish stops and begins a second run. This is the same technique used all over Florida from causeways and bridges.

Just as weakfish have a fondness for mullet and needlefish, so do the porpoises of Florida inshore waters have a fondness for weakfish. As soon as porpoises appear over the grassy flats, a wise fisherman will seek his weakfishing elsewhere.

The gray trout, or gray squeteague, shecutts, squit, chickwick, or sea trout, which reaches its greatest abundance north of Virginia, is a somewhat stronger fighter than the spotted sea trout. It does have the same tender mouth, however, and in general the same methods are used to catch it.

Weakfish usually arrive in northern waters in numbers early in May. The first fish appear in Peconic Bay, Long Island, about the middle of May, by which time most available charter boats have already been booked. The typical method of weakfishing in this area involves the use of such live bait as sandworms and squid or shrimp. Although the weakfish is essentially a bottom feeder, it can be attracted into range of the bait and held there by persistent chumming.

Gray trout can be taken equally well both day and night in the small bays off the New Jersey, Long Island, and Connecticut coasts. A typical technique of many charter-boat captains in this vicinity is to watch for schools of shiners, menhaden, and other baitfish during daylight and then return to the same area after dark. Almost always a large school of weakfish will have moved into the vicinity. The mouth of an inlet

to a bay is always a good spot for weaks at high tide and again during the outgoing tide. Any coves in these bays are also good fishing areas.

Many fine weakfish are taken from mid-August to mid-September by trolling with a small bucktail fly, a spoon, or a feather jig. A sinker of sufficient weight is added to troll the bait at a depth of from 10 to 15 feet, which is the zone where weakfish are most likely to be hooked. It's always a good idea, if several weaks are hooked in one area, to drop the anchor overboard and to start chumming and/or casting thereabout. Be careful to lower the anchor gently and then allow the lure to sink to about 15 feet before retrieving it very slowly.

There are periods, especially in midsummer, when bottom-fishing with a slack line and worms for bait is most productive. In these circumstances, a weakfish will usually hook itself. Always give the fish plenty of time to mouth the bait before striking and then do so firmly rather than abruptly. Some of the better baits for bottom-fishing are shrimp, bloodworms, sandworms, squid, and shedder crabs.

Breakwaters and docks are always good places to prospect for weakfish during the middle of the summer and especially on midsummer nights. During this period, be on the lookout for small fish skittering and racing wildly along the surface with no indication that larger fish are following them. Ordinarily this is a sign that weakfish are about, because unlike striped bass, bluefish, and other large fish in pursuit of minnows, weaks do not splash water or boil to the surface.

11

ATLANTIC GRAB BAG:

Codfish, Pollack, Black Drum, Sheepshead, Black Sea Bass, Tautog, Porgy, Summer Flounder (Fluke), Winter Flounder, Atlantic Halibut, Whiting

CODFISH

Most anglers along the north Atlantic seaboard have good reason to despise cold weather and winter. High winds, rough seas, and a stinging salt breeze make any kind of fishing extremely unpleasant.

Most sane fishermen sit this season out, but cod fishermen are not particularly sane. On the worst days of January and February a surprising number of "codballs" leave the comfort of warm living rooms to suffer on cold and slippery boat decks just to catch a mess of cod.

The codfish, found on both sides of the Atlantic Ocean, is one of the most important fish in the world. Early American colonists depended on cod for food and income. The species was so highly considered that it is pictured on the Colonial Seal of Massachusetts. Today the figure of a codfish still hangs in the Bay State legislature.

On the North American side of the Atlantic, cod range from the Arctic Ocean southward to Virginia. Preferring cold, deep water, they inhabit certain offshore banks almost the year round. South of Cape Cod they are sometimes found inshore, especially from November to April. (An exception is Coxes Ledge off Block Island, where cod may be found in July and August.) Generally they are most plentiful in water from 50 to over 250 feet deep.

Cod are extraordinary travelers. One tagged in Iceland was caught off Newfoundland two thousand miles away. All codfish seem to make extensive migrations to forage for food and to spawn. In addition, they make shoreward movements each fall and spring. Tagging has revealed that most cod caught in New Jersey and New York waters come from summering grounds in the Nantucket Shoals area.

The brown-spotted, yellow-bellied, chin-whiskered cod is known by many names, including Atlantic cod, black cod, rock cod, and scrod (this last is actually used to designate immature cod). Its scientific name is *Gadus callarias*, but no expensive or elaborate tackle is necessary to catch the species. The cost of a winter fishing trip on a party boat, for instance, may be as low as ten or fifteen dollars a day, bait included.

Cod are not terrific fighters, but you will still need sturdy (rather than elaborate) tackle because of the strong tides, deep water, heavy sinkers, and rocky bottoms you will be dealing with. Many fishermen prefer a simple, stiff, two-piece boat rod; others use regular surf rods.

The reel should hold 200 yards of monofilament line testing about 30 or 40 pounds. The best hooks are size 7/9 or 8/0 in Sproat or O'Shaughnessy types. These are knotted onto heavier (than the line) test nylon leaders, each about 24 inches long, then to a spreader or to a three-way swivel.

Many anglers use two hooks, with the bottom one tied about a foot above the sinker and the top one tied just about 2 or 3 feet above the first hook. Sinkers from a half to one pound are sometimes necessary to reach bottom depending on the depth of the water, the velocity of the current, and the tide.

Virtually any bait is good enough for codfish, including clams, shrimp, lobsters, mussels, conchs, starfish, sea urchins, sea cucumbers, worms, or pieces of cut bait. The bait most often provided aboard party boats is the surf clam or skimmer, the "innards" of a couple of these being placed on a single hook. Codfish entrails also can be used.

Some of the best codfishing along the Atlantic seaboard occurs almost within sight of New York City. Party boats are based at such nearby ports as Sheepshead Bay, Canarsie, Freeport, and Montauk. Other boats fish out of bases along the New Jersey coast. During mild winters they go out almost daily, even through January and February, but the most fruitful fishing months are November, December, March, and April. Most party boats, at least the larger ones, have heated cabins and small coffee shops on board. Many also rent fishing tackle. Even when the weather is at its worst, codfishing offers a pleasant change of pace.

More important than tackle is good warm clothing. The winter fisherman should wear woolen or insulated underwear, heavy outer clothing, a cap with earmuffs, large-size boots or overshoes which can accommodate extra pairs of woolen stockings, waterproofed gloves and waterproofed parkas or foul-weather gear. The more raw and cold the day, the more important it is to be dressed properly.

Cod prefer rocky, pebbly bottoms or mussel beds. Near New York, the Cholera Bank, Angler Banks, and 17 Fathoms are the best-known areas. Cod are also always found around sunken, offshore wrecks.

POLLACK

Winter codfishermen sometimes encounter a bonus in the pollack, a relative of the cod which frequents the same waters. Sometimes called Boston bluefish, the pollack, *Pollachius virens*, ranges from about Cape May, New Jersey, to Nova Scotia and perhaps beyond.

Pollack are taken on the same tackle and by the same methods as are cod along most of the Atlantic seaboard, but they have the fortunate habit of rising to the surface just before dark and just before daybreak at certain times of the year. When this occurs, pollack become excellent light-tackle fish and the fisherman who finds them on the surface, either while surf-casting or while fishing from a boat, is lucky indeed.

The best pollack fishing occurs in October and lasts well into November, a foggy time along the Atlantic coast when visibility can be poor. The presence of pollack is always easy to detect, however, because of the wild commotion they make chasing small fish on the surface. They are usually accompanied by gulls, which feed and circle above them.

Surface-feeding pollack, which average 5 pounds but which can reach 20 or 30 pounds, will strike different artificial lures. Large saltwater darting plugs are effective, as are feather jigs and bucktails when retrieved with short sharp jerks. Occasionally during calm weather, pollack feed actively and extensively on the surface at night.

BLACK DRUM

The black drum, *Pogonias cromis*, can be found anywhere from Long Island shores to the mouth of the Rio Grande. An important commercial species, it is also an important sport species along the Atlantic coast. The drum, closely related to the sheepshead or freshwater drum, is a heavyweight. The largest known specimen weighed 146 pounds; 50- and 60-pounders are taken every year.

The black drum may be the best musician of the entire family of drums and croakers to which it belongs. Many have voices so loud they can actually be heard some distance above the surface of the water. The drum's vocalizations are produced by special bandlike muscles vibrating against a taut air bladder. Whether drumming, as these sounds are called, indicates spawning and sexual activity or whether it's an expression of feeding contentment is uncertain. Some biologists believe that the fish are most vocal during spawning migrations. Males are said to drum very loudly, while the females have softer voices.

Thanks to its large pharyngeal teeth, the black drum is an avid eater of shellfish. In Texas it has a reputation as an oyster pirate, but it prefers a small clam that is very abundant in shallow bays along the Gulf coast. These clam beds are well known to fishermen as the best places to look for black drums.

Drums suck the clams up and out of the mud in which they burrow and crush the shells. Although they swallow many shell fragments along with the meat, some parts of the shell are discarded. Black drums are great gluttons who, when feeding, stand on their heads with tails out of the shallow water. Lucky fishermen frequently find them in this tailing position.

On the Texas coast, drums spend much time in inshore bays during both summer and winter. Sometimes the water in the passages to the deeper bays becomes so shallow that the drums have difficulty passing through and often are badly cut while going over these oyster "reefs." Drums are caught over the entire Florida coast but are most numerous along the north Atlantic coast. Small or puppy drums are taken there throughout the year, but the best period for catching larger fish begins in March.

Black drum tackle should be heavy. Because nylon leaders are no match for the oyster beds that drums frequent, heavy wire leader should be used. In addition to oyster beds, drums are frequently caught from bridges, piers, and along certain coarse sand beaches. North of Florida some hotspots are the Sea Islands of Georgia, near Beaufort, South Carolina, inside North Carolina's Outer Banks, and the vicinity of Cape Charles, Virginia.

Some consider flesh of large black drums to be coarse and tasteless. Elsewhere the fish is held in high esteem and is the main ingredient in delicious chowder and baked drum dishes. Black drums should always be filleted and skinned.

SHEEPSHEAD

The sheepshead, *Archosargus probatocephalus*, of the Atlantic and Gulf coasts is found anywhere from Texas to the Bay of Fundy but it is abundant only on the southern Atlantic coast. The greatest concentrations are found on the northwest coast of Florida.

A member of the porgy family, the sheepshead is closely related to the familiar scup or porgy, an important commercial fish northward from Virginia. It should not be confused with the freshwater sheepshead that is a member of the drum or croaker family.

The sheepshead is most often captured around wharves, breakwaters, and sunken wrecks. It has a weakness for crabs, oysters, and other shellfish which it crushes easily with its strong bridgework. In inlets it moves in and out with the tide and, at least in the southern part of this range, does not seem to migrate extensively. During the spawning season, which occurs in the spring, sheepshead assemble into schools and move into shallow water to deposit their eggs. Many are caught at this time.

The largest sheepshead of record weighed about 20 pounds, but the average is only about 2 pounds. Larger fish should be filleted and smaller

Sheepshead and channel bass are typical of mixed-bag fishing in warm saltwaters of North America.

ones cooked whole. The meat is white, tender, and pleasantly flavored.

A fisherman should look for sheepshead along rocky, irregular bottoms, over reefs not too far from shore, and inside channels. The most notable physical characteristics of the fish are the sheeplike lips and the protruding teeth. The inside of the mouth is equipped with grinding teeth which permit easy feeding on such bivalves as mussels and barnacles.

Sometimes the sheepshead is so fast in taking live bait that it is difficult to hook. Over reefs it will quickly seize baits the minute they are dropped to the bottom. One exciting way to catch sheepshead is to thoroughly chum an area with shrimp or bits of shellfish and, after the sheepshead have begun to feed actively, to cast with small ¼-ounce jigs. On light tackle it is a sporty fish.

BLACK SEA BASS

June through August the black sea bass, *Centropristes striatus*, is plentiful along our eastern seaboard. It is usually found in shallow water over rocky formations with weeds, ledges, sand-

bars, and reefs. During dog days the black sea bass may be the only really abundant fish. Striper, bluefish, or trout fishermen can always find bass even when these other species are uncooperative.

Averaging only a pound or two, but occasionally reaching 8 or 9 pounds, the black sea bass is strong and a pleasure to catch. On light tackle they never seem to stop fighting and, once caught, they can inflict cuts on a fisherman's hands with their very sharp fins. The best way to handle this fish and remove the hook is either to hold it firmly by the lower lip or to put fingers into the eyes to grip it solidly.

Black sea bass prefer sea clams or squid but will take almost any bait offered. Larger bass are taken by bottom-fishing from boats, while the smaller ones are usually taken from shore. In either case, it isn't necessary to use heavy tackle. Most fishermen use two or three baited hooks at one time.

The flesh of the sea bass is white, sweet, and firm and can be prepared like any other panfish. Large ones should be filleted and smaller ones cooked whole. Excellent in chowders, sea bass are especially good served with hush puppies.

TAUTOG

The tautog, *Tautoga onitis*, is equipped with extremely strong jaws and powerful, conical teeth far back in its mouth. With this double-barreled apparatus, the tautog feeds on the hardest of crustaceans and shellfish along the Atlantic coast. About the middle of May the tautog begins to move from deep water to feed and spawn in big bays and inlets along our middle Atlantic coast. This is a good time to fish for the species.

Fairly heavy tackle should be used for the tautog for two good reasons. In the first place, it is necessary to use considerable force to set the hook, and, secondly, once hooked, the fish will certainly take refuge among any rocks or underwater obstacles it can find. The tautog reel should hold at least 150 yards of 30-pound test line. This may seem heavy for a fish that averages only 3 or 4 pounds and seldom exceeds 20, but once in sanctuary among the rocks, there is no way to horse it out.

The first fishing of the season is done from small boats or party boats and the best water to explore is over rocky ledges, among rocks and shoals, and over mussel bars. Never look for tautog far from this type of habitat.

Early in the season a tautog is a reliable target for surf-casters where the flood tide covers up an isolated area of rock. It doesn't have to be a large area because half an acre of rocky "island" will hide many fish.

The most productive fishing months are April and May, and again from September until the end of October. When very warm or very cold weather arrives, the tautog goes into deeper water and does not return until spring or fall. Winter and summer it's found on the bottom in from 50 to 150 feet. Occasionally it will rise to chum.

Shore-fishing can be effective. Tautogs in search of food swim along rocky and weedy shores, where they tend to congregate in certain holes. Find such a place and it will afford fast fishing throughout the season, maybe for many seasons to come. A wide variety of baits are acceptable, but the best is a piece of cut crab. Sea worms, squid, and cut fish are also good.

The tautog is often called blackfish, confusing because blackfish is also another name for the pilot whale.

PORGY

The northern porgy, *Stenotomus chrysops*, called scup or northern scup, ranges from Maine along the Atlantic coast to South Carolina. The southern porgy, *Stenotomus aculeatus*, also called scup or southern scup, ranges from North Carolina to the Florida Keys and to Texas. Most abundant in southeast waters, it is prized as food fish everywhere.

The best fishing season for porgies runs from May through October. Throughout summer and fall, special porgy boats drift back and forth over long-established fishing grounds and on good days fill up with porgies. The fish caught at sea weigh 1 to 3 pounds; those taken in shallower bay waters usually weigh less. They bite best when the tide is slack or early during an incoming tide.

Strictly bottom feeders, porgies are found over shellfish beds, sandy bottoms, around wrecks, reefs, and the entrance to bays. Scups take any bait, but prefer shrimp, skimmers (the favorite), crabs, small pieces of squid and soft-shell clams.

No matter what bait is used, taking porgies requires a specialized fishing technique. The first trick is to find the bottom. Then lower your line and give quick, short jerks of the rod tip up and down, being careful that the bait does not rise higher than a foot above the bottom. Care must be taken not to move the bait too swiftly. Since porgies have extremely small mouths, the bait should be small. Once hooked, a porgy is a stubborn fighter with a tendency to turn broadside and bore to the bottom.

The porgy is a species anglers are likely to catch along the Atlantic coast.

Porgies rarely exceed 4 or 5 pounds. But while fishing the Bermuda reefs our party once caught several weighing more than 10 pounds apiece.

SUMMER FLOUNDER (FLUKE)

The summer flounder or fluke, *Paralichthys dentatus*, actually a halibut, dwells in shallow shoreline waters from Cape Cod to Georgia, but it is most numerous from New York to North Carolina. It frequents sandy and muddy bottoms of the Atlantic seaboard and is taken in muddy estuaries where the water is only moderately brackish.

Like all the other flatfish of both oceans, the summer flounder has its eyes and dark color on one side. In the case of the summer flounder this happens to be the left side as opposed to the winter flounder (a true flounder), which has them on the right side. The fluke can camouflage itself against any background. Placed on a red background it becomes red, on blue it becomes blue, and so on through all the colors anyone could use on the bottom of an aquarium.

Although the flesh of this flounder is dry, it has good flavor, especially when fried or baked. This is one of the fish that passes for fillet of sole in most fish markets.

The fluke is curious and will investigate any silvery or flashing movement in the water. Though it may not strike, a fluke will at least investigate a foreign object, and most of the time will suck it into its mouth. If it happens to be a lure, the fluke may be hooked, but a fisherman must strike back immediately. In no way does the summer flounder resemble any classic game fish, but still it is a strong, vigorous fighter. It feeds on both the bottom and the top and is caught in a variety of circumstances.

Summer flounder occasionally reach 25 pounds but the average specimen would weigh 2 or 3 pounds. The best way to find out if and where flounder are striking is to watch the outdoor columns in local newspapers. Another tip is to go fishing following a bad storm. Some fishes strike well during heavy weather, but fluke are among the species notorious for feeding after a storm. Also fish for fluke just before dusk and just after dark when they are most likely to surface; much sport is possible at these times by casting ⅛- or ¼-ounce feather or bucktail jigs.

Cast and retrieve these lures as slowly as possible, using a wire leader. One variation to the technique is to cast the jig behind a large wooden float, setting the jig about 3 or 3½ feet deep, and retrieving the combination in very slow sharp jerks.

WINTER FLOUNDER

The winter or blackback flounder, *Pseudopleuronectes americanus*, inhabits shallow water from northern Labrador to Cape Lookout during the coldest winters. Though absent during the summer, it is fairly abundant in winter in Chesapeake Bay.

Like other flatfish, it swims and rests on one side, in this case on its left side. It is caught in a similar manner to the summer flounder and on similar light tackle. New England fishing begins in March and lasts until the end of May when the best spots are "bottom holes" in the middle or near the mouth of a bay. The best period is on the outgoing tide. Fishing is productive until the tide changes.

Usually in June the blackbacks stop striking until fall, but they return in September or October and are plentiful along North Atlantic beaches and bays until it's too late and too unpleasant to fish them any longer.

There is no reason to use heavy tackle. A reel with 100 yards of 15- or 20-pound test line is good enough. Hooks in sizes 8, 9, or 10 with a 10-inch leader are sufficient. Best baits are blood- and sandworms, night crawlers, soft- or hardshell clams, mussels or tapeworms. A ribbon worm will often catch fish when other baits fail (reddish in color, this worm is found by digging into mud flats at low tide). The one drawback here is that you must use these worms when procured, as it is difficult to keep them alive more than a few hours.

ATLANTIC HALIBUT

Only a very few fishes, the swordfish, marlin, some sharks, and the tuna among them, exceed the Atlantic halibut in size. The largest member of the flatfish family, the Atlantic halibut, *Hippoglossus hippoglossus*, inhabits all northern seas, southward along our Atlantic coast to New Jersey. Like the winter flounder, its eyes and color are on the right side of the body.

Although large halibut brought into New England ports range in length from only about 4 to 6 feet and in weight from 50 to 200 pounds, a few weighing 300 and 400 pounds are taken every year. A 9-foot 2-inch jumbo weighing 625 pounds dressed was caught 50 miles from Thatcher Island, Massachusetts, in 1917.

The Atlantic halibut is voracious. Feeding mostly on crabs, lobster, clams, and mussels, it is able even to capture seabirds occasionally and is well known as a scavenger of refuse thrown from vessels at sea.

Although most Atlantic halibut are taken by commercial fishermen on set lines, it is possible to take them on sport-fishing tackle. They will strike a variety of baits, particularly in spring and summer, which seems to be spawning time along the New England coast. Once a halibut is hooked, it's a long hard drawn-out struggle rather than an exciting fight.

Small open watercraft such as this are ideal for fishing coastal waters for a variety of game and food fishes.

WHITING

The whiting, *Menticirrhus saxatilis*, belongs to the drum family of fishes, which includes the weakfish, channel bass, croakers, and others. It is found along the Atlantic coast from Maine to Florida, but it is common in the northern half of this range only in the summer.

From May through August, surf-fishing for the whiting is popular and rather good along New Jersey and Long Island shorelines. Best time to fish is during high tide, as it follows the surge inward toward shore. It is also caught during flood tides in bays and inlets.

Southward from North Carolina the whiting disappears from shallow inshore waters during cold spells, but it reappears when the weather warms up. In the Carolinas this species and a barely distinguishable relative are taken in abundance along the shore in winter or early spring.

The whiting is a light-tackle fish. An angler is most likely to be successful using shrimp, crabs, small mollusks, worms, or small fish for bait. It is possible to take them on yellow feather jigs, but the bait fisherman will have better luck. Whitings usually run from 12 to 18 inches, and 6 pounds is about tops for the species. The largest ones feed most actively at night. Whitings are rated highly as food fish.

12

THE PACIFIC SALMON

When Captain Robert Gray sailed his good ship *Columbia* into the great River of the West he found a tribe of Indians living in comparative luxury on the huge salmon which abounded in the stream he named after his ship.

The Indians were the Chinooks and the salmon they feasted on became known by the same name. Today the chinook salmon is the monarch of game fishes, as well as the base of a major commercial and sport-fishing industry. In some other Pacific waters it is known variously as the tyee salmon, spring salmon, king salmon, and quinnat salmon. But whatever the name, in the Columbia and other coastal waters, the chinook affords the finest of all sport-fishing.

Five kinds of salmon are found along the Pacific coast of North America. Besides the king, there are the silver, sockeye, chum, and pink. But 90 or 95 percent of all salmon taken on sport-fishing tackle are either kings or silvers and our discussion of the salmon family will be limited to these two species.

King salmon, which have the almost unpronounceable scientific name of *Oncorhynchus tschawytscha*, can be separated from silver salmon at a glance by checking the color of the fleshy lining over the crown of the gums where the teeth come through. In king salmon the lining is always blackish while in silver salmon it is white. The rest of the inside of the mouth of both kings and silvers is dusky or blackish.

Kings have been caught in the Pacific from San Diego all the way north to Alaska and the Aleutian Islands, and south along the Asiatic coast to Japan. On our side of the ocean, however, they're only rarely taken south of San Luis Obispo County, California, or north of Bristol Bay, Alaska. The Sacramento–San Joaquin river system is the site of the southernmost salmon run of any consequence.

Nearly every fisherman knows the story of how salmon, after spending several years in the ocean, return to their natal streams or rivers to spawn and die. Pacific salmon are spawned in flowing creeks and rivers often high in the mountains and as much as a thousand miles from the sea. In their first or second year the young salmon descend the rivers to the sea where they live on marine life until the spawning impulse strikes in their third, fourth, or fifth year.

Once in freshwater, a salmon rarely feeds. All his energies are concentrated on his stubborn

A good day's catch of king and silver salmon taken along the Oregon coast.

journey of birth and death, and anything that gets in the way will be fought off vigorously. Any object flashing in the water will anger a salmon, causing him to lunge at it. This is particularly true of spinners and wobblers, which, not surprisingly, have become nearly universal salmon lures.

In freshwater, Pacific salmon seldom hit a fly, as will their Atlantic cousins (the coho, however, will hit streamer flies in tidewater, bay areas, and sounds, often with reckless abandon). "Mooching" with fresh or cut herring for bait is the most popular method of angling in offshore and tidewater areas.

Since the commonly accepted life history of the Pacific salmon is full of misconceptions, it's worth considering a few important details here. Unlike silvers, which enter rivers only in autumn, king salmon enter streams and rivers during two different periods annually. Those entering during the spring run spend the summer months loitering in deep holes throughout the river system. They may even make a quick dash back to the ocean. In any case, they continue on to spawning grounds in the fall. On the other hand, kings that enter during the fall run move directly to inland spawning grounds.

Not all chinooks return to home rivers to spawn, although most apparently do. On occasion adult fish have been captured during their spawning run many miles from the ocean, only to be recaptured much farther downstream. In one case, an adult king salmon was caught 30 miles offshore from San Francisco almost a year after it had been netted and tagged 80 freshwater miles up the Sacramento River.

Most kings spawn when either three or four years old, but there are exceptions to this too. Males, especially, may spawn when they are only two, and some large females do not spawn until five or six. The average female king salmon will deposit from 3,000 to 4,000 eggs. The time it takes for eggs to hatch may vary from fifteen to twenty days, depending on water temperature. Hatching occurs sooner in warm water than in cold.

Young chinook salmon migrate downriver tailfirst—usually at night—within several months after hatching. During these migrations many of the young are lost as they drift or are sucked into irrigation canals. Still others are consumed by the multitude of predators along the migratory route. If they make it to saltwater, there is evidence that they disperse rapidly in the sea and travel for considerable distances. However, not much is known about their travels after they reach saltwater.

Any chinook salmon is a savage striker with a stout heart and tremendous fighting ability, which means that salmon fishing is a sporty

*The king of chinook salmon is the most popular
game species along the northwest Pacific coast.*

keep the trolled bait at the desired depth, which
is quite near the bottom.

The preferred trolling speed used by most
salmon experts is around 2 knots and the most
productive trolling depth along the California
and Oregon coasts would seem to be between
100 and 150 feet. Salmon fishing is best north of
Monterey Bay in California, but there is usually
excellent sport, at least for a limited period, out
of Avila, Port San Luis, Morro Bay, and San
Simeon.

Oregon's best salmon fishing occurs around
Coos Bay and in the vicinity of Astoria. In
Washington, the waters of Puget Sound and the
Strait of Juan de Fuca are world-famous. A
super hotspot is the Hope Island "slot" near the
mouth of the Skagit River, which has produced
an astounding number of trophy-size salmon
through the years. For one reason or another,
the Skagit River breeds an unusually large race
of kings, bigger on the average than those
hatched elsewhere, with the exception of a few
places to the north in British Columbia and
Alaska.

Many saltwater salmon fishermen of the
Northwest are partial to "mooching," a technique that calls for comparatively light tackle.
The rod is the type generally used for steelhead
with a long butt, a progressive taper, and a light
tip. Eight- to ten-foot glass rods made in two sections with a cork-handle reel seat for spin-casting reels or with the standard reel seat may be
purchased. The revolving spool is preferable to
the spinning reel since it is seldom necessary to
cast.

Trolling rods (which usually come in two
sections) are categorized according to the
weight of the rod tip. A beginner would do best
with a six-ounce rod equipped with a medium-
sized saltwater trolling reel filled with 200 to 300
yards of monofilament or braided nylon or wire
line. The trolling rod should be at least as long
as the terminal gear below the point (usually a
sinker) where the terminal gear is stopped, while
reeling in, by the tip-top guide. Local trollers
most often use a dodger or a flasher as an attrac-
tor followed by herring bait spoon or fly. The
best method for rigging up trolling gear using
the dodger or flasher is generally included on a
diagram contained with the newly purchased
gear.

proposition no matter how it's done. Yet the
fishery does seem to be declining almost every
year.

Most ocean fishing for king salmon is done
primarily by trolling with dead bait or with
quite a number of different artificials. Occasionally anglers will use live bait for still-fishing
or drift-fishing, a method more popular in the
ocean south of Monterey, California, than elsewhere.

Kings normally stay very deep, usually in
from 40 to 250 feet of water, except for certain
unpredictable occasions when they rise to the
surface to follow schools of baitfish. It isn't a
hard-and-fast rule, but generally salmon are
taken in shallower waters the farther north they
are found along the Pacific coast. Occasionally
off Ketchikan, Alaska, and thereabouts, they are
taken in water as shallow as 10 or 12 feet.
Nearly always a heavy weight is necessary to

Trolling in the Juneau area produced these fine kings to 50 pounds in southeastern Alaska. Anglers are John Moxley and Phil Baker.

"Mooching" probably originated on Puget Sound and is the most common form of local, light-tackle saltwater salmon angling. The terminal gear consists simply of a sinker and a one- or two-hook leader. Once the bait is lowered to the desired level, the action necessary to spin it in the water is supplied by winds, tides, oars, or a slowly running motor.

Special sinkers used in mooching are shaped like a canoe with a swivel chain or bead chain attached to each end. They are available in various weights but are most often used in the 1- to 4-ounce range. Most anglers use an 8- to 15-pound monofilament line and a leader about 6 feet long of 8- to 12-pound test monofilament.

Many fishermen jerk the bait away from the salmon. Usually a salmon bumps the bait first or just nips at it with the intention of crippling it before finally grabbing it. Give the fish time to take the bait. After the bumping stops, a heavy, steady pull tells the angler it is time to bring the rod up and reel quickly until a steady pressure is maintained. Handle the fish carefully, for they are very quick and will often run rapidly away.

Salmon gather in certain favored locations. Shallow water that drops into deeper water is sought by feeding and migrating fish. Tidal currents resulting from an abrupt change in depth will create a rip or an eddy where fish bait collect; salmon find this a good feeding area. Current or tide rips, where two bodies of different densities come together, are also productive. Splashing fish, skittering baitfish, and gulls diving into the water are all signs of the presence of salmon.

Washington, Ocean Beach, Puget Sound, and Juan de Fuca Strait resorts cater to the salmon fisherman. Boats with or without motors may be rented at resorts throughout Strait and Puget Sound waters. Tackle can be rented and bait purchased. Fleets of charter boats, accommodating from five to a dozen or more persons, cruise the more popular ocean fishing grounds daily, usually from early morning until mid-afternoon (7 A.M. to 3:30 P.M.). This is probably the best way for a novice to experience the thrill of salmon fishing. The skippers are capable guides, always ready to assist an uncertain angler.

Information on charter boats may be had by writing to the Chamber of Commerce of any fishing town or city you plan to visit. Reservations may be made for one or more persons, but should be made several weeks in advance, especially during the months of July and August. At presstime, the average cost per person on a charter boat was about $50. Tackle rented for $5 and bait was nominal. Of course these rates are subject to inflation.

Chinooks taken on hook and line will range from 10 to 30 pounds, with the average at about 20 pounds. Forty-pounders, however, are fairly common in Alaskan and British Columbian waters and they're not too rare in Puget Sound. Alaskan waters are known to contain kings running to 60 and 70 pounds, and on extremely rare occasions 100-pounders have been captured by commercial fishermen. A 126½-pounder appears to be the all-time record for the species.

Although heavy-tackle trolling is as popular as ever, more and more fishermen are switching to lighter tackle and different methods of fishing. Thanks to the pioneering efforts of the Tyee Club of Campbell River, British Columbia, the use of light tackle is spreading up and down the coast.

Both spinning and mooching are ideal for any of the sheltered waters from Puget Sound to Juneau, where it seldom gets too rough to fish from a small boat, the ideal craft for a moocher. These very simple methods take their cue from the way in which salmon attack a school of herring, slashing into it and crippling as many as possible. Then at leisure the predators return to pick up the wounded, which are moving in a

slow, uncertain manner. The idea in mooching and spinning is to make a herring perform in this same uncertain manner. If these baits are properly manipulated by the flexing of the rod tip and by movements of the tide, they're extremely deadly.

The typical salmon spinner or moocher uses a rod that is fairly long, say from 8 feet 6 inches to 10 feet, quite flexible, and with a fairly long two-handed grip. His reel can be either a conventional design or a spinning reel, as long as it's capable of holding at least 200 yards of 10- or 12-pound monofilament line. To this line should be added 8 or 10 feet of slightly heavier monofilament material.

A crescent sinker with a swivel on the leader end is attached to the line with a long loop and the leader is looped to the other end. This type of sinker offers little resistance to tidal current and has a keel effect that prevents twisting of the line when the bait spins.

The herring bait should be prepared or cut to imitate the action of the wooden plug baits with beveled or grooved heads. The way to do this is to cut off the herring head at an angle of about 60 degrees to the backbone, cutting diagonally downward to produce a beveled front. The herring's body is then rigged with two hooks as shown in the bait section of this book.

Spinning or mooching is successful wherever salmon can be found. In the inland passages of

A salmon chaser boat heading offshore to intercept early Pacific salmon runs.

the Pacific Northwest coast, kings seem to move back and forth constantly in search of schools of herring or candlefish. Occasionally they work near the shoreline or at least off points or peninsulas of land that jut out into fairly deep water. Sometimes where the sweep of tide isn't too great, it is advantageous to anchor the boat; elsewhere it's far better to drift with the tide. The best time for mooching appears to be just before flood tide and just after, when salmon are normally most active and when there is enough movement of the tide to keep the bait acting "alive."

Mooching is done as follows. The whole rig, herring bait and keel sinker, is cast out and allowed to settle to the bottom. Then, a yard at a time, the angler retrieves the bait upward at an angle, trying to imitate the fluttering, helpless action of a wounded fish. Obviously different weights of sinkers are needed to cope with various tide movements and with different depths.

The most commonly used sinkers for this purpose are crescent-shaped and come in sizes of from 1½ to more than 6 ounces, but ordinarily the 2- to 3-ounce sizes will be most useful.

During periods when the tide is slack or very slight and when baits seem to go dead, it is possible to mooch with the boat set at its slowest idling speed. Only experience can give a salmon fisherman the right touch for mooching, but once this is learned it becomes almost involuntary.

In some ways the silver salmon or coho is a more exciting game fish than its larger cousin the chinook. Since it's usually found near the surface, it can be taken on lighter tackle.

Silvers have been found in the Pacific Ocean from Los Coronados, Baja California, north to Alaska and south on the Asiatic side to Japan. Adults ascend almost all of the accessible streams from Santa Cruz north to Alaska to spawn. However, the most successful fishing is probably in the British Columbia area where the largest silver of which there is an authentic record was taken. This was a 31-pounder captured in 1947. The California record was a 22-pounder taken at Papermill Creek in 1959. The average landed by

sportsmen on hook and line would be under 24 inches long and run from 6 to 9 pounds.

Unlike chinooks, which sometimes enter streams in springtime, silvers always move upstream to spawn in the fall or winter, beginning in September and continuing through March. The bulk of the spawning actually occurs from November to January. Adult males enter the streams when they are either two or three years old, but females seldom return to spawn until they are at least three years old. All silvers, male or female, spend the first year of their lives in the stream or river in which they hatch and all adults die after spawning. This means, of course, that silvers spend a much shorter time in saltwater than do the larger chinooks. But during the time they are at sea, their growth is extremely rapid and, in fact, borders on the phenomenal when compared to their growth while still in the home stream.

Food study findings indicate that, in the ocean, cohos feed mostly on many kinds of small fishes, on a few crustaceans and squid. In saltwater, silvers are caught primarily by trolling with shiny spoons or the old favorite, beveled plugs. Less often they're taken by trolling with whole dead herring. They're usually found within 30 feet of the surface and therefore are within "range" of medium spinning tackle. The best trolling speed appears to be about 2 knots per hour.

Coho fishing is extraordinary sport off the Canadian Pacific coast, where it's often possible to catch them on standard bait-casting, spinning, or fly-casting tackle amid magnificent mountain scenery. The fish are very acrobatic and they fight with the same abandon, the same long runs, and with the violent leaps of the Atlantic salmon. In fall around Queen Charlotte Islands, the cohos gather in schools and there it is possible to take them by trolling large streamer flies—as used for large freshwater trout and Atlantic salmon—or small spoons or spinners. They also provide great sport in the bays of Vancouver Island, where the common technique is to drift-cast for them near the surface with light tackle and large bucktail flies or darting spoons.

A boat rigged with multiple trolling gear and downriggers for coho salmon fishing.

A salmon boat heads toward the open sea from La Push on the Olympic Peninsula.

13

OFFSHORE FISHES OF THE PACIFIC COAST:

California Yellowtail, Pacific Jack Mackerel, Black Sea Bass, Kelp Bass, Pacific Bluefin Tuna, Pacific Albacore, White Sea Bass, Pacific Bonito, Sheepshead, Bocaccio, Ocean Whitefish, Pacific or California Halibut

Ichthyologists figure there are about 30,000 to 35,000 different kinds of fishes living in the world today. About 18,000 or 20,000 are marine fishes while the remainder inhabit freshwaters. As many as 100 to 200 fishes completely new to science are discovered each year throughout the world.

About 700–800 different species of the world's total have been found in North American Pacific coast saltwaters. Many are offshore fishes. Some live near the surface; others, called demersal species, stay on the floor of the sea. Still others prefer living just halfway in between and are accordingly called mid-depth fishes.

Often the body color of a fish is a dead giveaway of the depth at which he normally lives. Bright or multicolored species usually inhabit inshore waters shallower than 150 feet. Brown, red, or black are typical colors of fishes living on or near the bottom in moderate to deep water. Offshore surface dwellers are usually blue or gray above and white underneath. Those that live at the middle depths, several hundred feet beneath the surface, often have light organs on

Heading out onto the open Pacific to fish for a great variety of offshore species.

The houndfish is among the strangest species an angler might hook in the Pacific.

their bodies or are aluminum-colored with crimson fins. There are exceptions, but these are good basic facts to remember.

The roster of Pacific marine fishes includes interesting and strange ones as well as the popular game species. For example, there's a flatfish that makes a slow stalk along the bottom and rears up to strike its prey like a cobra. In this manner it can capture crabs with unusual skill. Another strange one is the goatfish with tastebud-equipped chin whiskers to sweep the bottom in search of dinner. Anglerfish dangle enticing lures from built-in fishing rods and the attracted victims are helpless to escape against the "current" created when the anglerfish opens its over-sized mouth.

Senoritas operate fish delousing stations in and around kelp beds. Sheepshead, kelp bass, and other fishes periodically take advantage of the senoritas' services and swim close by for a complete "examination." The patient cooperates by languidly raising its fins, flipping gill covers, or even by opening its mouth at the appropriate time. So long as the senoritas are near their delousing stations, they are safe from attack, but if they wander away, they become fair game for other fishes.

California has been a pioneer in the conservation and management of saltwater fishes. As long ago as 1931, bag limits and size limits were placed on popular game species. Closed seasons on species in danger were inaugurated as early as 1901. California is one of a handful of states that require a valid angling license to fish in saltwater.

CALIFORNIA YELLOWTAIL

The Pacific or California yellowtail, *Seriola dorsalis*, is one of ten members of the international jack family known to inhabit North American waters. In one year as many as 350,000 yellowtails were taken by sport fishermen alone. The commercial catch runs into several hundred tons annually.

Most yellowtails caught along our Pacific coast originate around Cedros Island, Baja California. Here yellowtails spawn when they are about two or three years old and at a weight of from 7 to 10 pounds. A three-year-old female may carry 1,500,000 eggs during the spawning season, which runs from June through September. Most activity occurs in early August. Yellowtails are great migrators and, once mature, travel long distances, averaging as much as 200–300 miles to reach California waters.

Yellowtails have been reported from Monterey Bay to Cabo San Lucas, Baja California, and north throughout the entire Gulf of California. Most will weigh between 10 and 20 pounds and be between three and seven years old when hooked.

Hardly delicate in their feeding habits, yellowtails forage avidly on anchovies and sardines in southern California waters. Farther south they add pelagic red crabs, squid, and similar items to their diet. They can be caught on a wide variety of live baits.

Ordinarily yellowtails are found in greatest abundance around the offshore islands, and also around kelp beds of the southern California coast. Anglers trolling for albacores during midsummer frequently receive a yellowtail bonus if they drift or troll past floating patches of kelp with a feather, nickel-finish spoon, or an artificial squid. Yellowtails strike best on a fast rather than slow troll.

During summer and early fall months large schools of yellowtails are frequently observed "breezing" near the surface of the water, or cruising aimlessly about. In winter and early spring, however, they're found deeper, practically never on the surface.

Fishermen often see yellowtails engage in a peculiar maneuver, which, for lack of a better title, can be called "let's attack the shark." A dozen or more yellowtails will find a shark, usually a blue shark, and then appear to attack it from all sides—nudging, pulling at its fins, biting and bumping it. But the shark is not really in trouble. The yellowtails are only removing external parasites from the shark's body. A lure cast near the yellowtails will bring an immediate strike.

PACIFIC JACK MACKEREL

Jack mackerel, *Trachurus symmetricus*, are caught along the coast from British Columbia to Acapulco, Mexico, but are rare south of Magdalena Bay, Baja California. They are an entirely pelagic, schooling species, often found near the surface and close to the mainland shore, to islands, or hovering above offshore banks.

It is a bonanza for fishermen when schools of large jack mackerel suddenly appear in any given area. The most dependable bait is a large live anchovy, fished near the surface on a small hook and light monofilament line. The jack is excellent for the light spinning enthusiast.

Jack mackerel have very weak mouths and often wage a strong-enough fight to tear loose from the hook. Others are lost when fishermen attempt to hoist them aboard without a net or a gaff. The best jack-fishing period off California is usually July through September, but fish may appear in numbers as early as May.

The catch from southern California party boats reaches 200,000 a season. Extremely prolific, a typical jack female will spawn more than once during the season. The eggs float freely in upper layers of the ocean, usually within 300 feet of the surface. At average ocean temperatures, the eggs hatch in four to five days. The spawning takes place over an extensive area as far as 80 to 250 miles from shore.

The Pacific jack mackerel—also called jack mackerel, mackerel jack, horse mackerel, and Spanish mackerel—does not grow to impressive size. A 20- to 22-inch fish is a good one.

A similar fish, the Pacific mackerel, *Pneumatophorus japonicus diego*, is often confused with the mackerel. Also a pelagic, schooling species known to range from the Gulf of Alaska to Banderas Bay, Mexico, it seldom weighs more than a pound.

Mackerel readily strike small jigs, small spoons, small spinners, plugs, cut bait, and live bait. It is difficult to find a fish that will be more active on extremely small tackle. But such a fish can be a nuisance when the anglers on a crowded passenger boat are looking for larger game.

For a fisherman who likes to spin with extremely light gear, this mackerel is made to order because it's very easy to attract. An angler after jack mackerel should simply chum by grinding any smaller fish, such as sardines or anchovies, and allow the bits of chum to drift away with the tide.

BLACK SEA BASS

The black sea bass or California bass or California jewfish or giant bass, *Stereolepis gigas*, is a relative of the striped bass, kelp bass, other saltwater basses, groupers, and cabrilla. This giant fish ranges from Monterey, California, southward and into the Gulf of California.

Most abundant at Anacapa, San Nicolas, and Los Coronados islands and between Oceanside and San Clemente on the mainland, black sea bass prefer a rocky bottom just outside of a kelp bed where the water varies between 19 and 25 fathoms deep. But they can frequently be found in inshore areas from 5 to 10 fathoms deep where the bottom is sandy. These inshore blacks average smaller in size.

Black sea bass do not mature until they are eleven to thirteen years old, between 50 and 60 pounds. A 320-pound female ready to spawn was found carrying an estimated 60 million eggs that weighed 47 pounds. The main spawning season occurs from July to September.

Because of their size and extremely bulky shape, black sea bass may appear slow and clumsy. Actually, they are capable of catching some of the fast fishes of the Pacific in a short chase, as is evident from the wide variety of items found in their stomachs. Included in a bass's diet would be mackerel, jack mackerel, sheepshead, ocean whitefish, sand bass, cancer crabs or red crabs. Once the stinger of a stingray was found inside the air bladder of a large bass. It had become embedded there after piercing the stomach.

The mouth of a large bass is yawning enough to consume a medium-size fish in a single gulp. Black sea bass probably exceed 7 feet 6 inches in length and 600 pounds in size. There's no way to estimate the longevity of this fish, but California biologists recently examined a 435-pounder and determined that it was between seventy-two and seventy-five years old.

There is no shortcut to landing a black sea bass once hooked. Most sea bass specialists use a double-built swordfish or marlin rod with a 22-ounce tip; a number 14/0 hook; about 500 yards of 70-pound test line on a 10/0 (600-yard capacity) heavy-duty, deep-sea reel, and wire or cable leader testing about 100 to 150 pounds and about 6 feet 6 inches long.

The bait can be almost anything, but one favorite is a small barracuda or mackerel, split and tied to the line with a section of nylon. This is done to hide the hook with the point left embedded near the tail. Besides mackerel and barracuda, black sea bass readily take sand dabs, smaller bass, large sardines, queenfish, or a fillet of any of the other fishes that live in the same water. The bait need not be fresh and anglers prefer it a bit ripe from sitting in the sun.

Sometimes the strike is barely noticeable, but a wise fisherman plays out a small amount of line anyway, just in case. As soon as this much slack is taken up and the line taut, he sets the hook sharply.

The secret to landing this species is to maintain all the pressure the tackle will stand. If the fish is given any slack at all, the bass will shake its head violently from side to side. Either the hook will be pulled free or the line will snap.

Sport fishermen can afford to copy a trick used by market fishermen to catch big blacks. The tail is chopped off a large live sardine or jack mackerel or ocean whitefish. The idea is to inhibit the swimming ability of the baitfish and at the same time permit the release of blood into the water where a hungry bass may be lurking. More often than not he'll sniff it out.

KELP BASS

Although kelp bass, *Paralabrax clathratus*, also known as rock bass, sand bass, calico bass, bull bass, and cabrilla, do not compare in size to black sea bass, they are an extremely fine game species. Unfortunately, this almost sedentary fish becomes scarcer every year, even though commercial fishing has been prohibited since 1953.

Kelp bass are mostly caught around kelp beds on live anchovies or sardines fished near or just under the surface. Recently more fishermen have been catching them on trolled plugs, spoons, and streamer flies because these fish will take a variety of artificials. Best catches are made with yellow or brown plugs or streamer flies. But more important than type of bait is knowledge that kelp bass are almost never caught far away from a kelp bed. Many kelp beds where bass are most plentiful are not visible from the surface of the water.

Kelp bass are distributed from San Francisco south to Abreojos Point, Baja California. They are not abundant north of Point Conception, California, but at kelp beds elsewhere within their range, usually the most abundant game species in residence.

Calico bass, a common name for a smaller kelp bass, can be caught practically the year round. But the period from May to October is best for the larger variety, frequently called bull bass.

The kelp bass and black sea bass have cousins along the Pacific coast worthy of mention here. First is the broomtail grouper, *Mycteroperca xenarchus*, a colorful, spotted fish also called the garrupa (in Mexico), gray broomtail, pinto broomtail, or spotted broomtail. Especially plentiful in scattered spots off Baja California, it can be taken on strip baits, live baits, or trolled spoon lures. The broomtail grouper has been caught up to 75 pounds, but probably grows larger.

Another bass cousin, this one reaching a weight of 125 pounds, is the gulf grouper or garrupa de baya, *Mycteroperca jordani*. Less colorful than the broomtail, it is more abundant south of San Quintín Bay and in the Gulf of California. Only a few have been taken north of San Diego. Largely a bottom feeder on live bait, it will take an artificial lure trolled slowly.

The sand bass, *Paralabrax nebulifer*, can be taken the year round south of Monterey on various kinds of strip baits, live anchovies, queenfish, small sardines, shrimp, and mussels. It feeds on the bottom and reaches almost 2 feet in length. The spotted bass, *Paralabrax maculatofasciatus*, also called spotted cabrilla or pinto cabrilla, reaches about 1½ feet in length. It ranges from Point Conception, California, southward in nearly all bays, sloughs, and stream entrances to Mazatlán, Mexico. It is taken on a wide variety of live and cut baits.

PACIFIC BLUEFIN TUNA

An important event for California sportsmen begins each year with the sudden announcement: "Tuna off San Diego!" When word spreads that schools are streaming north toward Catalina waters, hundreds of party boats, charter boats, and private craft suddenly appear and roam these offshore waters. And the excitement, which follows from the docks of San Diego to Los Angeles, is something to see. All at once

these offshore waters are filled with ravenous schools of bluefin tuna making their annual and mysterious northern migration.

There are big and small tuna, but it makes no difference to sportsmen. Even the 20- to 30-pounders can strip a reel in seconds. The California party boats are excellent vehicles for catching many species of fish found offshore but they are made to order for the bluefin tuna run. All contain ample bait tanks which can hold an average of 15 pounds of live anchovies for each angler. When the tuna are active these anchovies are used up rapidly.

Party boats always leave the dock long before dawn. The entire trip to the tuna "grounds" is a time for vast speculation. Every experienced boat captain knows well the vagaries of bluefins. He knows that some days the deep blue channel will be alive, but suddenly they are gone. New and bigger schools can appear and disappear with almost magical suddenness, and every fisherman on board hopes this will be *the* day.

If the bluefins move in to gorge on huge baitfish schools around the Channel Islands, it's a day never forgotten. The party boat will reach the scene before daylight and the captain will study the current and swing his craft in a wide circle while a bait tender tosses live anchovies or chum overboard. The first wild swirl out on the dark surface of the water means that the tuna are coming in!

Immediately the bait tender ladles out more chum. Everyone on board pitches a live anchovy bait in the path of the tuna. Then they wait and the suspense is terrific.

Fishermen go down to the sea for many reasons. One is to enjoy nature's magnificent changing spectacle. I remember standing aboard a party boat as the sun came up over mainland mountains, revealing a clear blue and calm Pacific Ocean. The whole scene was exquisite. But suddenly a school of tuna reached the first baits tossed overboard. We could see the shadowy blue forms moving underneath them. Then came the first lightninglike strike, and somebody's rod bent nearly double.

Those bluefins were crazy and hungry. Several reels began to sing at once and line vanished from all of them. Although every fisherman is expecting a strike when tuna are feeding all about him, the strike still comes as a sudden electric shock. The rod tip is whipped downward and at once the reel is thrown into gear as a fast-moving fish strips off 100 yards and maybe even 200 yards of line on the first wild run. When he finally stops, you begin to pump, but not for long, because in a few seconds the big bluefin will be off again.

The more tired the tuna becomes, the deeper it goes and the tougher it is to pump it upward to the boat and to the gaff. To catch just one 30-pounder on light tackle is a hard day's work; a full morning of this kind of action is enough to send an angler home sore and tired, but happy.

The Pacific or California bluefin tuna, *Thunnus saliens*, is one of three tunas which inhabit Pacific coastal waters. Although adults have been taken as far north as Shelikof Strait, Alaska, to Cabos San Lucas, Baja California, they are seldom numerous north of Los Angeles or south of Magdalena Bay. A pelagic species, bluefins appear seasonally, sporadically, and unpredictably.

Although the Atlantic bluefin attains a weight of 1,800 pounds and more, the largest known Pacific was a 297-pounder caught off Guadalupe Island, Baja California. The largest California bluefin on sport-fishing tackle was a 251-pounder caught off Santa Catalina. Average-size tuna nowadays run between 10 and 45 pounds.

Although some days bluefins strike with abandon, they are more reluctant to take a baited hook than any other tuna or tunalike fishes. They are seldom caught on trolled lures or trolled baits.

A tuna foraging near the surface wants a large, live, and lively anchovy in which the hook is not visible. No leader or swivels are used because it's believed that the tuna will not strike any baits thus rigged. There are times, however, when tuna lose almost all their wariness; this is especially true of bluefins in mixed company with albacore or skipjacks, when the competition for food is especially keen. An angler lucky enough to find such a mixed school of fishes will do very well with either live anchovies or firecracker sardines.

Occasionally, bluefins are located at depths of 100 to 150 feet where they aren't as selective as they tend to be in shallow water. A fisherman can use a sinker weighing as much as 2 ounces and a larger hook without alarming them.

The first Pacific tuna was taken off Santa Catalina in 1898 by Fredrick Holder. Although

Heading for blue water off southern California where great fishing exists the year round.

he was using the crudest kind of tackle and a knuckle-buster reel without mechanical drag, he still managed to land a 183-pounder. It remains one of the most remarkable bluefin catches of all time. Holder surely started something. Shortly after his historic catch, the famous Catalina Tuna Club was formed and among its earlier visitors were Zane Grey and Gifford Pinchot. Mostly these early pioneers trolled (instead of using live bait), and the tuna they hooked were usually of large size. In 1909, George Farnsworth introduced the unorthodox system of trolling by flying a kite. This was moderately successful and has been copied in Atlantic waters, where it works better. More and more the bluefin is becoming a light-tackle fish in the Pacific, where a few serious anglers have made some astonishing catches.

Bluefins are likely to show up along the California coast from May through September. Some of the most productive areas are in Santa Monica Bay, near the kelp beds between San Clemente and Oceanside, around Santa Catalina, San Clemente Island, and Los Coronados.

Two other tunas are found in Pacific coast waters. These are the big-eyed tuna, *Parathunnus mebachi*, and the yellowfin tuna, *Neothunnus macropterus*. The yellowfin occurs southward from Santa Barbara along the coast of Baja California to Central America. It is present around the Hawaiian Islands but otherwise is not common north of Mexico. It is taken in a manner and on tackle similar to that used for taking bluefin tuna.

PACIFIC ALBACORE

Not long ago Japan notified California Department of Fish and Game officials that an albacore had been caught about 145 miles east of Tokyo. The fish carried a spaghetti-type plastic tag affixed to the fish nine months before in California. It had traveled 4,600 miles and had gained 4½ pounds. It had traveled more than 500 miles a month—almost 18 miles day.

But that is no isolated example. Other albacore tagged and released off California also have been captured by Japanese fishermen. California-tagged albacore have been recovered off Midway Island out in the Pacific and in waters around Hawaii.

These recoveries prove that the albacore, also called longfin or long-finned tuna, is among the most widely traveled, the finest, and the fastest traveling game fishes. *Germo alalunga* is distinguished from other tunas of the West coast by the extremely long pectoral fins which reach two thirds of the way back to the tail.

The life history of the albacore is as mysterious as its unpredictable wanderings over the Pacific. Spawning probably does not take place near our coast. No Pacific albacore larvae have ever been identified in our waters or elsewhere in the Pacific. There are indications, however, that albacore spawn in mid-ocean, possibly north and west of the Hawaiian Islands, because large specimens caught in this area during late summer, very deep, had nearly ripe eggs in their ovaries. Contrary to belief on party boats and around fishing docks, the albacore is not a hybrid or "mule." It is a distinct, far-ranging species.

The albacore's diet varies, depending on the depth of the feeding area and on the foods most easily available. The stomach contents of most albacore caught reveal small fishes mixed with squid, octopuses, and shrimplike organisms. Recent research has indicated that of every hundred albacore caught, fifty-one are hooked in waters with temperatures ranging between 60 and 64 degrees F. An additional thirty-seven of these fish are taken in temperatures of between 65 and 70 degrees F. In other words, 90 percent were taken in waters between 60 and 70 degrees, a fact that has simplified the finding of albacore schools.

The fishing technique for albacore is much the same as for tuna, except that they can be taken far more often on artificial lures. Nor are they as selective of live baits. The first albacore of the season are taken in mid-June, and a few remain in United States coastal waters until the last half of February. Year in and year out, the best action occurs during August and September.

Like many other fishes, actively feeding albacore will strike almost anything. At times they even seem to catch the bait in midair. On other days nothing seems to work.

Many charter-boat captains are expert at finding albacores when there is no sign of them on the surface. This means probing around with a long line in depths from 100 to 300 feet. It isn't nearly as action-filled as surface fishing, but it is productive. Some years most schools of albacore seem to migrate northward along the coast either deep enough so that the sport fishermen do not find them or beyond the range of sport boats.

An angler's best bet is to watch the outdoor columns in local newspapers to learn of the arrival of albacore in local waters. They first appear off Baja California. Although there are records of albacore from Clarion Island off the coast of Mexico, the fish are rarely caught south of Magdalena Bay. Gradually they move northward along the coast, reaching the south coast of Alaska in the late summer and fall months. Fishing in-between is good off Oregon and Washington.

The largest known albacore is a 93-pounder taken by commercial fishermen on long line gear, though larger fish have probably been caught and gone unrecorded.

WHITE SEA BASS

Nine kinds of croakers are found along the Pacific coast. One of the most important is the white sea bass, readily distinguished from all other croakers by greater size when mature, and by the four or five dark and vertical bars on their flanks when young. There is also a raised ridge on the midline of the belly at all ages. The white sea bass is also called white croaker, king croaker, weakfish, sea trout, or *Cynoscion nobilis.* It is taken near kelp beds, over shallow submerged banks, and on the edges of banks with such live bait as sardines, anchovies, small mackerel, and strip bait. Sea bass will take lures trolled at a fairly slow speed.

The recommended hook size is from number 1 to 2/0. Although white sea bass are not ordinarily as wary and shy as some other Pacific offshore fishes, they can become quite selective. Occasionally sea bass will strike only fairly large, live Pacific mackerel. Other times a live squid is the only successful bait.

Once white sea bass were far more plentiful than today. Large numbers were taken years ago in the San Francisco Bay area, but their presence there is now a thing of the past. Spawning is presumed to take place in late spring and on into the summer months. The shore areas in Santa Monica Bay, Belmont Shore, Dana Point, Oceanside, Coronado, and similar localities appear to be important nursery grounds for white sea bass. But in many of these same areas the white sea bass population is seriously threatened by pollution.

Large white sea bass have been taken as far north as Juneau, Alaska, though ordinarily they do not range far beyond San Francisco. Southward they extend along the coast of Baja California and into the Gulf of California. Larger fish frequently gather into large, loosely grouped schools, and are most common over sandy bottoms and around the offshore margins of kelp beds on the mainland coast. They are most numerous offshore around San Clemente and Santa Catalina.

An adult white sea bass is a strong fighter and anything over 10 pounds will give tackle a good test. The largest known is an 83¾-pound fish taken off San Felipe, Mexico, in 1953. That must have been an extremely old fish because 40-pounders taken in Mexican waters will average about twenty years old.

Many saltwater species of fish are vastly more active at night than in daylight and the white sea bass is one of these. Fishing for big whites at night is among the most unforgettable experiences available to an angler along the Pacific coast; still, this technique is not yet fully exploited.

To angle at sea in the middle of the night for any game species is wonderfully exciting. Summer nights on the Pacific are often calm except for the activity of fishes and marine animals that suddenly surge to the surface. Sometimes the activity is so great that the sea appears to be boiling. At such times white sea bass lose much of their caution. They not only venture closer to a boat in darkness, but also feed nearer the surface and strike any lure or live bait with more abandon.

Even on those nights when action is slow and fish are not striking, there is a restful fascination to sitting quietly on board and waiting for the unexpected to happen.

PACIFIC BONITO

Many fishermen consider the Pacific or California bonito, *Sarda chiliensis,* among the finest fighting fish for its size in the ocean. And with good reason, because here is a fish with a voracious appetite—which at times will strike any conceivable bait or object tossed in its path. Once a school is aroused, a bonito will attack a dead or a live anchovy, a sardine, squid, jig, a freshwater plug, practically anything. One bonito has been known to take two different baits trolled behind a boat at once.

The California bonito is a handsome member of the mackerel family, which also includes the wahoo and sierra mackerel. The only other member of the family found off the United States coast is the Monterey Spanish mackerel, a very rare summer visitor.

Bonitos are the only tunalike fishes with oblique dark stripes on their backs. They appear in almost every section of the eastern Pacific, ranging from Vancouver Island, British Columbia, to Panama and along the South American coast to Chile. They are a school species usually observed within a few miles of shore along the mainland and around islands. Only occasionally are they found far at sea.

Most bonitos are taken by anglers trolling (usually for other fish) with chrome jigs, plastic squid, or feather jigs. When a single bonito is caught and hooked, it is possible to hook others by casting near the hooked fish. By keeping one fish hooked all the time, one after another bonito can be taken until a fisherman becomes too tired to continue. A bonito of 4 or 5 pounds on light or medium spinning tackle is a game fish of unbelievable endurance. Its strength is amazing to freshwater anglers who hook a bonito for the first time.

There are numerous reports, none verified so far, of bonitos weighing up to 40 and even 50 pounds. The largest verified bonito is a 28-pounder taken off Baja California. Most bonitos weigh between 3 and 10 pounds; anything over 10 pounds is extraordinary. Bonitos are important along the Pacific because they are valuable baitfish for other sport fishing.

Spawning occurs all along the West coast at odd intervals between January and May. The free-floating eggs require three days to hatch and the resulting small fish are usually first observed by the livebait haulers when they reach 6 or 8 inches in early summer. After one year they may weigh as much as 6 or 7 pounds. Young bonitos from 6 inches to more than a foot long are the best baitfish. The larger sizes are especially desirable for marlin, tuna, and black sea bass.

SHEEPSHEAD

The sheepshead of the Pacific, *Pimelometopon pulcher*, one of three members of the wrasse family along the West coast, is among the plug-uglies of the fish world. As though its caninelike teeth and its lantern jaw are not enough, the male sheepshead develops a forehead hump during the breeding season. His scientific name means "beautiful fat forehead."

Even the body colors of the sheepshead are weird. At all stages, ages, and sexes, sheepshead can be distinguished from the other wrasses by their unique coloration. The young of both sexes are a solid orange-red except for roundish black blotches. Adult females are a dull red or rose, and adult males have a bluish black head and tail with a red midsection. Both males and females have light or whitish chins when full grown.

Most abundant near the bottom, particularly around dense kelp forests, sheepshead are taken from 29- to 100-foot depths, though they are occasionally caught in shallower water. They also tend to congregate along rocky shores, especially near mussel beds. Never abundant north of Los Angeles, they have been taken from Monterey Bay to the tip of Baja California and throughout the Gulf of California.

Male or dog sheepshead are said to reach more than 30 pounds, but most sheepshead caught by fishermen are less than 15. They are taken on 3/0 to 5/0 hooks baited with mussels, rock crabs, lobster, shrimp with the shell on, clams, abalone, and fish strips.

Although they seldom strike a trolled or cast lure that is retrieved in a normal manner, sheepshead can often be tempted to strike even a shiny bare hook or a small metal jig that is jiggled up and down in an enticing manner within a few inches of the bottom. They are expert bait thieves and their large jaw-teeth can cause the hook to slip out after an angler strikes.

Any fisherman who hooks a sheepshead is in for a strong, tugging battle. It can end in disaster when the fish runs through or around kelp or ducks beneath a rocky ledge. It's possible in some rocky areas to hook sheepshead all day long but never land one. The best fishing areas are around kelp beds south of Point Conception, California, and around the offshore Pacific islands south of Santa Cruz Island.

Skin divers have often reported what they believed to be the same sheepshead frequenting a particular reef, rock outcropping, or other underwater landmark over the course of several years. There are so many similar reports that it is almost safe to assume that sheepshead do not wander about very much. This is especially true of large, adult fish.

Commercial fishermen consider sheepshead a nuisance and believe they are destructive to lobsters, abalones, and other kinds of shellfish. According to skin divers, sheepshead do spend time trying to live up to this bad reputation. On the other hand, while a sheepshead's stomach is usually filled with such shellfish as lobsters and abalones, many a large black sea bass has been found to contain a sheepshead in its innards. Lobster fishermen frequently use sheepshead as bait in their traps but sheepshead often reciprocate by entering a trap and eating all the lobsters inside.

Until recent years the flesh of the sheepshead

was considered inedible and perhaps even poisonous. This meant that many fishermen didn't bother to take their catch home. Actually, the flesh of a sheepshead is white, firm, and rather mild in flavor. When fried in thin fillets, it is difficult to surpass on the table, and chunks of sheepshead meat make a delicious fish chowder or fish salad.

BOCACCIO

All together there are fifty-two members of the rockfish family native to Pacific coast waters of North America. The bocaccio, *Sebastodes paucispinis*, is one of the most numerous. It reaches a length of 36 inches and a weight of 21 pounds, but an extremely good fish would be half that size.

Almost any rocky or rubble bottom from 250 to 750 feet deep is likely to yield a good catch of bocaccios. The secret lies entirely in finding the right type of bottom.

The usual fishing rig consists of from four to six hooks above a sinker heavy enough to take all to the bottom on a fairly straight course. The rig can be fished from a large specially built reel attached to the rail of a boat, or from a large capacity reel as used for large billfish and tuna. Because of the depths (adult bocaccios sometimes go as deep as 1,000 feet), it takes considerable time just to lower the line and haul it up again. So the bait should be sufficiently tough to remain on the hook while being chewed by bocaccios and other deep fishes. Squid makes an ideal bait.

Once the angler finds the bottom, he should leave the rig there long enough to catch a fish on every hook. This is difficult because the impulse is to strike immediately when a nibble is felt. Bottom fishermen have caught bocaccios from Queen Charlotte Sound, British Columbia, to Ensenada, Baja California.

Another rockfish caught in great numbers is the olive rockfish, often confused with kelp bass. It reaches a weight of 7 or 8 pounds, and some kelp beds around Santa Barbara and San Nicolas islands are almost paved with them. Olive rockfish have been taken as deep as 480 feet.

Another important rockfish is the blue, which ranges from the Bering Sea to Santo Tomas, Baja California. It never reaches more than a few

pounds in size, but can be caught in quantity near rocky shores, around breakwaters, sunken ships, piles of rubble and similar localities along the entire California, Oregon, and Washington coasts. Best baits are mussels, clams, crabs, shrimp, or squid. For their size, blue rockfish put up an excellent battle on light tackle.

Vermilion rockfish have been caught from Vancouver Island south to Baja California. They reach 30 inches, about 15 pounds, and occur in water 180 to 500 feet deep over irregular, rocky or rubble bottoms. Vermilion rockfish usually make up a majority of the bag of southern California anglers. The same rig, bait, and technique can be used as for bocaccios.

Because a good rockfish hole may yield a dozen or more kinds of rockfish any day, rockfishing is colorful, interesting, productive, mysterious, and good exercise. And it yields very unusual fish. The strangest member of the rockfish family is the sculpin, which reaches a maximum weight of about 4 pounds and is an excellent fish for chowders and soups.

Fishermen should handle sculpin carefully because the sharp fin spines—dorsal, anal, and pelvic—are mildly poisonous and can cause an extremely painful wound if the skin is punctured. Immersion in hot water in which Epsom salts have been dissolved will help alleviate the discomforts from a sculpin wound. If undue swelling, nausea, dizziness, or fainting follow, a doctor should be called immediately.

OCEAN WHITEFISH

The ocean whitefish, *Caulolatilus princeps*, no relation of the freshwater whitefish, is the only member of the blanquillo fish family known to inhabit California waters. It reaches 20 pounds but seldom exceeds 10 and is caught from Point Conception south to the tip of Baja California, then throughout the Gulf of California. The same or a closely related species is also found off Ecuador, Peru, Chile, and the Galápagos Islands.

Whitefish live mostly at depths of from 30 to 300 feet where the bottom is rocky. They will eat almost anything, including crabs, shrimp, many crustaceans, small octopuses, squid, and bottom-feeding fishes.

Once he has hooked a whitefish, a fisherman is·

in for a thrill because even a small ocean whitefish wages a strong battle. In a good whitefish hole, a rig with from two to four hooks can be used to catch that many fish at once. The best spots are offshore islands south of the Santa Barbara County line. Cortez and Tanner banks are also good. Spring, summer, and fall months are excellent. The winter months provide good fishing, but in much deeper water.

PACIFIC OR CALIFORNIA HALIBUT

Found all around the world is the flatfish family, consisting of flounder, soles, and halibut, all of which are delicious on the table and curious in appearance. Their compressed bodies with both eyes on one side make adult flatfish easy to recognize.

After flatfish spawn, their eggs develop into normal-looking small fish, but gradually one eye begins to "migrate" or shift to the other side of the head and the young fish settle to the bottom. There they spend their entire lives lying on one side, with both eyes on top, while feeding on small fish and bottom-dwelling invertebrates. Usually the bottom side of the fish becomes white and the top side matches the ocean floor. A flatfish can even change its color and pattern as it changes location.

The left-eyed California halibut is the largest species of the flatfish family known in North American waters. There are numerous reports of 70- and 80-pounders, but the accepted record is a 61½-pound fish, which measured 5 feet in length.

Unlike many of its relatives which depend mostly on crustaceans, halibut feed largely upon anchovies and similar small fishes. Impossible as it must seem, they have been observed jumping clear of the water to catch anchovies from schools traveling near the surface. In turn, halibut are preyed upon by angel sharks, electric rays, sea lions, and Pacific bottlenose dolphin.

Once the California Department of Fish and Game tagged 7,000 halibut and 350 tag recoveries were made. Only one fish had traveled more than one mile.

California halibut are most abundant on sandy bottoms shallower than 10 fathoms. Some of the largest halibut tend to congregate around dense

The halibut is a great food fish caught with bait right on the bottom. Halibut reach 300 pounds and possibly more.

beds of sand dollars just outside a pounding surf. They are found from the Klamath River south to Magdalena Bay, Baja California. At times they are abundant in the fast-running channels of Morro and Mission bays and at other times are caught in strong surf along open, exposed beaches or in areas where rocky bottoms and rugged shoreline are broken up by small sandy areas.

Pacific coast waters include two other game fishes of importance. One is the sablefish, *Anoplopoma fimbria*, the only member of the sablefish family inhabiting the coast. Adult sablefish live on the bottom, preferably in blue clay or hard mud areas near submarine canyons and depressions from northwestern Alaska to the tip of Baja California.

The record sablefish probably exceeded 50 pounds, but most weigh less than 30. Tagging studies reveal that they do not travel very far.

Sablefish are sometimes abundant in inshore waters and smaller individuals are even caught in the surf. But more live in deep water from 450 to about 1,000 feet. They seem to migrate into deeper waters during winter and in summer are most likely to be found in shallower water. They will strike chunks of salted mackerel or fresh squid with equal abandon. Although not very strong fighters, they more than make up for it, in some cases, with heavy weight.

Another important Pacific coast species is the lingcod, *Ophiodon elongatus,* which exists from northwestern Alaska to Central America, but is not abundant south of San Francisco. It inhabits deep areas near the bottom, generally close to rock piles and kelp beds, especially where there is a strong tidal current. About 350 feet is the ideal depth at which to find lingcod, which reach lengths of 5 feet and weights of 70 pounds.

A totuaba comes aboard in the Gulf of California, Baja California.

14

INSHORE ALONG THE PACIFIC COAST:

Corbina, Surfperch, Greenling Seatrout, A Miscellany of Pacific Coast Fishes

From Point Barrow, Alaska, to Panama curves a shoreline of approximately 4,000 miles, including all bays, river estuaries, and the Gulf of California. Included in that distance are some 2,500 miles of surf available to any shore angler. Most of this surf line, except in Mexico, is paralleled by excellent highways. Motorists can scan this vast expanse of water and wonder where and when to fish. First consider a partial list of fish available to the saltwater inshore fisherman along the Pacific coast: opaleye, surfperch (many varieties), bass, cod, cabezon, croaker, corbina, several kinds of rockfish, halibut, flounder, sole, sculpin, sheepshead and dab, striped bass and salmon. Remember these are only the major, widely distributed varieties. Elsewhere other fish can be taken in limited areas. A good example is the game and spectacular roosterfish of the Gulf of California.

For the man with limited time or knowledge of the waters there is one sure way to locate a productive spot and this happens to be true on any coast anywhere. Watch for the bait and tackle shops and boat liveries located along coastal highways. Such establishments are fairly sure signs that good fishing exists nearby and they also serve as good sources of fishing information.

Still tackle and bait stores are not your only recourse. There are other reliable ways to find productive waters on any shoreline. On a mostly rocky shoreline look for a short stretch that is smooth and sandy. Any fish in the vicinity which prefer a sand or open-type bottom will congregate there. Or on a long, uninterrupted stretch of smooth sandy beach, look for a place where the breakers occur consistently 30 to 50 yards out and where there is one large breaker

Halibut taken casting from the shore near Bahía de Los Ángeles, Baja California.

rather than a series of small ones. Many game fish lie just outside that one big breaker to feed on food released by an incoming tide.

When the shoreline is all rocky, unbroken by smooth stretches, look for a spot where you can get beyond the breakers into deeper water. Such a place might be a pier, seawall, breakwater, or natural ledge extending beyond the surf line. Many breakwaters enclose harbors and extend for miles into deep water. They are good fishing spots and the rough going on foot keeps them from being as overcrowded as many sport-fishing piers tend to be. Watch also for small estuaries where freshwater streams empty into the ocean, and concentrate on the area where sweet water blends with saltwater.

Try all freshwater inlets north of central California for striped bass, steelhead, and salmon. For rockfish and rock bass, try the surf on rocky, rough shores; the sandy shores from central California south for perch, halibut, and dab, smelts, sheepshead, and bass. Most coast surf-fishing is concentrated in southern California and Mexico.

At many piers near towns on coastal highways

you can rent small boats and motors. There is usually excellent fishing, not accessible from shore, to be enjoyed nearby. These spots are mainly behind seawalls, kelp beds, reefs, or sand flats farther out. If there is a seawall, fish close to the wall, using a medium weight to get the bait down. If you are dealing with a kelp bed, fish at its edge, dropping the bait to the bottom then raising it about a foot. At seawalls there are many mussels, small crabs, rock worms, and crustaceans which lure larger game fish.

Always watch for gulls and terns wheeling and diving. Birds milling anywhere usually means baitfish close to the surface and that in turn means game fish attracted to the baitfish. So fish where the birds are fishing.

Wherever you fish along the West coast, seek advice about tackle and bait from local sources. In general, you want a rod with at least an 8-foot tip and a 30-inch two-handed butt, a free-spool reel with star drag and 200 yards capacity of 20-pound monofilament. You'll need sinkers from ½ to 8 ounces, wire leader material, swivels, and hooks from size 6 to 5/0, depending upon which fish you are trying to catch.

Your bait will be whatever local experts advise (at least to begin) or whatever is available. However, there is a way to discover the best bait for yourself. Attach three hooks to the line, each on an 18-inch leader and spaced about 3 feet apart. Put the weight beyond the hooks at the end of the line and a different bait on each hook. Try mussels, cut fish, shrimp, or sand crabs on alternating hooks. Whichever bait is most productive is the one to use on all the hooks. In the absence of advice to the contrary, fish on a rising or full tide, early or late in the day.

Use pear-shaped weights on a rocky bottom, pyramid-shaped weights on a sandy or mud bottom. If you find breakers are bringing your bait back, you need more weight. The best all-around bait for fishing the surf as well as in rocky areas is a shrimp with its skin removed.

This is a good spot to talk about the inshore fishes and how they have adapted to their habitats. The shape of a fish's body is usually indicative of the kind of habitat in which it lives. For example, the typical open-ocean types of fishes, such as tuna, mackerel, and bonito, are streamlined and cigar-shaped because they rely on speed to capture food and to escape enemies.

The sand beach at Waldport is only one place on the 400-mile Oregon coast where many inshore species can be caught.

Bottom dwellers, on the other hand, are of two different types. Either they are flattened out, such as the halibut, sole, flounder, and ray, or they have short, bulky bodies with large pectoral fins for quick short movements, such as the sculpin, rockfish, and greenling.

Most inshore areas are turbulent and under bombardment by breaking waves. A part of this inshore area is covered with water at high tide and is high and dry at low tide, with occasional tide pools along rocky coasts. Especially suited to this area are fishes with slender, elongated bodies able to entwine or hide among seaweeds and rocks, to seek shelter in holes and crevices from the force of the water and from enemies.

Other small fish with slender bodies tend to hide in cavities under ledges and among seaweeds. Because of their shape, deep-bodied fishes such as the surfperch, half-moon, and California sargo are difficult for most predators to swallow. When these fish face head on into the force of the water, they offer little surface for resistance.

CORBINA

Maybe the surf-caster is the aristocrat of saltwater fishermen. His arena is a clean, soft beach scoured by the surf, where the noise of breakers is always present. There is no other sport exactly like it, whether the surf is on the Pacific or on the Atlantic coast. As many surf anglers go out

to savor the natural beauty, to obtain a suntan, or to strengthen mind and muscles as to catch fish.

The surf-fisherman is cut from a different mold than his gregarious cousin who enjoys fishing with others on a party boat. The surfer likes solitude. He finds his own fishing hole, baits his own hook, and fights his fishes single-handed. And from Point Conception on the California coast south into Central America, including the Gulf of California, one of his most frequent adversaries will be the corbina.

The corbina or corvina, *Menticirrhus undulatus*, is among the most difficult of the surf fishes to hook. There are times when an entire school will actively feed on soft-shell crabs all around a fisherman's bait, ignoring the sand crab with a hook in it. Some say that hooks that are too large keep the fish away. Others maintain that the corbina is spooked by a too heavy and too stout leader. Possibly it's a combination of both and perhaps the corbina is just extremely selective.

A single fleshy, chin whisker on the lower jaw distinguishes the corbina from all the other croakers, except the yellowfin which shares the same waters with its close cousin. The corbina has only one or occasionally two weak spines and its body is rounded. A bottom fish, the corbina lives along sandy beaches and in shallow bays. Occasionally it is found in muddy estuaries where freshwater enters saltwater, a condition that occurs most frequently in Central America. Corbinas travel in small schools in the surf in from only a few inches of water to depths of 50 feet. The average depth in which a fisherman can expect to find them is about 6 feet. They move offshore into deeper water during winter and when spawning. But they tend to move closer inshore during high tides at night.

In August 1945 a 7¼-pound corbina, which measured 28 inches, was taken at San Onofre and this remains the largest verified record in California. However, corbinas twice this size have been captured in the Gulf of California and along the coast of Costa Rica.

Male corbinas mature at about two years of age and females at about three years of age. The spawning season extends from June through September but is heaviest during late July and early August. This activity apparently takes place offshore, as ripe females are seldom found in the surf zone by fishermen.

About 90 percent of the corbina's diet consists of sand crabs, with the remainder composed of clams and other crustaceans. Nearly all feeding is done in the surf, sometimes in water so shallow that the corbina's back is exposed. After scooping up mouthfuls of sand and then separating the food from it by sending the sand through the gills, the corbina spits out bits of clamshell and other foreign matter, swallowing only the meaty parts. This mouthing of food explains why fishermen are seldom rewarded with a really hard strike. The angler must have a good sense of touch or highly developed intuition to detect the slow bite of a corbina.

An experienced surf-fisherman's tackle includes a 6-ounce or smaller pyramid or triangle sinker, whichever size is heavy enough to hold against the undertow or current of the tide. This is tied to a 48-inch 2-pound leader with two loops on the leader a foot apart. Two shorter leaders, each about 8 inches, are attached to the loops and to these are knotted No. 1 or No. 2 short shank hooks. Most fishermen bait with sand crabs, but there are times when pileworms or rock worms are effective.

A surf-caster always keeps a wary eye on the weather, but the element that really hinders him is a strong onshore wind. Most surfers prefer to fish on an advancing or flood tide, or at least an early-morning low tide. This gives him a chance to collect the mussels, sandworms, or sand crabs he needs.

An early low tide also gives an angler a chance to select his spots. These are the deep holes or depressions along any beach which will be under some depth of water at later high tide. It is always extremely valuable—and this point cannot be stressed enough—to locate these hollows or depressions before actually fishing. If they are not discovered before the tide comes in it is necessary to do much extra casting and probing with a heavy sinker to discover such spots. Good surf-fishing depends very much on finding the right holes.

Once a good corbina or croaker hole is located, whether in the surf or fishing in a bay, a unique method of baiting or chumming can be used. Open a dozen or so mussels and, without removing the meat, toss them into likely holes or depressions. This will attract numerous small fishes and the commotion will in turn attract corbinas. A hook baited with a mussel is then dropped within a short distance down the tide from the bait.

The goal here is to arouse the competitive feeding instinct among fishes. If one fish in a school can be tempted to strike, others will become wildly excited and probably begin striking with abandon. Corbinas are especially susceptible.

During the warm period of midsummer a wise corbina fisherman tries his luck at night. Most surf fish are very active night feeders and the corbina is no exception. Furthermore, there is evidence that they are attracted by a light, especially on a very dark night. A Coleman-type lantern is like a magnet and is likely to bring corbinas close to the caster if any are feeding nearby.

Corbinas and all croakers feed closer into the beach at night. An angler cannot see the fishes feeding as in daylight and must work by the touch system. But sometimes at night it's possible to hear fish feeding close to shore, which has accounted for many extremely fine catches.

Besides the corbina and yellowfin croaker, several other members of this family deserve mention. Most important is the white croaker, which ranges from Vancouver Island southward to the tip of Baja. Like the corbina it is a school fish with a preference for sandy areas in the surf zone, in shallow bays and lagoons. Mostly it's found in depths of 10 to 100 feet.

The spotfin croaker, which reaches a weight of 12 to 15 pounds in Central America, is a more widely traveled fish than his cousins. These croakers appear sporadically along the California and Mexican coasts in large runs, mostly in midsummer, then disappear suddenly. Schools of large spotfin cruising offshore are seldom touched by sport fishermen.

SURFPERCH

Twenty different kinds of surfperch have been identified along the Pacific coast. The most common ones are the barred, calico, and redtail, which are similar in habit and often confused with one another. The barred surfperch are usually found in the surf along sandy beaches, where they congregate in certain holes or depressions along the bottom. They constitute about 50 percent of the surf angler's bag in southern California, but their range extends from Vancouver Island southward to the tip of Baja California. The largest taken in California was a nine-year-old weighing only 4¼ pounds. Any fish over 3 pounds is an extremely good one, since the average catch will weigh a pound or less.

Barred and all other surfperches are viviparous, which means they give birth to living young. As many as 113 embryos and as few as 4 have been found in female surfperch, but the average is about 33 per individual. The fertilization of the eggs is entirely internal; these eggs hatch and the young develop in saclike portions of the oviduct. The young surfperch are usually born between April and July, and are about 2 to 3 inches long at birth. Some mature when they are only 6½ inches long, between one and two years of age.

An analysis of stomach contents of barred surfperch caught by fishermen revealed that their diet, like the corbina's, is 90 percent sand crab, with the remainder of their diet consisting of other crustaceans, particularly bean clams.

Thousands of barred surfperch have been tagged by California Fish and Game biologists and results revealed that, like corbinas, they travel very little. Their average movements are less than 2 miles and only one had traveled 30 miles from the place it was tagged.

The tasty, white-meated, barred surfperch can be taken any time of the year, any time of the day or night. The largest are usually taken in midwinter (January is the best month). Best baits are soft-shelled sand crabs, bloodworms, mussels, and pieces of mackerel. In some areas, entrails of freshly caught sardines are used. The barred surfperch in particular will readily strike certain artificial lures. Small jigs are effective, so are small streamer and nymph flies, such as the Pink Shrimp. Fly-casting on relatively calm days is a sporting and lively proposition.

The most consistent area for barred surfperch are sandy beaches between Point Mugu and Pismo Beach, but there are other hotspots. Calico surfperch fishing is best along beaches of Monterey Bay while redtails are most abundant northward from San Francisco. Some especially good areas are along the coastlines of Humboldt and Del Norte counties.

Other members of the surfperch family taken in numbers along the Pacific are: the walleye, which is especially abundant around open rocky coasts and fishing piers; the black perch, which ranges from Bodega Bay to Abreojos Point, Baja California; and the shiner perch, which reaches a maximum of 8 inches and is taken from shore, docks, piers, rocks.

Another fish, the opaleye, which superficially resembles the surfperch, is a year-round resident of rocky shorelines and kelp beds between Monterey Bay and southern Baja. Opaleyes live in caves and among seaweed-covered rocks in shallow water, but are also found at mid-depths and in offshore kelp beds. Spin-casters and fly-casters have found they are extremely game, dogged, light-tackle fish. They occasionally reach 6 pounds. Opaleyes will bite on mussels, sand crabs, and pieces of other fish.

Another Pacific coast fish that resembles the surfperch is the half-moon. Half-moons have been caught as far north as Eureka, California, but are most abundant on the southern California coast and in the Gulf of California.

The greatest number of half-moons occur around the Channel Islands where they are year-round residents of kelp beds, shallow waters, and rocky shorelines.

The largest known half-moon weighed under 5 pounds but 1- and 2-pounders are most commonly caught on fresh-cut anchovies, sardines, or squid. Pier fishermen account for many, but spin-casters using artificial lures have very poor luck. Half-moons are excellent to eat because their flesh is white and mild in flavor. Frequently found in the same waters and caught by the same methods used for half-moons are kelp rockfish and grass rockfish.

GREENLING SEATROUT

There are many interesting and brightly colored fishes along the Pacific coast, but one of the most striking is the greenling seatrout, *Hexagrammos decagrammus*, one of those rare instances in which the male and female are marked and colored differently. Two other closely related greenlings share the same waters: the rock greenling and white-spotted greenling.

Greenling seatrout live entirely on the bottom in very shallow water, especially along rocky coasts, around jetties and kelp beds. They range from Kodiak Island, Alaska, to La Jolla, California, but are rare south of Point Conception. The largest seatrout recorded in California measured only 21 inches long and weighed about 3½ pounds, but larger fish have been caught along Washington and Vancouver Island coasts. Its diet consists mainly of sea worms, crustaceans, and a wide assortment of smaller fishes.

An excellent food fish, the greenling seatrout can be difficult to land. Once hooked, it will dive into crevices, caves, or seaweed and somehow snag the lure or cut the line. Successfully landing a greenling seatrout is a feat worthy of mention, especially since the greenling is so beautiful and unusual in appearance.

Most greenling are taken on cut fish, clams, mussels, shrimp, squid, worms, and crabs. Greenling themselves are excellent bait for many other fishes, especially the lingcod, which is taken in deeper water. The best greenling hole in California is said to be the south jetty at Eureka.

A MISCELLANY OF PACIFIC COAST FISHES

Almost anyone who fishes the inshore waters eventually catches the California sargo or Chinese croaker, the only member of the grunt family in this part of the world. Sargos are found close to shore and in all bays between Point Conception and Cabo San Lucas, and in the Gulf of California, in water only a few feet to 130 feet deep. Sargos reach a maximum weight of about 4 pounds. They were introduced into the Salton Sea in 1951 and since then have reproduced and seem to be established.

A weird resident of Pacific inshore waters is the shovelnose guitarfish, which lives on sand or mud-sand bottoms from central California southward through the Gulf of California. They are gregarious, occur in large numbers in some areas, and are found the year round throughout most of their range.

The largest-known shovelnose guitarfish was a 5-footer that weighed 40½ pounds, taken in San Quintín Bay, Baja California. Individuals over 3 feet long are uncommon. Shovelnose guitarfish bear young alive, with as many as 28 being carried by a single female parent. Little else is known about their life history. Guitarfish ordinarily are caught by anglers seeking other fish. They will take live or dead bait, clams, mussels, and crabs, just about anything edible.

One member of the eagle ray family exists in Pacific waters: the bat ray, which is relatively abundant from Oregon south to Central America. It can be distinguished from other rays by a sting and a distinct head, which is elevated above disclike wings. Bat rays reach large size; a 209-pound specimen was taken at Newport Bay and there are unconfirmed reports of larger bat rays, including one taken along the Mexican coast which was said to weigh 340 pounds. Many bat rays are hooked but never landed because they are hooked on tackle much too light for them by anglers concentrating on some other game fish. The big rays are most numerous in San Diego Bay, Newport Bay, Alamitos Bay, Morro Bay, Elkhorn Slough, San Francisco Bay, and Humboldt Bay.

A few southern California fishermen fish specifically for bat rays because they are strong and wage an interesting fight. Commercial fishermen despise them because of the damage they do to nets. Oyster growers would like to see them completely exterminated. One ray can almost completely destroy a whole oyster bed overnight.

An extremely common fish in quiet coastal waters, bays, and sloughs with muddy or sandy bottoms from Cape Mendocino to the Gulf of California is the diamond turbot, a right-eyed, porcelainlike flounder. They live in water from a few inches to 100 feet deep, but are most common in 4- to 10-foot depths.

Diamond turbot, which rarely reach a weight of 3 or 4 pounds, are easy to catch on small pieces of clams or shrimp impaled on extremely small hooks. Mission Bay and Newport Bay in California are good for this species, taken the year round. Considering their size and shape, they put up a good fight on light tackle.

A close relative of the diamond turbot is the starry flounder, an inhabitant of sand, mud, and gravel bottoms from central California north to Alaska and the Bering Sea, then east along the north Alaskan coast to Coronation Gulf, northern Canada. It is also found in the Aleutians and western Pacific from Kamchatka to Japan and Korea. It even enters freshwaters and has been taken 75 miles up the Columbia River.

Starry flounder have been caught in water only a few inches deep to 900 feet. Although they reach 20 pounds, the average starry flounder will average 2 pounds. Most live exclusively on sea worms, small crustaceans, copepods, and amphipods. As they grow larger, they eat crabs, clams, sand dollars, and similar marine life.

Some of the best starry flounder fishing occurs on Oregon and Washington beaches, where they are most readily caught between January and March on sardines, clams, shrimp, and squid.

One of the stranger Pacific coast fish, the cabezon, belongs to the large family of sculpins. Males sometimes reach a length of 3 feet and a weight of 25 pounds, while females attain a much larger size. Cabezons are caught from northern Mexico to Puget Sound, with the majority being taken in the northern half of that range. Among the most sought-after fishes of rough and rocky shorelines, cabezons will take abalone trimmings, mussels, clams, squid, shrimp, sea worms, and cut or strip bait, as well as live, swimming bait when available.

The cabezon is another rock dweller that is much more difficult to land than to hook. As soon as it is hooked, every cabezon will try to retreat into the shelter of a rock, cave, or seaweed bed. Once inside it's virtually impossible to pry it loose on sport-fishing tackle.

These unique fish with oversize fins, stout bodies, and wide heads are found year round on rocky bottoms from shallow tidal pools to depths of more than 250 feet. Their average depth off Oregon is about 35 feet. They normally lie motionless on the bottom and never stir except to grab something to eat.

Although the flesh is often a bluish green when fresh, cabezons are excellent food fish when filleted, skinned, and fried in deep fat. But one important word of caution: *Never eat the roe!* The eggs are poisonous and will make anyone violently ill.

The monkey-faced eel, which despite its name is not a true eel, is one of the strangest fishes along the Pacific coast or anywhere else. The body shape and absence of pelvic fins distinguish it from all common inshore fishes, except the rock eel. It varies from a dingy black to a brownish green and has one or more reddish spots on the flanks or belly. This color combination makes the fish all the weirder in appearance.

Monkey-faced eels up to 3 feet in length have been taken and there are reports of monkey-faced eels reaching 4 or even 5 feet, although the catch in California and Oregon is smaller. They are found from the Oregon-California border southward to San Quintín Bay, Baja. They inhabit rock pools between the tide lines and seek cover in crevices, caves, and other secluded places. Even skin divers rarely see them moving about in open waters.

These fish can be taken wherever rock areas rim the ocean, either in bays or along the outer coast of central and northern California. Some favorite spots are the rocks north of Crescent City, California, between Bodega Bay and Dillon Beach, between Stinson Beach and Muir Beach, around the Golden Gate and Shell Beach and near Pismo Beach. Low tide is the best time to fish and although they will strike all year, the best weather for this fishing probably occurs during the summer months.

The method used to catch monkey-faced eels is as unique as the fish. The main tool is a bamboo pole about 10 feet long, at the small end of which is a wire leader about 6 inches long with a

No. 4 hook fastened to the end. The end of the pole with the baited hook is inserted into likely crevices and cracks in a process called "poke-poling." The usual bait is shrimp, but mussels, clams, marine worms, and sardines work well. As soon as a fish is hooked, it is jerked immediately from its hiding place.

Monkey-faced eels are cleaned in exactly the same way as are freshwater catfish—by skinning first. They're excellent eating.

15

SHARKS

Sharks were swimming in the oceans 300 million years ago, long before dinosaurs stalked the earth. Since then many animals have evolved and become extinct, while sharks have hardly changed at all. No mere relics of bygone eras, sharks are well adapted to and thrive in their modern environments. Probably the main reason for the evolutionary success of sharks is their remarkable ability—unique in the entire animal kingdom—to orient themselves in an open sea and find prey. How they do it remains a mystery, but their success speaks for itself.

A good bit of fishing for sharks goes on all around the world. Some serious anglers consider them great game fish; others, considering them a nuisance fish, would cut a line before dueling with any hooked shark. It remains true, however, that the largest fish ever taken on hook and line are sharks. Landing these giants represents an extraordinary amount of hard work as well as exhausting sport.

A 2,664-pound great white shark caught in 1959 by Australian Alf Dean is the officially recognized world record, though it is not the largest fish ever taken on rod and reel. In 1977 an even bigger shark was caught by Clive Green of Brisbane, but it was not officially recognized by the International Game Fish Association. Using 130-pound-test tackle off Albany, Western Australia, Green caught a great white shark that measured 16 feet in length, 10 feet 2 inches in girth, and weighed 3,388 pounds.

Boating the fish took five long and difficult hours. Under the strain of the fight, the gamefishing chair collapsed, tumbling Green onto the deck. Before the first gaff could be planted the shark was brought close more than twenty times, only to tear the wire leader out of the crewman's hands each time. Three gaffs in the shark's jaw and a wire noose around its tail finally subdued the fish. During that fishing expedition, Green also "lassoed" two other great white sharks alongside the 45-foot fishing cruiser. According to Green, "The action was quite unbelievable. One fish about 2,500 pounds was close to coming into the boat. We had six feet of its tail in the boat, and it reared eight feet into the air attacking our boat with terrifying savagery. After these fish quieted down, we released both unharmed."

Because of the completely sinister appearance of the sharks and their even more sinister reputation, almost nobody has any affection for them. But in recent years, more anglers do recognize their value as a genuine sport fish, and even as a fairly high quality food fish. Some sharks, in fact, are so good to eat that their meat is routinely sold as swordfish. A few of the sharks, such as the mako, are crazy enough jumpers to be ranked with the finest game fish in the sea.

There are about 200 species or subspecies of the international shark family; 47 of these have been taken in the Atlantic coastal waters of North America, 29 species on the Pacific coast. Some live in deep water, some in shallow water. Some are pelagic. Some travel in schools. A number of species are dangerous while others are quite harmless. Some even venture into brackish water or shallow freshwater.

The largest shark in the world is the whale shark, which is known to reach 25,000 pounds in weight. Despite its bulk, the whale shark is completely harmless.

Sharks differ from other fishes in that their skeletal structure is composed of cartilage rather than bone. In addition, sharks lack scales, and most are equipped with sets of formidable, oversize teeth unlike those of any of the bony fishes.

Many fishermen believe that all sharks constitute a menace and should be destroyed. They have been known to attack human beings, of course, but so have swordfish, barracuda, groupers, and even triggerfish. And sharks do consume a vast quantity of game fishes, but this is only a phase in nature's relentless balancing act. The truth is that sharks are valuable, even indispensable residents of the sea.

No matter what the prevalent feeling about sharks may be, the fact remains that more fishing for them goes on now than was the case ten years ago. Perhaps because sharks are so extremely numerous in Australia, shark fishing there is very popular and very highly regarded. In North America it's more popular on the California coast than on the eastern seaboard. Although California sportsmen are likely to catch any of twenty different species, two—the common thresher and the blue shark—are the most sought after.

The common thresher is one of five members of the thresher family, so named because of a tail almost one half its total length. The common thresher runs from bluish gray to brownish gray on the back, shading to white on the belly. It has a small mouth and relatively small, weak teeth for a shark, but there are about forty teeth in a row in each jaw.

The common thresher isn't limited to California offshore waters. A pelagic species living in clear blue water, it's found in nearly all temperate and tropic waters around the globe, sometimes far offshore. It is often observed on or near the surface and as deep as several hundred feet.

All sharks are very interesting, somewhat mysterious creatures and the common thresher is no exception. Though little is actually known about it, the thresher is believed to reach a length of from 20 to 25 feet and a weight far exceeding 1,000 pounds. There is evidence that it doesn't mature sexually until it is at least 14 feet long. The young are born alive and usually about two to four at a time. An 18-footer caught off Newport Beach in 1954 contained four young sharks weighing from 11 to 13½ pounds apiece and measuring from 4 feet to 4 feet 6 inches long.

Though the average thresher taken in California waters will measure from 5 to 8 feet long and average less than 100 pounds, commercial fishermen in 1948 reported two threshers which weighed in at 1,094 pounds and 968 pounds. The best places to find threshers include the San Francisco Bay area, the inshore coastal waters between Point Conception and Hueneme, Santa Monica Bay, and in Los Angeles Harbor. They seem most abundant during summer when they are observed swimming slowly on the surface or even jumping clear of the water.

When hooked on light or medium tackle, some thresher sharks will put on a display of aerial jumping not unlike a marlin of the same size. Others do not jump and depend on a subsurface, brute-strength fight which can tow a fishing skiff for many miles.

Best baits for threshers are live sardines, anchovies, and mackerel, but there are examples of the fish taking artificial lures or salmon plugs. No matter what bait is used, it is important to use a stout wire leader of 10 to 20 feet. Such leaders are a necessity in every type of shark fishing—to cope with the teeth of the shark and because an ordinary nylon line will wear through after long rubbing against the abrasive hide of a shark.

There is no known record of an unprovoked

attack by a common thresher shark upon a human being. Because of its habit of sometimes swimming on the surface and waving its large tail above the water, it has been mistaken for some strange kind of sea serpent.

Another shark familiar to California sportsmen is the blue, which belongs to the requiem shark family and which is a close relative of soupfin and tiger sharks. It is readily identified by its brilliant blue topside, which fades to white below. Found in all temperate and tropic seas of the world, the blue shark is occasionally common off southern California but rarely appears north of Point Conception unless currents of abnormally warm water bathe that area. Often it is observed swimming on the surface some distance from shore.

The blue shark is not considered a dangerous man-eater, but no doubt is responsible for some attacks on swimmers and skin divers. It should be approached with caution because of its great abundance and because it is so quickly attracted to blood.

An 11½-footer is the largest blue shark of authentic record, but no doubt the species grows to much larger size. Most of the blues taken in California waters are shorter than 6 feet and weigh less than 50 pounds. Interesting to note is that during a recent southern California shark derby, all of the hundred blue sharks taken were male. This may indicate a geographical distribution or segregation of the species by sex, at least during part of the year.

March through October, blue sharks are easy to capture off the southern California coast. They are not as exciting or difficult to land as threshers, and it is possible to handle even the largest on light tackle. But once a blue is brought to the surface, it twists and rolls in such an ugly manner that wire leaders become tangled almost beyond further use.

In natural surroundings, blues feed on crustaceans, fish, squid, and octopuses. They will also take flying fish and pelagic crabs. Blues also have the reputation for being readily attracted to garbage from ships and they will gorge on anything small enough to swallow.

Along our Atlantic coast, the mako is considered the most desirable shark. Found in abundance in such widely separated parts of the earth as off New Zealand, Ceylon, Cuba, Puerto Rico, and northward along the Atlantic coast to about New Jersey, it is the only shark sought by North American charter boats.

A large mako is certainly a formidable adversary. It reaches 800 pounds or more, and is difficult to land because it mixes a deep, dogged fight with sudden and spectacular jumps. There have been cases where it made a last-ditch attempt to turn upon the man trying to gaff it alongside a boat.

You should use heavy tackle for makos. The best recommended outfit is a 6-foot overall boat rod with a 36-ounce tip, 18- to 20-inch butt and a reel with a capacity for from 800 to 1,200 yards 130-pound or heavier test line. Use such whole live baits as menhaden, mackerel, whiting, or herring on 10/0 to 14/0 Sobey hooks. A stainless steel cable or piano-wire leader should be at least 15 or 20 feet long.

The largest mako shark of which there is a record was a 1,000-pounder measuring 12 feet which was caught near Mayor Island, New Zealand, in 1943, on 130-pound test line. A far more remarkable catch, however, was the 261-pounder taken in 1953 by Chuck Meyer off Montauk, New York. Meyer's line tested only 12 pounds!

Another shark familiar to Atlantic fishermen is the strange and awesome hammerhead, named for the elongated nostrils that give its head the shape of a hammer. It is thought that this unique feature enables the fish to use its head as a rudder and to make sharper turns in pursuit of prey than any of the other sharks.

The hammerhead is often seen swimming with dorsal and caudal fins above the surface and can be found almost anywhere in warm waters on the high seas. I have also found and hooked hammerheads, and big ones too, far inshore around the Isle of Pines, Cuba, while fishing for tarpon and bonefish.

Few fishes have as remarkable a sense of smell as the hammerhead. Since it is able to scent blood at a great distance, it is generally the first shark to arrive when a hooked fish is badly hurt and begins to bleed. Chances are that most of the game fish lost to sharks are lost to hammerheads.

Though the average hammerhead caught offshore will average from 8 to 10 or 12 feet in length, they are known to reach almost 18 feet. No completely accurate weights for the largest fish are available, but it's assumed that they will reach 1,500 pounds. Ordinarily the food of a hammerhead consists of sea clams, fish, and barnacles, but you can hook a hammerhead simply by tossing or trolling a large chunk of fish or meat close to its mouth. Hammerhead females produce extremely large, live families. Thirty-nine young were found in one hammerhead caught off the Texas coast.

The great white shark that furnished Alf Dean with the current record for largest rod and reel fish also occurs in warm temperate waters along the Atlantic coast. Occasionally found as far north as eastern Nova Scotia, it prefers a diet of sea turtles and large fish and has been known to attack man, whales, and sea lions on many occasions.

The stomach contents of the great whites have included the following: a Newfoundland dog (in Australia); two 6- to 7-foot sharks inside a 15½-foot female (Florida); and a 100-pound-plus sea lion (California).

A close relative of the white pointer is the porbeagle. This heavy-shouldered fish reaches a length of about 12 feet and occasionally ventures as far north as Nova Scotia. It is mostly a nuisance because it gets into commercial nets when following schools of menhaden, herring, or shad. The largest porbeagle on record is a 366-pounder taken in 1960 near Montauk, New York.

Tiger sharks are most plentiful in Australian and New Zealand waters, where the world's record 1,422-pounder was taken in 1958. But occasionally the large brutes with the sickle-shaped teeth wander north along our Atlantic coast as far as Maine. Tigers will average about 12 feet in length, but there are a few reports of individuals that reach 30 feet. They feed mainly on sea turtles, on large fishes and other sharks. They're greatly feared as man-eaters around the world, especially in the West Indies.

A most familiar species along our entire Atlantic coast is the sand shark, a sluggish fish that swims leisurely with tail and dorsal fin above the surface and sometimes reaches 6 feet and 300 to 400 pounds. It's gray in color, spotted brown or olive, with a fin occasionally edged in black. Found as far north as the Bay of Fundy, Canada, during the summer months it swims close to shore and into river mouths. As soon as cold weather sets in, it forsakes these northern waters for balmier climes farther south along the Atlantic seaboard.

The sand shark is a poor man's big game fish. When hooked and fought from shore, a 200-pounder can provide all the thrills of hooking a fish of equal size offshore in a boat. This fish is not particularly fast, but it is strong enough to strip several hundred yards of line from a reel before being stopped.

Some coast sportsmen fish specifically for sand sharks, and the tackle they use is quite heavy. A surf or boat rod with a 400- to 600-yard capacity reel full of 45-pound test line is suitable. The hook should be no smaller than from 9/0 to 12/0 and the leader should be a 15-footer. A whole fish such as menhaden or mackerel is extremely good bait.

Sand shark specialists chum with menhaden, either fresh or frozen. Although almost any chummer fish will attract sharks, menhaden seem to be most effective. To prepare the menhaden for chum, use a meat grinder, small hand ax, or sharp knife. Cut it into tiny bits. Chum with the outgoing tide in deep water off a beach near an inlet or off a rocky formation or jetty.

Sand sharks strike readily day and night, but you will probably fare better at night. If you're lucky enough to land one, be extremely careful when handling it. A blow from the tail of a 100-pound sand shark threshing about can easily break a man's leg or smash his fingers.

Some coastal sportsmen like to leave out a heavy setline on a dock, bridge, or shore in the hope of hooking a giant such as a shark, jewfish, or sawfish. This line—usually rope, most often quarter-inch nylon—is left unattended. You need an extra big swivel and your leader wire should be heavy cable, No. 15 single-strand wire, or a shark hook and chain leader.

The key to this rig is an old (but not rotten) automobile or truck inner tube. This is tied to the rope, close to the point where you anchor the rope firmly to a piling or tree. Tie your line to one side of the inner tube, allow some slack, then tie to the other side of the tube, directly opposite the first tie.

Once the shark is hooked, the stretch of the tube "plays" him. Without the tube to absorb shock, your fish might break the rope or pull loose from the hook. Use only the stoutest hooks obtainable. It is a deadly way to hook sharks from shore, without constantly attending a line.

Angler Bob Stearns of Miami catches a medium-size shark on plug-casting tackle in the Florida Keys.

16

SALTWATER TACKLE

In the past, the term "saltwater tackle" referred to a specific fishing rig consisting of a certain cumbersome rod, heavy reel, and braided line. But today saltwater tackle can mean anything from a medium fly rod weighing a few ounces to boat rods with 14/0 reels which altogether may weigh 40 pounds. In other words, the modern way to both success and enjoyment in saltwater fishing anywhere is to match the tackle to the target.

SPINNING

Today, the most versatile of all fishing methods is, without a doubt, spinning with open-face spinning outfits. It is the method used by a majority of saltwater anglers for a wide variety of angling situations. Spinning differs from other tackle in one main respect: a spinning reel has a fixed spool that does not revolve, as contrasted with all other fishing reels on which the spools do turn. When cast, spinning line pulls off the end of the spool, and when retrieved, the line is wound onto the spool with a pickup mechanism.

The main value of this, especially for less expert anglers, is that it almost completely eliminates the tangles and backlashes so common with revolving spools. A beginning saltwater fisherman can pick up a spinning outfit and after just a few minutes of practice cast well enough to catch fish.

There is another small advantage. Assume you are right-handed. With a spinning outfit you cast with the right arm and retrieve with the left hand. In any other kind of casting you cast with the right arm, but then shift the rod and reel to the left hand so that you can retrieve (turn the reel handle) with the right hand.

So maybe the logical question is: Why not use spinning tackle all the time for all saltwater fishing? However versatile it might be, even the largest or heaviest spinning gear made is not suited for lines heavier than, say, 20-pound test, although up to 30-pound test might be used on a spinning reel in a pinch. Also, conventional plug-casting tackle is vastly superior when very accurate casting is necessary (as in mangrove channels for snook or tarpon) or for casting topwater lures. Spinning tackle is ideal with lines

a

b

c

d

These are typical reliable saltwater spinning reels that are very popular today: a is a Shakespeare Sigma; b is a Penn 716Z; c and d are manufactured by Daiwa; e is the Garcia 9200.

e

in the 12- to 15-pound test category; beyond that, plug-casting is usually better. On the other hand, plug-casting does not work well for casting lures of ¼ ounce or less, as in some shallow waters.

For saltwater, spinning rods vary from 6½ or 7 feet (the shortest and lightest) to from 9 to 12 feet long. Most modern rods are of fiberglass, graphite, or a similar material. Graphite is costlier and perhaps most widely used by experts because it does more work with less arc in the rod. In other words, it provides more power for less rod weight in the hand. Most graphite users believe the rods are more sensitive to both lure action and the softer strikes of some fishes. However, graphite seems to be less durable, with a tendency to break more easily than glass.

The lightest spinning rods (6½–7 feet) are meant for use with lines of 6- to 10-pound test, in other words, for saltwater panfishing with light lures or small natural baits. Rods ranging from 7 to 8½ feet vary a great deal in action, but they are meant for lines from 8- to 12-pound test. These are good all-around saltwater rods, suitable for inshore casting and trolling, plus some light bottom fishing. For deep jigging, offshore fishing, and inshore for tarpon, consider a 7½- to 9-foot rod with 10- to 20-pound line. Still longer spinning rods (to a maximum 12 feet) are used for surf-fishing, on open party boats, for pier or bridge fishing, with 12- to 20-pound test lines.

When acquiring a saltwater spinning rod, look for a few important features which reveal a rod's quality. The guides should be of stainless steel or aluminum oxide ceramic, both of which are smooth and hard, thus eliminating line friction and heat. (Always keep a close check on guides for signs of grooving or wearing.) All reel seats on rods should be of corrosion-resistant material and of screw-locking design. Anodized aluminum seats are the lightest in weight. The finish on rods should be an epoxy coating, not just a varnish dip. A double wrap is the most durable way to affix guides onto the rod, although single wraps under a good epoxy finish may serve just as well. Very colorful and decorative wraps may be attractive and actually sell an angler on a particular rod, but have no real functional value.

A bewildering amount has been written about different rod actions, fast and slow taper, fast and slow tips, parabolics, etc. But most of this information will serve only to confuse many anglers; essentially it all boils down to the fact that the best rod is the one that feels best in your hand when you are casting. It's also worth remembering that no one particular rod is absolutely the best for more than one specific kind of fishing. An angler can lose his mind searching for something that does everything. It's far better to try out several different spinning rods before actually buying one.

One of the basic choices to be made when selecting a spinning rod is between one- and two-piece models. A well-made two-piecer with tight-fitting ferrules is not significantly weaker than a one-piece stick. Today's two-piece rod probably won't fail, even after prolonged use with strong fish, but the chance that a break could occur at an inconvenient time is never entirely eliminated. The major advantage of a two-piecer is ease of storage and transportation. If this is not a consideration for you, use a one-piece rod. Otherwise take advantage of the takedown feature.

Regardless of size, today's spinning reels are functionally the same. Still, for use in the salt, reels can be separated into three categories: standard, intermediate, and heavy. Standards—the most commonly used—have a capacity of about 200 yards of 10-pound line, but can be used with lines from 6- to 12-pound test. A wise angler might carry extra spools with different-weight lines to be interchanged on his one standard reel. The approximate capacity of intermediate reels is 200 to 250 yards of 12- or 15-pound line. The lighter the line filling the spool, the more of it the spool will hold. The heavy reels are meant to handle lines of 12- or 15-pound test and upward. A wise rule to follow in reel selection is to select a spool capacity of 200 yards of the heaviest line you are likely to use or need. Or in the extreme, consider a capacity of 300 yards if you're seeking especially powerful, far-running fish on your spinning gear.

The more frequent and demanding your fishing, the greater the need for a reliable, high-quality reel. Here are some important points or features to consider in any acquisition. The reel should have a solid or substantial feel about it and be crafted of corrosion-resisting material: stainless steel or anodized aluminum. It should have a skirted spool which permits working the reel bail by hand or by turning the reel handle. In addition, skirted spool almost totally eliminates the old nuisance of line getting beneath the reel and spool and wrapping hopelessly around the reel shaft.

Saltwater reel bails of stainless, heavy-gauge material should snap open and close positively into position. The line roller (which should be kept clean and lightly oiled) should be of hard corrosion-resistant material, should turn easily and not wear out the line. A ball-bearing action is desirable although not all good reels feature it. Probably the greatest necessity of a saltwater reel is for a smooth, conveniently adjustable, positive drag made of multiple discs inside the spool. Test any reel you buy by stripping off long lengths of line at various drag settings to be certain it is smooth and not grudging or irregular in its response.

Closed-face spinning reels (which are also called spincast, bunghole, and push-button reels) are often used in saltwater. The spool on these is fixed inside a cone-shaped housing. These reels fit onto plug-casting rods, are virtually foolproof for beginners, but have so many drawbacks that we do not consider them suitable for anything except the lightest fishing in saltwater for smaller fish.

BAIT-CASTING OR PLUG-CASTING

Developed originally for freshwater bass, bait-casting, which depends on a small revolving spool reel, has evolved into an important angling system. Not long after the advent of spinning just following World War II, it seemed that plug-casting might die. But today it is more popular than ever with a large elite of bait-casting fishermen in the salt. For this writer as well, it is a very satisfying way to go fishing.

Bait-casting rods for saltwater run from 5½ to about 7½ feet. They come with either straight or slightly offset handles, the latter usually being (for most anglers) a little easier to cast, though the straights are generally preferred for fishing in the salt. In straight-handled rods, the shaft (stick) extends all the way down through the handle to the butt assembly. The reel is held in place with knurled screw rings, in the same manner as spinning rods. Summed up,

the straight handle is the one for really serious saltwater fishing for heavy powerful fish.

Good-quality rods are available in many actions, from very light action capable of handling 10-pound test lines and lures as light as ⅜ ounce, to stiff rods, almost without any action at all. The latter are suited to setting the hook solidly into fishes with very hard, bony jaws. Bait-casting rods are made of the same materials as spinning rods. One kind of rod in common saltwater use is the two-hander with an extra-long, straight butt for two-handed casting. These are called popping rods, especially along the Texas coast.

Trouble-free pleasurable plug-casting isn't possible without a good reel. Nor is handling large game fish. Any saltwater plug-casting reel worthy of consideration should have a free spool, an anti-reverse and star drag. When you cast, the free spool (which you activated by pressing a button) disengages the spool from the gears. In other words, when you cast, only the spool (and not the gears or the reel handle) turns. But when you begin the retrieve, the gears automatically reconnect. Either braided or monofilament line can be used on free spool reels, but saltwater anglers today prefer mono about ten to one.

For saltwater fishing, a plug-casting reel must have greater line capacity than for freshwater: about 200 yards of the heaviest line you expect to need. The top plug-casters nowadays figure a reel should carry 200 yards of 15-pound test line, which is the ideal weight for this system, or even more of 10-pound test mono.

For general reference consider the following match-ups in bait-casting tackle for different kinds of fishing. A good all-around saltwater choice might be a 5- to 6-foot rod with a reel containing 200 yards of line to cast lures from one-half to one ounce. A 6- to 7-foot medium action rod, same reel, will throw lures up to 1½ ounces. A heavier 6½- to 7-footer with stiffer action will deliver baits up to 4 ounces and is suitable for deep jigging as well as pier, jetty, or party-boat fishing.

There is still another reel, called either a service or a small boat reel, which probably fits into this plug-casting category. These are larger, usually hold much more line, have star drag, level wind, and free spool. While these are cheaper and do not cast as well as the best plug-

a

b

c

d

*Typical saltwater plug-casting reels: a and b are
Garcia Ambassadeurs; c is a Shakespeare Sigma;
d is a Daiwa Procaster; e is a Daiwa Millionaire.*

e

casting reels, they are popular with anglers who do a lot of mixed fishing—trolling and bait-fishing as well as casting artificial lures.

BOAT FISHING OR TOURNAMENT TACKLE

Almost all boat tackle is designed for trolling or still-fishing and is not meant for casting. This category includes both the everyday, workhorse gear which can put a lot of fish in the boat without great finesse, as well as tackle designed to meet tournament standards or regulations, set by the International Game Fish Association (hereafter IGFA). IGFA is the official record-keeping agency for saltwater fishing. Any fish submitted for possible inclusion in the record book is categorized in the following line-test classes: 6-, 12-, 20-, 30-, 50-, 80-, and 130-pound test. Not only do many anglers fish with lines within these categories, but the categories have been widely accepted as (more or less) standard and handy guides for describing saltwater fishing tackle of different sizes. So when somebody refers to 12-pound tackle, he means an outfit (rod and reel) which is matched to fishing with 12-pound test line. The terms class tackle and IGFA tackle are also used frequently. But buy any tackle well matched to whatever line will do the most efficient job of hooking, playing, and landing fish.

Nearly all sticks or blanks are of solid or thick-walled tubular fiberglass. The better ones (often the most expensive, too) have roller guides and a roller tip. Others have only a first-roller guide, with ring guides out to a roller tip. IGFA class rods also feature slotted butts so they can be used either in a fighting (waist) belt or in a fishing chair gimbal. Rod butts are of hardwood, fiberglass, or anodized aluminum with machined reel seats.

Reels can be broadly classified into two types. The less-expensive models have separate star-drag and free-spool lever mechanisms, while the more expensive ones combine the two in a single lever. When the lever is all the way back, the reel is in free spool (only the spool revolves); when all the way forward, there is maximum drag on the reel. In between is a wide choice of drags. The single-lever reel has its greatest advantage when fishing for the largest of the ocean game fishes because the drag can always be readjusted during the course of a duel with the fish.

In the past, saltwater boat reels were categorized as 1/0, 2/0, 2½/0, and so on up to 12/0 and 14/0 reels. The higher the number, the larger the reel. The numbers would also give a rough idea of the line for which it is best suited. For example, 2/0 to 3/0 reels handled 20-pound test line fairly well; 30-pound test worked with 3/0 and 4/0 reels; 10/0 to 14/0 reels usually were filled with 130-pound test line, although some latitude was possible.

Experienced ocean fishermen consider 350 to 400 yards of line as being adequate in the 12- to 30-pound classes, or nearly twice that length in lines heavier than 30-pound test. It is prudent to have more line on a spool than at first seems necessary to compensate for wear, abrasion, and rerigging often on the business end near the bait. Some kinds of big game fishing can be extremely punishing to line on a busy day.

SURF-FISHING TACKLE

Almost any kind of tackle, except heavy boat tackle, can be used in the surf somewhere. Everything depends on the surf itself, whether it is calm or wildly breaking, deep or shallow, beach or boulder-strewn. Generally, though, surf-casting tackle means gear that will deliver heavy baits, lures, and sinkers for long distances, even out and beyond faraway breakers.

So-called surf rods are long, from a minimum of about 8 feet to almost twice that length of fiberglass, with very long handles (two feet or more) and stout tips. A consensus of veteran surfers is that 10- to 11-foot rods are suitable for almost all situations along U.S. coastlines. A surf-caster is more likely than other saltwater anglers to build his own rod, usually to get exactly the outfit required to throw up to 5 or 6 ounces of lead sinker. Most specialists own and use several different surf rods, at least one being a very stiff, heavy outfit and another lighter one meant just to handle small school fish.

The main difference between surf reels and others already described is that all have wider spools. Surf reels also feature free spools and star drags. The reels are filled with braided nylon, which is often called squidding line, testing from

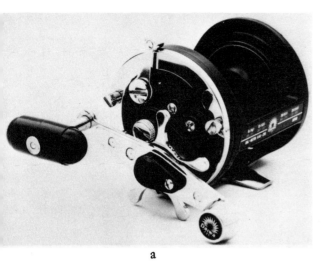

a

b

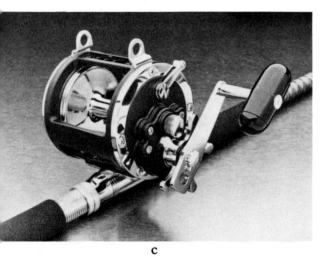

c

d

e

Typical ocean or trolling reels: a, b, *and* c *are Daiwa Sealines;* d *and* e *are the Penn Senator and Penn International.*

18 to 54 pounds, but with 27 and 36 being by far the most popular. These strange sizes are survivors of times past when linen lines were used. More than a few surf-casters prefer to use the largest spinning reels, rather than surf reels, with monofilament line. Which is best is clearly a matter of personal preference.

FLY-FISHING TACKLE

Fly-casting differs from other kinds of casting in one main aspect. The fly line rather than the lure or bait or sinker is cast. In other forms the lure is the casting weight. Theoretically fly-rod lures are weightless, but in fact (and especially in saltwater) are of very light weight. Fly-casting originated in the dim, distant past as a technique for freshwater trout fishing, but in modern times it has become more and more popular with saltwater anglers in search of greater challenge. Although to some it may seem ludicrous, attempting to take heavy species of the seas on such seemingly frail tackle, in recent years fly tackle has accounted for some astounding catches of everything from trophy tarpon to sailfish and marlin. In 1979 Bob Sterns boated a 117½-pound Pacific sailfish on a fly rod and 15-pound leader tippet off the Costa Rican coast. It is a world record for the species on fly tackle.

For a long time—and to some extent even today—many fishermen have shunned fly-fishing because of the mystique surrounding it. Too many early fishing writers described it as a technique for experts (themselves) only. But that has proved to be not true. Fly-casting is just as easy as any other technique to learn, and often more satisfactory, once learned. In a few instances, fly-casting is the best way to catch meat for the galley chef, but its greatest appeal must lie in the great challenge it offers the sport fisherman.

When first selecting fly tackle, the main concern is balance—proper matching—between rod, reel, and line. For saltwater use, fly rods range from 8 (for the lightest work) to 10 feet in length, the sticks being made of tubular fiberglass or graphite. Some of the advantages of graphite over fiberglass are mentioned in the spinning section. Graphite rods have a "faster" action, i.e., the rod has most of the action at the tip section, with a fairly stiff butt. Glass rods tend to have a "slow" action, meaning that the rod's action is better distributed over the entire length of the rod. Anglers just starting to fly-fish usually find a slow action to be best. More experienced saltwater fly-casters carry at least two rods, fast and slow, in the same lengths for use in different situations.

Probably the best all-around saltwater fly rod is a 9-footer, referred to as a medium salt, with 9- or 10-weight fly line. Manufacturers now use a standard table of numbers to indicate line weights and almost all factory rods indicate the proper line to be used. For heavier fish (tarpon, sailfish) the recommendation is for a 9- to 9½-footer with 11- or 12-weight fly line. A minor mismatch between line and rod is not a catastrophe, but it certainly does not improve casting. Example: if a rod is designed to use 10-weight line, it will cast properly with *any* kind of 10-weight line: level, tapered, or weight forward.

Nowadays most fly-casters use some kind of tapered lines for extra distance and ease of casting. The double taper line has a fine tip, a thicker center or belly section, and a fine rear part, next to the backing on the reel. It is designed for presenting very small flies delicately and has its greatest application in freshwater. A weight-forward, or bug or torpedo taper, swells abruptly to a thick portion about 20 feet long, just after a short fine tip. The rest of the line (nearest the reel) is as fine as the tip and is called shooting or running line. The weight-forward tapers are meant for long casting of heavy or bulky flies with a minimum of false casting necessary. All fly lines are only about 100 feet long.

Lines also come in floating and sinking types. Though floating lines are the most often used today, the more difficult to handle sinking lines are coming into their own for those species of fish found in deeper water. The best bet for a novice fly-caster, we repeat, is a level floating line (which also happens to be the least expensive), from which he can graduate once the mechanics and timing of fly-casting are thoroughly mastered.

More than anything else, a fly-fishing reel serves to conveniently store line and backing. Since saltwater species are likely to make runs longer than the length of any fly line, every reel must be filled with line (called backing), say, from 150 to 250 yards of 20- to 30-pound monofilament. (Use a uni-knot or nail knot to affix your fly line onto the backing line.) The ideal saltwater fly reel is single action (no gears, the spool turns once with every turn of the reel handle), with line plus backing capacity to match the type of fishing, and with an adjustable drag. Some large-capacity saltwater fly reels of good quality are inexpensive and are among the best values in fishing tackle.

Some final thoughts on fly-fishing: the advice of an expert on selecting tackle and using it properly is more important here than with the other types of saltwater fishing. A balanced rod, reel, and especially line will mean the difference between enjoyment and failure.

17

LINES, LURES, ACCESSORIES, AND TECHNIQUES— PLUS A WORD ON TIDES

SELECTING A MONOFILAMENT LINE

Dozens of industrial firms manufacture various types of nylon, with each type being specifically formulated for a certain use. Because of the standardized procedure, most line manufacturers produce a fishing line that offers similar performance benefits, so much so that anglers find it difficult to distinguish among various lines. And even though each manufacturer's label claims his line contains some or all of the same properties, fishermen have no way of knowing how these properties have been balanced or how they will affect the line's performance. So how does the serious angler select a premium monofilament fishing line?

First, you have to know what type of conditions you'll be facing, what type of fish you're going after, and what type of equipment you'll be using. Then you can determine which of the seven critical line properties, or which combination, will be most beneficial to your fishing needs. To help you make that decision, here's a rundown of the seven critical properties.

Break Strength

What you see isn't always what you get. Lines are sold by the break strength and the label might read 6-, 8-, or 10-pound test and so forth. But that's not the actual break strength of the line. Nationally known brands usually break above the label rating. This is because all nylon monofilaments lose strength when they are immersed in water. Depending on the nylon, some lines will be 10 percent weaker or more.

The label designation for premium monofilaments is based on wet strength rather than dry strength. Some manufacturers take advantage of this by "underrating" their lines. They do this by merely selling line of larger diameter and heavier break strength with a label that lists it as a lower pound test than it really is. The result: A fisherman may think he's getting a 20-pound test line, but in reality he's getting the break strength of a 15-pound test. Underrated lines typically have larger diameters and excessive stiffness.

Stretch

When a fish hits and runs on a nylon monofilament line, the line's break strength is put to the test. And so is its ability to stretch. Strength and stretch go hand in hand under actual fishing conditions. The stretch serves as a shock absorber to keep the line from breaking. But once stretched to capacity, the line will break.

So how much stretch should a line have?

Fishing line with too much stretch may appear to be really tough when dry. Put it in water and it will stretch like a rubber band, making it difficult for the fisherman to set the hook. A line with very little stretch is just as bad. This type of line may have a high break strength compared to its diameter, but it will lack shock absorption and be brittle. Good premium fishing lines should have a proper balance of strength and stretch, with neither property being exaggerated. When one property is increased to the extreme, problems occur. Knot strength poses a more complex problem. You can find lines that have excessive stretch coupled with good knot strength, but they perform poorly under fishing conditions. If you want to maximize knot strength, you must begin the manufacturing process with the right nylon molecules.

Trilene® is probably the best nylon for fishing purposes. The nylon alloys provide exceptional knot strength, because the unusually tough, abrasion-resistant surface layer on these alloys (visible under an electron microscope) helps prevent knots from slipping. That's why getting maximum knot strength starts with the brand of line you buy and ends with the kind of knot you tie. Even the best lines can be severely damaged by a poor knot. That's why learning how to tie

a consistently strong fishing knot will be time well spent. But exercise a little caution when dealing with knot strength. A line's wet knot strength should be the determining factor when you're getting ready to tie on your favorite lure.

Uniformity

If you could test a 100-yard length of any nylon monofilament inch by inch, you would discover that some areas are stronger and others weaker. That's one reason why a 99¢ spool of mono may not be the bargain you think it is. Economy-grade line is much less uniform than premium monofilament. Even among the premium grades there is a difference. Be cautious. Monofilament line is like a chain. It's only as strong as its weakest section. Uniformity varies from brand to brand. If you measured the diameter of two different brands of line at frequent intervals, you would find that variations do exist. It takes great skill in the manufacturing process to produce a nylon monofilament line with consistent uniformity.

Stiffness

Under actual fishing conditions, especially in cold water, you can easily recognize the effects of stiffness. Wiry lines seem to have a mind of their own. They coil and spring off the reel in loops and snarls. These stiff lines can cause misfires even among fishermen using the best rods and reels.

Suppleness and lack of "memory" or "curliness" have proved to be two of the most significant features of the Trilene® nylon alloys. Fishing lines constructed from these nylon alloys provide greater casting performance and more natural lure presentation—key factors that directly affect fishing success. All this is worth considering if castability is important in the type of fishing you do.

Abrasion Resistance

Abrasion resistance is that property which protects the line from nicks, cuts, and scrapes. It guards the line against damage inflicted by rocks, logs, fish teeth and gills, and other underwater abrasive surfaces. Simply put, abrasion resistance helps keep the line from becoming weak.

Measuring abrasion resistance in a fishing line can be misleading. Laboratory tests cannot come close to simulating actual fishing conditions. You must make the decision: How important is abrasion resistance in the type of fishing you do? To answer that question correctly, you must judge a line's abrasion resistance with respect to the balance of the other critical line properties. And those properties may suffer if abrasion resistance is the only factor used to select a line.

Color

Color is one property in fishing lines that you can see and measure. Some fishermen believe a line should be invisible underwater. Others think you should be able to see the line above the water at all times. But no matter which line you prefer, one thing is quite clear: Regardless of color, there is no such thing as a totally invisible nylon monofilament line. Since fish are capable of seeing any fishing line, it's wise to remember that a line's appearance is important above and below the water's surface.

Another aspect that comes into play is the color of the water itself. Water colors vary greatly, from the transparency of a windowpane to blue, green, and even chocolate, and should always be taken into account when selecting a line color. Before we do so, however, let's look at how lines are colored by the manufacturer.

Lines can be colored three ways. The cheapest way is to simply dip the monofilament in a dye solution, making sure the dye penetrates the surface of the monofilament. This method is fast, but the color fades quickly when the line is exposed to natural sunlight. And since most anglers fish during the daylight hours, this type of coloring isn't practical.

Secondly, powdered colorants can be added to the nylon pellets prior to melting. This gives the line a uniform, rich-looking appearance and good fade resistance. Even better is the third method whereby chemicals are made to react with the nylon molecules. When this is accomplished, the color becomes chemically spliced into the nylon, producing high-visibility colors that are long-lasting and fade-resistant.

The human eye can see some colors better than others. Any hunter knows about Blaze Or-

ange, while fishermen are well aware of the effects of fluorescent fishing lures. If you were to look at a rainbow of colors going from dark blue to green, yellow, orange, and red, you'd discover that your eye responds best to colors in the yellow-green spectrum.

When fluorescence is added to a fishing line, it makes it easier to see. The line soaks up light from the sun and then discharges it, making the line brighter and more visible. A fluorescent fishing line seems to glow above the water's surface. But contrary to what you might think, fluorescent lines continue to glow underwater too. Some line colors will actually spook fish.

For that reason, choose fluorescent lines carefully. While a fluorescent lure might be desirable in order to attract fish, a glowing fluorescent line can have the opposite effect. Fluorescent colors range from bright gaudy yellows and oranges to more subdued blue shades. Research studies indicate that fluorescent blue/green lines work better, even though they do continue to glow underwater.

In waters where bass feed on shad minnows and other baitfish, studies have shown that fluorescent blue/greens can attract fish. The same research demonstrated that bright yellow lines appear to alarm bass, contributing to lower catch rates when used.

Underwater Trilene® research indicates that clear monofilament works best in very clear water where fish have a tendency to spook easily. The same nylon alloys with a high-visibility blue/green fluorescent coloration seem to be the appropriate choice when you have to watch your line for signs of a subtle strike.

No one has written the final word on line colors yet. But natural, uncolored nylon monofilament has become more popular. The only drawback is that most uncolored lines are milky. The new Trilene® nylon alloys, however, offer unusual underwater clarity in a natural, uncolored monofilament. A clear line is always a wise selection when you are in doubt about water conditions and colors.

SELECT THE LINE THAT'S RIGHT FOR YOU

Now that you're better acquainted with the six critical properties of a line, you're ready to choose a premium fishing line. But before you do, think about all the factors involved. Type of fish. Location. Water conditions—clear, open, muddy, heavy vegetation, submerged trees, rocks, etc. Equipment—tackle, lures, reel, rod. And which combination of the six critical line properties would prove to be the most beneficial.

One line can't match every fishing condition you might face. A line that claims to possess just the right balance of all six properties isn't practical. It's a compromise. Some conditions require a line with high abrasion resistance. With others, castability is more important. But the one element that every good premium line should have is overall strength. Because strength is the most important performance feature of any fishing line.

Examine the data. Consider a line's overall strength. Refer to the six critical properties. Think about the type of conditions you fish. And keep in mind that a line with a smaller diameter is less visible to the fish and offers more spool capacity and better total performance.

SPOOLING UP

Engineers designed your reels to be fished with a full spool of line. A properly filled spool will give you longer and more accurate casts, better drag performance, a wider range of drag settings, and more line to successfully play a fish. Even the best reels misbehave when spools become less than half full.

There are advantages in having the dealer fill your reel using a line metering machine because it spools line evenly and under the proper tension. But you also have the option of buying bulk spools or filler spools and filling your own reels.

Deciding on the proper pound test line is easy if you consider two things: the type of fishing you plan to do and the size of the reel you will be using. If you are going to fish for big fish or in waters full of obstructions, you'll need heavier line. Line diameter must also be matched to the reel spool.

HOW MUCH LINE IS ENOUGH?

If you fill your own reels, the most reliable way is to slip a pencil through the center of the bulk spool and have someone hold it while you crank the line off the spool and onto the reel, allowing the bulk spool to rotate freely.

Overfilling can be just as troublesome as underfilling. Put too much line on the spool and it will balloon off and tangle. To prevent overfilling, here are a couple of tips to help you determine when you have correctly filled your reels. On bait-casting reels and other conventional models, fill them until the line reaches the point where the top of the spool begins to flare outward. The line on a correctly filled spinning reel should stop within 1/8″ of the lip. Spin-casting reels should never be filled above the level of the spool.

Reel spools should always be filled under uniform minimum line tension. Applying excess tension has the same effect on a spool as wrapping a rubber band around your finger. Each succeeding wrap causes more and more compression on those underneath. Too much keep can actually burst or permanently warp a metal reel spool.

Some reel spools with large capacities can be very expensive to fill completely with line, especially since you might need several hundred yards. Advanced anglers have a remedy for this situation. They wrap a core of heavier braided line around the reel, tie it off, and then put the monofilament on top of it. The braid acts as a cushion and reduces the pressure on the hub of the spool.

When you do change the line on your reel, jot down the date and the line's pound test on a piece of tape and stick it on the reel foot. This will serve as a handy reminder just as the sticker in your car tells you when the oil was changed last.

SETTING THE DRAG ON YOUR REEL

Have you ever noticed how some fishermen always seem to catch big fish on small diameter lines? One reason is that they use the best, most uniform monofilament they can find. But the basic reason for such success is that they have mastered the art of using the drag on their reels.

Drag is the adjustable device on a reel which limits how easily line may be drawn from the reel. Advanced anglers know that the right drag control can help put them in command of any fishing situation. And mastering drag control should be just as important to you.

To keep the line from breaking, the drag assembly on your reel must yield line while still allowing you to maintain control. Once you know how to set the drag correctly, you'll also be able to play a strong fish on a light line successfully. The key is to set the drag properly before you start fishing. Here's how it's done.

Put the reel on the rod and run the line through the guides. While holding the rod at a 45-degree angle, as if you were fighting a fish, have a friend pull the line. As the line is pulled, adjust the drag-setting knob or wheel until the line flows at a moderate line tension. If you need additional drag while you're fishing, place your hand against the reel spool.

If you have a scale, hang the end of the line on it and measure the amount of tension, with the rod *pointing directly at the scale*. The Trilene® Research Team recommends the drag be set at 25 percent of the rated break strength of the line.

There are a few points worth remembering about drag control. It takes more force to start a drag slipping than to keep it slipping. When you first set the hook, you'll have maximum drag resistance. As the fish runs, drag resistance drops. Test your reel's drag design and become familiar with it. Know how much knob adjustment to make and how to decrease drag on a strong, running fish.

Many people are surprised to learn that a reel's drag resistance increases as a long-running fish empties the reel. The common mistake is to tighten the drag in an attempt to stop the fish. Usually, the line breaks before the fish stops.

What you should do is loosen the drag as the fish takes more line. This reduces tension on the line and will also extend the life of your reel's drag control. And it's another reason to start with a full spool of line.

Spotting a faulty drag is easy. Watch the rod tip as a friend pulls the line. If it bounces up and down, the drag assembly is either defective, needs lubrication, or is improperly set and poor for fishing. With a well-lubricated, properly set drag control, the rod tip should dip toward the

direction of the pull and remain almost stationary as additional line is pulled off.

If you expect top performance from your reel's drag, you must take care of it. Inspect it after each trip and clean the drag assembly frequently. (Silicone spray can work wonders in smoothing out a sticky reel drag.) Grit and dirt can destroy the smoothness of any drag. And a faulty reel drag control can undermine the best line and tackle.

KNOTS—HOW TO MAKE THEM WORK FOR YOU

Fishing knots have frustrated anglers for a long time. Some tie whatever knot comes to mind. The advanced angler knows, however, that the right knot, properly tied, can often prevent the loss of a fish. He has learned that the basic overhand knot is always a poor choice because it weakens the line considerably. In some monofilaments, an overhand knot will cut the line break strength by 50 percent.

Knots serve specific functions. That's why it's wise to know which knot is best for a specific use. Some knots are used to connect line to terminal tackle, secure line to a reel, join two lines, or form a loop in the end of a line. But a handful of knots will cover most of your fishing needs, because they lend themselves to strong ties every time.

Understanding when and where to use each knot can be crucial. Some knots work better with large-diameter lines and others with lighter monofilaments. There are even knots that can be used to join two lines of unequal diameters.

Good knots will fail if they are not tied correctly. The Trilene® Research Team discovered that a knot in monofilament will begin to slip just before it fails. Knowing this, it makes sense to draw a knot up as tight as you can. The drawing process should be slow and steady. Use water as a lubricant to reduce friction and help the turns in the knot slide easily.

Caution: Experiments have shown that some people's saliva can weaken knots in monofilament line.

If you cinch up a knot too fast, you can generate enough heat to weaken the knot. Speaking of heat, some fishermen insist on burning the tag end of the monofilament with a cigarette or a lighter. They reason that a "knob" on the end will help prevent slippage. This practice actually causes more harm than good. The flame frequently burns the knot or heats it, reducing the break strength of the line.

After you have tied a knot, examine it closely. If it doesn't look right, cut it off and retie it. If you think it might be weak, pull on it. It's better to have a knot break or slip in your hands than when you're depending on it to hold a fish.

When trimming the tag end, use a pair of cutting pliers or nail clippers. But be careful. Anglers sometimes nick the knot or adjacent line while trimming and they end up weakening the knot and/or the line.

To help you understand the following instructions, a *tag end* is the part of the line in which the knot is tied. Think of it as the shorter end of the line. It also refers to the excess line that remains after a knot is tied.

Distinguished from the tag end, the *standing part* is another name for the main length of line or the longer piece. A *turn or wrap* is one revolution of line around another. It simply means passing the tag end around the standing part.

TRILENE® KNOT TYING CHECKLIST

Before you start practicing your knots, here are some helpful tips to keep in mind.

1. Clip off any damaged section of line before you make a new tie. Usually the last 2 feet.

2. Check the hook or lure eye for barbs or rough spots.

3. Use plenty of working line when tying a knot.

4. Tie your knot wet. This allows the knot to cinch up smoothly without kinking or weakening the line.

5. Tighten the knot with a steady even motion without hesitation.

6. Pull your knot up tight.

7. Don't trim too close. Leave at least ⅛ inch of your line at the knot.

The following knots have been selected because they are relatively simple to tie, reliable, and they provide good knot strength. And with a little practice you'll tie them with confidence.

Trilene® Knot

The Trilene Knot is a strong, reliable connection that resists slippage and premature failures. It works best when used with Trilene premium monofilament fishing line.
The Trilene Knot is an all-purpose connection to be used in joining Trilene to swivels, snaps, hooks and artificial lures. The knot's unique design and ease of tying yield consistently strong, dependable connections while retaining 85-90% of the original line strength. The double wrap of mono through the eyelet provides a protective cushion for added safety.

1. Run end of line through eye of hook or lure and double back through the eye a second time.

2. Loop around standing part of line 5 or 6 times.

3. Thread tag end back between the eye and the coils as shown.

4. Pull up tight and trim tag end.

Improved Blood Knot

The Improved Blood Knot is used for tying two pieces of monofilament together of relatively equal diameters.

1. Overlap the ends of your two strands that are to be joined and twist them together about 10 turns.

2. Separate one of the center twists and thrust the two ends through the space as illustrated.

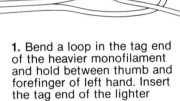

3. Pull knot together and trim off the short ends.

Albright Knot

The Albright Knot is most commonly used for joining monofilament lines of unequal diameters, for creating shock leaders and when a Bimini Twist is tied in the end of the lighter casting line. It is also used for connecting monofilament to wire.

1. Bend a loop in the tag end of the heavier monofilament and hold between thumb and forefinger of left hand. Insert the tag end of the lighter monofilament through loop from the top.

2. Slip tag end of lighter monofilament under your left thumb and pinch it tightly against the heavier strands of the loop. Wrap the first turn of the lighter monofilament over itself and continue wrapping toward the round end of the loop. Take at least 12 turns with the lighter monofilament around all three strands.

3. Insert tag end of the lighter mono-filament through end of the loop from the bottom. It must enter and leave the loop on the same side.

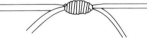

4. With the thumb and forefinger of the left hand, slide the coils of the lighter monofilament toward the end of the loop, stop 1/8″ from end of loop. Using pliers, pull the tag end of the lighter mono tight to keep the coils from slipping off the loop.

5. With your left hand still holding the heavier mono, pull on the standing part of the lighter mono. Pull the tag end of the lighter mono and the standing part a second time. Pull the standing part of the heavy mono and the standing part of the light mono.

6. Trim both tag ends.

Palomar Knot

The Palomar Knot is a general-purpose connection used in joining monofilament to swivels, snaps, hooks and artificial lures. The double wrap of mono through the eyelet provides a protective cushion for added safety.

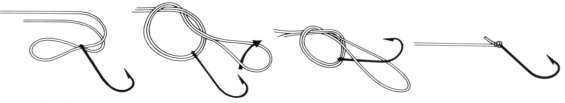

1. Double the line and form a loop three to four inches long. Pass the end of the loop through hook's eye.

2. Holding standing line between thumb and finger, grasp loop with free hand and form a simple overhand knot.

3. Pass hook through loop and draw line while guiding loop over top of eyelet.

4. Pull tag end of line to lighten knot snugly and trim tag end to about ⅛″.

Arbor Knot

The Arbor Knot provides the angler with a quick, easy connection for attaching line to the reel spool.

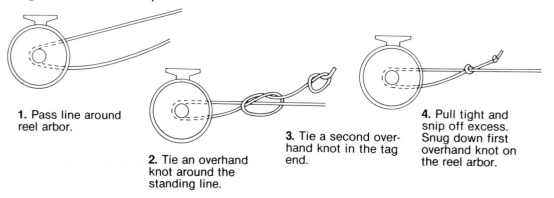

1. Pass line around reel arbor.

2. Tie an overhand knot around the standing line.

3. Tie a second overhand knot in the tag end.

4. Pull tight and snip off excess. Snug down first overhand knot on the reel arbor.

Double Surgeon's Loop

The Double Surgeon's Loop is a quick, easy way to tie a loop in the end of a leader. It is often used as part of a leader system because it is relatively strong.

1. Double the tag end of the line. Make a single overhand knot in the double line.

2. Hold the tag end and standing part of the line in your left hand and bring the loop around and insert through the overhand knot again.

3. Hold the loop in your right hand. Hold the tag end and standing line in your left hand. Moisten the knot (don't use saliva) and pull to tighten.

4. Trim off the tag end.

PROPER LINE CARE

There are many factors that can contribute to a lost lure or lost fish, but nothing causes more trouble than a damaged line. Knowing the condition of your line, and how to take care of it, will increase your fishing enjoyment. But how does an angler know when his line needs to be replaced?

Keeping track of the length of time the line is used is one way to determine when you should replace it. The best way to do this is by keeping a record of your line changes on your reel foot. When you replace the line, just jot down the day's date and the break strength of the line on a piece of paper. By keeping this handy reminder on a reel stick-on or in your tackle box, you'll know the age of the line on every reel, its pound test, and when you should replace it.

Yet you can't judge a line's worth by time alone. Many factors can affect a line. Even the best monofilament will become fatigued and weaken when subject to hard use. Repeated stress, excessive abrasion, lengthy exposure to sunlight, and improper storage can all damage a fishing line. But, by spotting the trouble early and using some preventive measures, you can keep your monofilament in peak condition.

All monofilament lines—economy as well as premium—are adversely affected by sunlight, heat, humidity, abrasion, faulty equipment, and chemicals. No matter which line you use, take care of it properly. It's the most important link between you and the fish. Here are five factors that can have an adverse effect on your line. If you detect one or more of these, it's time to replace your line immediately.

In some fishing conditions, you can't avoid getting hung up and losing lures. Each time you snag your line on submerged trees, rocks, or heavy vegetation, you're damaging it. In an attempt to work it free, you end up stretching the monofilament beyond its resiliency (elastic limits) and the line gets weaker. When this happens, and you break off, make sure you remove several yards of line before rigging up again. This will prevent reuse of any damaged section of the line.

Monofilament that suddenly looks dull and "fuzzy" should arouse your suspicions. Check it by running it between your lips. This should enable you to detect even the slightest nick or wear spot. One nick inflicted by a rock, a fish's gill cover, or underwater debris becomes a focal point. This weak section can cause the break strength of the line to drop by 50 percent or more. For example, 10-pound test could break at 5 pounds and you'd never know why.

High-energy waves from sunlight destroy monofilament by smashing nylon molecules. Over a period of weeks of continued exposure, the outer layer of exposed line weakens progressively. Your only clue might be that the line color has faded and the surface looks dull and chalky.

The best place to store line is at room temperature, away from chemicals, water, and direct sunlight. Filled reels and spare spools should never be stored where there is excessive heat. That's why a car's trunk or back-window ledge is the worst place to keep line. The heat in these areas can ruin even the best lines.

Lines should not be stored where they will come in contact with chemical vapors. They should be kept away from ultraviolet light as well. Nor is it a good idea to store monofilament in areas with excessive moisture. And beware of tackle dealers who display their lines in store windows.

FAULTY EQUIPMENT

The Trilene® Research Team has found that faulty rod guides and burred reel surfaces rank as the two most common causes of line failure. Run a brand-new monofilament over a diamond-sharp, cracked carbide or ceramic guide or tip-top and you've ruined the line. To prevent this, you should periodically inspect the hazard spots that are present on every rod or reel. Among them you'll find roller pins, shrouds and eyelets on push-button reels, rollers on open-faced spinning gear that are grooved or fail to roll, corroded or poorly polished surfaces on rollers and rod guides that are not perfectly smooth.

If you've wondered how a soft monofilament line can make a groove in a hard, chromed-steel guide or ceramic guide, the answer is quite simple. Wet monofilament collects a mixture of water and sand grit on its surface. These fine silica particles, coating the line, become a cutting compound. With repeated use in dirty waters, the line will slowly but surely cut through the hardest rod and reel surfaces.

Make it a habit to check the line guides frequently, especially the tiptop and the first or stripper guide nearest the reel. The tiptop and the stripper are maximum stress and wear points. Because of their importance and delicate nature, use a cotton-tipped swab or a piece of nylon stocking to detect signs of wear. Run them through and around the guides. If they don't become snagged, inspect that area with a magnifying glass. Don't try to polish the defective area. Damaged guides should always be replaced.

PLAYING THE FISH—HELPFUL TECHNIQUES

Playing a fish demands a give-and-take battle. That's why saltwater anglers are so fussy about the line they use and the knots they tie. Experience has taught them that they cannot put adequate pressure on the fish unless the line can withstand the strain. But besides the knots and line, there are several fishing techniques that can help you play fish more successfully. These techniques involve various stages throughout your struggle with the fish—setting the hook, dropping the rod tip, pumping, "bowing" to the fish, working the fish in close, netting, gaffing, and landing the fish.

SETTING THE HOOK

The best way to drive a hook into a fish is to use a series of short, sharp jerks in rapid succession. The rod can either be swept upward or kept low and moved sideways, parallel to the water. Always wait for the line to become tight or reel up the slack and take as much stretch out of the monofilament as you can before you set the hook. Hook-setting on a slack line warns the fish before you can generate enough force to set the hook.

To set the hook effectively, the line must be in good condition. Nicks, cuts, or frayed sections frequently cause monofilaments to fail. When a line pops during hook-setting, it might not be the fault of the particular brand of line you are using, but rather the condition of the

line on the reel. The instant you hook a fish, expect it to react with an explosive run for freedom. This sudden surge can strain tackle and line. Don't try to stop the fish and don't tighten the drag. Let the fish run until it tires. Then start working it back toward you.

DROPPING THE ROD TIP

A hooked fish's instinctive defense is to seek the safety of a submerged tree or thick vegetation, or to wrap your line around a rock. Your job is to stop him. That takes skill, determination, and quick reflexes. If the fish reaches its goal, you lose. If you apply too much line tension, the line breaks. An effective tactic is to drop the rod tip, back off on line tension, by loosening the drag, and then try to pull the fish back in the same motion. The key is to cushion the shock on the line without yielding to the fish. Sometimes a sudden release in line tension will cause a running fish to stop. When he does, that's your cue to regain control.

PUMPING

In fighting a fish, beginners often let excitement cloud their judgment. They continue to crank the handle in a frenzied manner. With bait-casting reels or conventional spool reels, this maneuver doesn't create a problem. But with spinning and spin-casting tackle, it will twist a line faster and more severely than any fish ever could. Here's why:

Every time the handle makes one revolution, several twists are put in the line. Some bails revolve as much as five times for every turn of the handle, and the line twist can become a serious problem very quickly.

Rather than using the reel to winch the fish toward you, a more effective approach is to use the rod as a lever and guide the fish toward you. This is called "pumping" and anyone can do it. Simply lift the rod smoothly from a horizontal to nearly a vertical position. When the rod is at about one o'clock, or a 75-degree angle, lower the rod tip swiftly and smoothly while you take in the slack line you just created. If the fish is near the surface, you can also pump effectively by sweeping the rod horizontally instead of lifting it vertically.

Veteran saltwater anglers often use a technique they call "short stroking." Short stroking involves using an extremely short amount of lifting with a very quick pumping action. Advocates of this method believe that this action keeps the fish from getting its head down and diving.

BOWING TO THE FISH

Certain species of fish are spectacular jumpers and can add pressure to the line. When you're confronted with a jumping fish, exercise caution. Push the rod toward the fish, creating controlled slack in the line. As the fish falls back into the water, you can regain control. Called "bowing to the fish," this technique helps to eliminate the chance of a fish landing on a taut line or surging forward against the line with its full weight.

WORKING THE FISH IN CLOSE

The most critical point in the struggle occurs when the fish is close to the boat, shore, or you (if you happen to be wading). Weaknesses in the line aren't as critical when the fish is far off because there is more stretch in the line to cushion the strain. But when you bring the fish closer to you on a shorter length of the line, its nicks and other types of wear become much more significant, and there isn't much line to absorb the shock. Some fishermen blame failure on the line when all along the fish and line could have been saved by using the proper technique.

LANDING THE FISH

How many times has a friend tried to help you land a fish by grabbing the line above the leader and yanking the fish upward? The result is usually disastrous, right? The fish shakes its head, surges or moves off, causing the line to break. Some anglers would blame the line, accusing it of being weak or defective. The truth is that, by grabbing the line, your friend prevented the rod from acting as a shock absorber. It was simply the wrong thing to do.

A similar thing occurs when someone tries to lift a fish into the boat. The problem is compounded by jerking the fish's head upward once the leader has been reached. Fishermen forget that fish in water weigh less than in the air. When anglers lift a fish out of water it seems to get heavier. Be careful. This effect puts added strain on the line.

To avoid such frustration, just remember: Whether you use the rod or handle the leader to lift it into the boat, get the fish tired first. Swim the fish toward you, and then, without losing momentum, lift it smoothly and in the same direction it was swimming. When done without any sudden jerks, this tactic has a chance of being successful. But lifting should only be attempted when there is no other way to land the fish.

NETTING OR GAFFING

Netting or gaffing a fish can be routine if you follow a few basic rules. Fish can't swim backward, so always net them head first. Get the net wet, hold it in the water at about a 45-degree angle to the surface, and then lead the fish into it. As the fish enters the net, lift it up and into the boat or onto the bank.

Gaffing is a bit more difficult. The gaff must be moved in position under the fish or across the fish without letting the handle get in front of the line or leader. Otherwise, a sudden surge by the fish would cause the line to rub against the handle and such friction could cut the line. When you do strike a fish with a gaff, make it a positive, controlled thrust. Strike the fish and lift it into the boat—all in the same motion.

AFTER LANDING A FISH

When fish are biting and the first one has been landed, the temptation is overwhelming to get your line immediately back in the water to catch another. Yet it's far more sensible to stop and check the line for cuts, nicks, or other signs of weakness. All lines are vulnerable to fatigue. You can't see it. But fatigue starts to show up in a line that's been worked hard. Advanced anglers with a reputation for catching more and bigger fish make it a practice to cut off a few yards of line periodically and rig up again. If they doubt the line's ability to hold up through another battle, they simply change reel spools.

Carrying a replacement spool filled with fresh line makes sense. This might sound extravagant, but the expert fishermen are always prepared for surprises. They expect the next cast to hook a trophy. That's why they don't take chances. They've learned it pays to give their line the attention it deserves.

SALTWATER LURES

Such a vast number of saltwater fishing lures are now available on tackle shelves that it's almost impossible even to catalog them. Still, hundreds of new models are introduced every year.

Some models survive because they are successful—they really attract fish. Others survive because they attract fishermen. But those that attract both fish and fishermen survive the longest and sell fastest. In any case, a saltwater angler who sets about buying every lure that will take fish would probably spend his entire life, and all his money, doing so.

The truth is that it's possible to stock up on a completely adequate assortment of saltwater lures at relatively modest cost. One secret, I think, is to ignore all the "gimmick" designs and

flashy colors. Occasionally, some of the unique actions or finishes on plugs or lures are very effective, but on eight or nine days in ten, lures finished in solid white or yellow will be the most effective. The action of a lure or the depth at which it's fished is far more important, I believe, than the color.

The basic saltwater lure as well as the oldest of them all is the jig. This is a simple and inexpensive product that is really nothing more than a lead-headed hook wrapped with feathers, hair, nylon, rubber strips, metal foil, or a combination of these. Almost any game fish in saltwater from the tiniest grunt to the heaviest marlin will strike a jig of the proper size fished at the proper depth.

Two things, therefore, influence the selection of jigs: the approximate size of the fish to be caught and the depth of the water to be fished. That means, if you fish the surf one day, the reefs the next day, and a bay the following day, you will need a wide selection of different size and weight jigs to get along.

For casting with either medium spinning or plug-casting tackle, jigs from ¼ to ⅝ ounce are suitable. For fishing in extremely shallow water as for bonefish, jigs in the ⅛- to ¼-ounce size are best.

When you move out to deep water offshore,

Selection of casting and trolling lures, from deep-running to surface types, manufactured mostly for Pacific coast fishing. However, most of these will work just as well in the Atlantic.

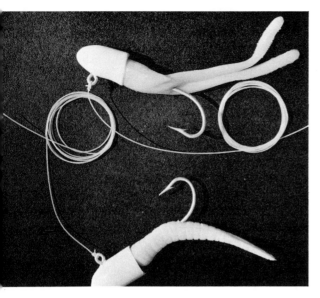

Casting jigs with plastic tails and metal heads work well on a great variety of saltwater game species.

perhaps for kingfish and similar species, you'll need more weight. In this case 1- to 2-ounce jigs are best, and occasionally those even heavier are necessary. The largest of all are those used when trolling for big game fish with heavy tackle.

Another basic type of saltwater lure is the plug made of plastic, wood, or glass and designed to imitate a small baitfish. Some plugs are designed for use underwater and others for use on the surface. There are exceptions to this rule, but generally the plugs without the built-in action are best in saltwater.

Among the surface plugs, some are cup-shaped to pop or bubble loudly on the surface while others are of the darter or silent type. Still a third type of surface plug includes those with whirling metal blades or propellers to increase the surface commotion.

At times when deep-trolling for snook, tarpon, channel bass, kingfish, and cobias, you'll find a lipped plug with a fast vibrating action to be extremely effective.

In addition to the jigs and plugs, every saltwater angler's tackle box should include a few spoons of various sizes and weights. Certain fish such as open-water barracuda and bluefish are particularly partial to these slivers of flashing metal.

TIDES

Ocean tides are regular, predictable fluctuations of ocean water levels caused by gravitational pull of the moon (and to some extent the sun) on the earth. In some parts of the world the fluctuation is very small; elsewhere it is great, varying as much as 30 feet between high and low tides. Along most seashores there are four tides each day and these tides repeat themselves about every two weeks. A high tide follows a low tide in approximately six hours and so forth.

This regular flow, or surging of water, along our coasts and into every bay and saltwater lagoon, even far up many coastal rivers, produces an inexorable current. Just as freshwater fishermen must understand and take advantage of

Plug-casting outfit with a selection of surface lures for tarpon, snook, and other saltwater game species.

river currents, saltwater anglers must carefully watch and understand the tides. No other single factor is so important to fishing success. Tides can either confound or greatly benefit saltwater fishermen: Depending on the place, fish can be very active on a high or flood tide, and quite inactive on a low or ebb tide. Elsewhere, however, the exact opposite may be true.

Being able to predict tides has an immense advantage in planning trips. To make this possible the federal government annually publishes a book, *Tide Tables for the East Coast of North and South America.* (There is another edition for the West Coast.) It sells for $5.35 and is available from the National Ocean Survey, Riverdale, MD 20840. In addition, local tide tables are published in many newspapers and journals, and tide table cards are distributed free by marinas, manufacturers of tackle and fishing equipment, and even by beer companies.

Tides affect fishing in countless ways. High tides flood vast areas of shallow flats and for several hours (before falling) create a very fertile fishing area. Low tides leave the same flats high and dry. Tide is very difficult to detect offshore, but affects fish and fishing nonetheless. As a rule of thumb, most rivers, and river mouths, which drain into the sea are hottest to fish on a falling tide because schools of forage fish or baitfish are retreating down current to where larger species wait to feed on them. On the other hand, many channels or cuts where the tidal current is strong are most productive during a rising or flood tide.

18

NATURAL BAITS FOR SALTWATER FISHING

Albacore Principally a game fish, it is used whole or cut for marlin, sailfish, and other large game fish.

Alewife Adult alewives measure about 1 foot, are caught in large numbers by commercial fishermen. Also called spring herring.

Anchovy The anchovy is considered one of the best baits along the Pacific coast for yellow-tail, halibut, barracuda, and other fish. Difficult to keep alive on a hook, anchovies give off oils that make them extremely attractive. Those caught along the Atlantic coast are used for striped bass, weakfish, and others.

Baitfish Many baitfish are used in saltwater fishing. *Silverside Minnows* or *Spearing, Killfish, Herring, Sardine,* and *Sand Launce* are all used at times. Large fish, such as mackerel, bonitos, dolphin, flying fish, butterfish, and silver hake, are used for big game fishing. Most baitfish can be bought in fish markets, from commercial fishermen or bait dealers. They can be caught in seines, drop nets, cast nets, minnow traps, or on hook and line, and kept alive, either in large

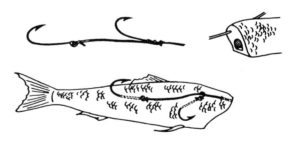

Plug-cut baitfish. When cut and rigged as shown, a herring or mullet can be cast and manipulated like a plug. Great rig for tarpon, big snook.

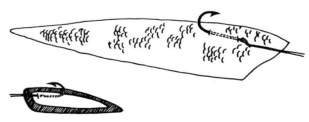

Cut spinner bait, which can be used in conjunction with a keel sinker.

tanks or in bait cans, or frozen, chilled on ice, or pickled in heavy brine. Live baitfish can be hooked through the lips, back, belly, or sides. Dead ones are hooked by running the hook either through the eyes or mouth and gill opening, then into the body near the tail.

Balao or *Ballyhoo* A member of the halfbeak family, resembling the needlefish, and used as a bait for tarpon, barracuda, amberjacks, and especially sailfish. Found in southeastern United States.

Barracuda Small barracuda are sometimes used whole in fishing for large game fish, or as cut bait for smaller fish.

Billfish Common name for *Needlefish*.

Blackbelly A common name for glut herring, found in abundance along the Atlantic coast. See *Herring*.

Black-tailed Shrimp A bait shrimp found along the Pacific coast.

Bloodworm Found in mud flats along Atlantic and Pacific coasts. Sometimes measures more than 8 or 10 inches in length. The name refers to red-hued bodies. When handled, they shoot out a long proboscis with four tiny black jaws. Both bloodworms and clam worms can be found along rocks and sandy bottoms, at low tide on flats or sandy basins. They can be kept in a cool

TWO REGULATION RIGS FOR TROLLING WITH BALAO

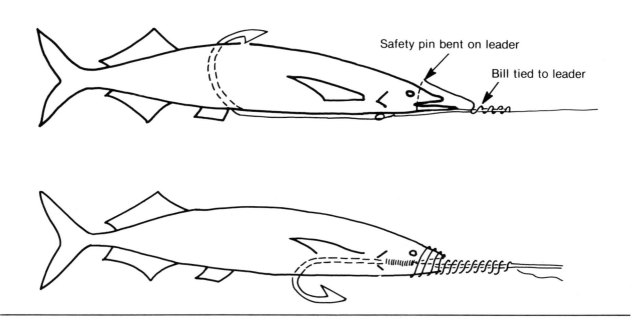

REGULATION RIG FOR TROLLING WITH STRIP

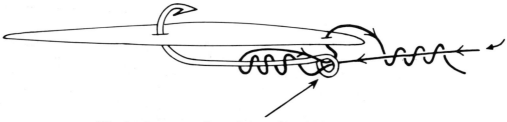

Wire leader passes through eye of hook,
twists around shank three times,
passes back through eye, then through strip,
and finally twists forming safety pin.

Techniques for rigging balaos for trolling.

bed of rock moss or on ice. For hooking fish such as rockfish, bass, and weakfish, use a single worm, whole or cut in pieces. Two or three get best results for blackfish, croakers, and nippers.

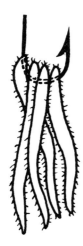

How to hook sand- or bloodworms.

Blue Crab Also called blue-claw crab and edible crab, the blue is large, dark, white-bellied with long bluish claws, red at the tip. Hind legs are paddlelike to propel it through the water. Blue crabs are found in bays, inlets, rivers, and have a preference for mud bottoms. They can be caught in nets and will live for several days out of water if kept cool. Hook the hard crabs in the underside of the top shell. Soft-shell crabs can be tied to hook. Crabs make the best bait for bluefish, weakfish, tautogs, and many other varieties.

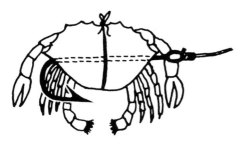

How to hook a dead soft-shell crab.

Blueback Another name for glut herring, used as bait along the Atlantic coast.

Bonito A common sport fish, sometimes cut in strips and used as bait for sailfish and marlin, or used whole for swordfish, blue marlin, sailfish, tuna, and other big game fish.

Brazilian Shrimp Common shrimp caught commercially in the Atlantic.

Buckram Term for a crab past the soft-shell stage but not yet hard. The shell caves in when pressed. Sometimes called leatherback, paperback, or peeler crab.

Bunker Another name for *Menhaden.*

Butterfish A baitfish sometimes used for weakfish, tuna, and other saltwater game fish.

Catfish Saltwater catfish are used as bait for black sea bass, marlin, tarpon, jewfish.

Cherrystone Clam Local name for the East coast commercial hard-shell clam.

Chum Various shellfish and baitfish crushed or ground up, either placed in a chum pot or thrown overboard to lure fish.

Clam Includes *California Razor Clam, Cherrystone, Long Clam, Nannynose, Ocean Clam, Pismo.* These bivalve mollusks are among the most popular baits. Many kinds are used, but the big *Surf Clam,* or sea clam, and the hard-shell clams are most common. Surf clams are found along the ocean and surf. Hard-shell clams are found in the more protected bays and sounds, can be dug with clam hoes or forks on tidal flats. Clams can also be bought from bait dealers and in fish markets. You can keep them for several days in a cool spot or on ice. For longer periods, they should be submerged in saltwater in a sack or other container. Open them with a knife or hit them against a hard object to get at the soft, meaty parts. For big fish such as cod, rockfish, and channel bass, put the meat from a whole clam or two clams on a hook. For tautogs, scup or porgies, sea bass, flounder, and other small fish, cut the muscular foot of the clams into sections.

Clam Worm These marine worms appeal to most saltwater fish. The clam worms (sandworms) and *Bloodworms* are the two kinds usually used. Clam worms have a brown, bluish, or greenish iridescence, rounded backs, and flat, pink or red undersides, with two rows of "legs" along the sides. Both clam worms and bloodworms can be dug with clam hoes or garden forks at low tide on tidal flats. For large fish, such as rockfish (striped bass) and weakfish, hook a single worm, or even two or three for best results. For smaller fish, such as tautogs, scup or porgies, flounder, and croakers, a worm can be cut in half or quarters.

Conch Univalve mollusks, most prevalent in tropical regions, where the soft bodies are removed from their spiral shells and used for bonefish, groupers, grunts, and snappers.

Crab Many crabs make good bait. Most popular are *Blue, Lady, Sand* (or *Green*), *Fiddler, Hermit, Red-Jointed Fiddler,* and *Hairy Hermit.* All live in the ocean and bays among rocks and weeds, in burrows or empty snail shells. You can catch most by hand in shallow water or with crab nets and traps. Soft-shell crabs make the best bait. Crabs usually can be kept alive several days out of water in a cool environment. For longer periods, they can be kept in cages submerged in saltwater. Hook the hard crabs through the back or side with the hook entering the underside and coming out on top. Soft-shell crabs can be tied to a hook with fine thread. Crabs will take striped bass, channel bass, bluefish, weakfish, flounder, tautogs, and many other saltwater fish.

How to hook a green crab near the base of the tail.

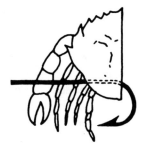

How to hook a live fiddler (or similar) crab.

Cut Bait Bait made by cutting large fish into strips.

Earthworm Sometimes used for striped bass, flounder, eels, and other saltwater fish.

Eel Favorite bait for striped bass. Found along the Atlantic coast in basins, tidal drainage rivers, freshwater ponds and lakes, they may reach 1½ feet in length. Slim and snakelike, with color varying from gray to yellow on the back, white on the belly. Though eels are generally fished dead or cut in sections, live eels are used for striped bass. Eel skins are frequently attached to metal or rubber rings and used as casting or trolling baits. Either the whole eel or the eel skins can be kept in brine solution. Jewfish, weakfish, and a great variety of saltwater species will take this bait.

Fiddler Crab Common crab used for bait.

Flying Fish Common baitfish used for tuna, sailfish, swordfish. It is frequently skittered along the surface.

Flying Squid Another name for the short-tailed squid found along the East coast from Cape Cod to Florida.

Ghost Crab Crab found along the East coast from Long Island south.

Green Crab Common name for sand crab. See *Crab.*

Halfbreak Another name for *Balao*, which resembles the needlefish and is used for tarpon, sailfish, and others.

Hermit Crab Crab that lives in abandoned shells of snails, is bait for bonefish, sheepshead, blackfish, permits, and snappers. Heat or crack the shell to get the crab and remove the claws.

Herring One of most common food fish in Atlantic and Pacific waters. Generally less than 12 inches in length, herring are used either dead or alive, but they are difficult to keep alive on a hook or in tanks. Can be hooked through the lips, through the belly, or attached to special herring rigs, which hold them securely but do not kill quickly. Used dead, they are hooked through the lips and if trolled the hook may be spooned into the body cavity. Strips, chunks, or ground-up herring make good chum.

Hickory Shad Large herring often used as bait.

Hog-Mouthed Fry Small minnow used for chumming and bait for many species in Bermuda.

Icefish Another name for *Smelt.*

Inkfish Another name for *Squid*.

Jumping Mullet Common name for striped mullet found along both coasts.

Killfish Favorite baitfish for fishermen along the Atlantic. Seldom over 6 inches, they travel in large schools, can be caught in bays, tidal creeks, rivers. Fishermen like them because they live a long time on the hook. They can be carried in damp seaweed, but it is best to keep them in water or on ice. Good for bass, weakfish, bluefish, sea bass, and especially summer flounder or flukes.

King Mackerel Sport fish used as cut bait or whole for larger fish.

Lady Crab Also called calico crab; found along the East coast and the Gulf of Mexico.

Leatherback Another name for *Buckram Crab*.

Limpet Small univalve mollusk found along both coasts, attached to rocks and other underwater objects. Soft body is removed from shell and used.

Lobster Good for striped bass, blackfish, and many saltwater species but expensive to purchase as bait.

Mackerel Commonly caught for sport, but commercial fishermen sell small ones as bait. Fished alive for large game fish such as tuna; the large ones are cut in strips and used for striped bass, bluefish, weakfish, flounder, or other species.

Marsh Fiddler Another name for mud fiddler crab found along the East coast and mud flats.

Menhaden Also called bonyfish, bugfish, chebog, bunker, greentail, hardhead, porgy, or razor-belly shad. The menhaden, or mossbunker, is one of best baitfish along the Atlantic and Gulf coasts. It is flat, oily, and often reaches more than a foot in length. Most menhaden are caught in purse seines and can be bought. Small menhaden are used whole; large ones are cut into steaks or filleted. Also ground up and used in chumming. Menhaden will catch bluefish, striped bass, weakfish, channel bass, mackerel, sharks, and many others.

Moon Snail Large snails found on both coasts. The meat is removed from the shell and used as bait for bottom feeders.

Mossbunker Another name for *Menhaden*.

Mullet Includes jumping mullet and silver mullet; a very popular fish along the Atlantic coast. Found in most bays, inlets, and surf, where they are caught—mostly by commercial fishermen—in seines or cast nets. Small mullet are used whole for bottom fishing; larger ones are rigged and used in trolling for sailfish. Big ones can be cut up. Mullet are especially good for striped bass, bluefish, channel bass, weakfish, and tarpon.

Mussel Includes bay mussel, fan mussel, mudbank mussel. These black, blue, brown, or olive-colored bivalves are well known and can be seen clinging to rocks, pilings, or the bottom of the saltwater bays. They are gathered at low tide in deep water. Larger mussels are best for bait, but even these are soft and difficult to keep on a hook. For some fish, such as tautogs, the

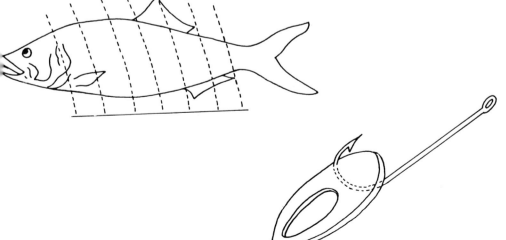

Top cut bait is the menhaden. Here's how to cut it and use it on hook. Use the head and entrails for chumming.

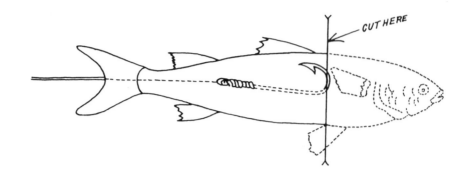

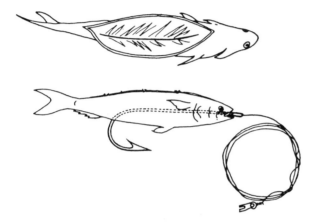

Above: *Mullet or grunt rigged for bottom-fishing. This can be cast without dead fish coming off the hook. It's a good hooker, too. Mullet is cut in half in front of the dorsal fin and a wire leader with hook attached is threaded through. Thus the hook point is exposed and the hook bend supports the weight of the bait.*

Left: *Mullet prepared for trolling. The fish is split down the back, the backbone removed and discarded. The hook is placed as shown, the back is sewed up and the eye of the hook sewed to the mouth.*

shell of a mussel can be cracked, but not removed, to make it stay on the hook better and to keep other fish from stealing the bait. Removed from the shell, mussel meat can be tied around a hook with fine thread. Mussels will catch flounder, croakers, corbinas, and many others.

Needlefish Also called longjaw or sea pike, these elongated, slim fish look like freshwater gar. They swim rapidly, close to the surface, and often can be caught in a dip net. They are fished alive for marlin, tuna, sailfish.

Octopus Closely resembles *Squid,* q.v.

Oyster Used for bottom feeders—sheepshead, flounder, etc.

Pacific Sardine Also called pilchard; frequently used like herring, for striped bass, yellowtails, and other game fish.

Pacific Smelt Known as whitebait, these are good for salmon, white sea bass, barracuda, yellowtails, halibut bonitos, and smaller tuna.

Periwinkle A small snail found clinging to pilings, seaweed, and other underwater objects. Most periwinkles are too small to be used, but since they are so prevalent, some of them can serve in a pinch.

Pilchard Another name for *Pacific Sardine.*

Pinfish Small sunfishlike panfish used alive for tarpon, black sea bass, tuna, and other fish.

Pinhead Small anchovy; usually hooked through the mouth.

Pismo Clam Though collecting Pismo clams is a sport in itself along the Pacific coast, they also make good bait.

Prawn A prawn is a shrimp, also called mud shrimp or pin shrimp. Prawns can be netted with a small dip net. Chum them for weakfish, bass, bluefish, blackfish, and scup. Hook through the tail to keep alive to take white perch, mackerel, flounder.

Razor Clam A clam with an elongated shell, resembling a straight razor.

Saltwater Crayfish See *Spiny Lobster.*

Sand Bug Called sand fleas, beach bugs, sand crabs, mole crabs, and mole shrimp, they look like small, tan eggs with several hairy legs on the underside and may reach 1½ inches in length. At ocean beaches from Cape Cod to Florida and along the Pacific, you find them burrowing in sand where waves break. They leave the sand when a wave comes in but quickly burrow again when the wave recedes. Dig with your hands or scoop with a special long-handled, wire-mesh trap. Sand bugs can be kept alive in a container filled with damp sand. To hook a sand bug, run the hook into the underside and out through the top shell. One bug is enough for small fish, while several lined up on a hook are best for larger fish. Sand bugs will take striped bass, channel bass, bonefish, sheepshead, tautogs, pompano, corbinas, croakers.

Sand Launce These fish are found in great abundance on both East and West coasts, above the tidewater mark, where they can be dug. They congregate in schools, are generally seined, and can be kept alive for considerable periods. Small ones are fished whole; large ones are cut in pieces. Excellent for bluefish, striped bass, and other sport fish. Also called sand eel.

Sardine A common name for Atlantic herring.

Scallop The soft part of the scallop makes good bait. A good trick for anglers is to crack the shell, trim the meat, and salt it down in an airtight container to preserve and toughen for a later fishing trip.

Sea Worm Also called mussel worm, pileworm, ribbon worm, rock worm, and tapeworm.

Shad Another name for *Menhaden*.

Shedder Crab A day or so before a crab sheds its shell the old shell loosens and can be peeled off. At this stage, the crab is called a shedder or a peeler. You can test this by breaking off the movable part of a pincer; if the shell breaks away leaving a soft inner portion exposed, this crab is a shedder. Almost all bottom-feeding fish can be caught with these crabs.

Shiner Another name for *Menhaden* or for *Silverside Minnow*.

Short-Tailed Squid East coast squid generally found in deeper water than common squid.

Shrimp All species of this abundant crustacean are used for bait—from the big, edible shrimp found in fish markets to the smaller sand shrimp and prawns often sold by bait dealers. Catch your own with seines in shallow water of bays, sounds, and inlets. Keep alive in water or on ice in rockweed or sawdust. Shrimp and prawns should be hooked through the tail. Use for striped bass, channel bass, weakfish, bluefish, bonefish, sheepshead, snappers, groupers, and most saltwater fish.

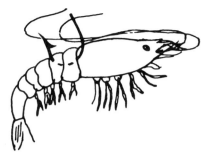

Edible shrimp hooked through the back. Keep the barb up.

Sand shrimp hooked near the tail.

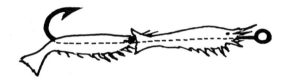

Two shrimp on a hook.

Silverside Minnow Saltwater minnows abundant along the East coast, caught in nets or traps.

Skimmer Clam Another name for surf clam, common along the East coast.

Smelt Includes icefish. They occur in tidal creeks, inlets, and into freshwater streams, where they spawn. Sometimes they reach a foot, but most are less than 6 inches. Good cod bait.

Snail Snails large and small can be used as bait. Moon snails or sand-collar snails found along the Atlantic and Pacific coasts are often left high and dry on shore or can be picked up in shallow water.

Soft-Shell Clam An extremely good bait along the East coast south to North Carolina but it is most numerous north of Massachusetts. Also occur along West coast as far south as Monterey, California.

Soft-Shell Crab Immediately after they shed

shells, crabs are called soft-shell and are highly prized as bait.

Spinners Strips cut from the sides of sardines or herring in pennant or triangular shape.

Spiny Lobster Common in warmer waters along both coasts, sometimes called saltwater crayfish. Caught in baited traps or seined. In many areas there are restrictions as to seasons, size, and number. Can be kept alive in cages in saltwater. Hard head and body parts are frequently kept and used as chum, and the tail as a bait.

Squid Includes blunt-tailed squid, inkfish, sea arrows. Among the best all-around saltwater baits. Usually found in deeper waters but sometimes close to shore. Usually caught in pound nets, traps, trawls, and seines, they can be caught by hand or in dip nets when close to shore. Or you can buy squid, fresh or frozen, from fish and bait dealers. Squid are difficult to keep alive, so are usually preserved on ice, frozen, or pickled in brine. The whole squid is used for striped bass and hooked with one, two, or more hooks through the body and head. Small portions and strips are used for sea bass, cod, bluefish, and other small fish.

The head of a squid hooked for bottom-fishing.

How to hook a squid for bottom-fishing.

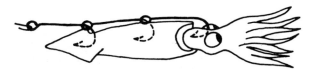

Three-hook squid rig. It will take a great variety of fish.

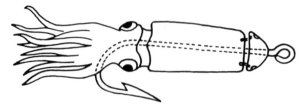

Lead-head jig in combination with squid.

Stone Crab Formerly used for bait, now scarce, due to commercial demand.

Top Smelt Pacific coast silverside minnow.

Whelk Includes channeled whelk, waved whelk, knobbed whelk; all are large, 2- to 4-inch univalve shells. May be trapped or picked up in shallow water. Good, tough bait for cod fishing; sometimes combined with softer bait like clam. May be cut up for tautogs, porgies, sea bass, other bottom fish.

Yellowtail Jack When alive, very effective for barracuda, sharks.

HOW TO RIG LIVE BAIT

A most important skill of saltwater angling is properly preparing a natural bait. And that can mean much more than simply impaling it on a hook.

Quite often a fisherman must cut, clean, or even sew baits onto a hook to obtain the kind of action that will tempt the fish he is seeking. Just for example, a minnow impaled for still-fishing or drifting is almost worthless for trolling because the fisherman is trying to achieve an entirely different effect when he trails the bait behind a moving boat.

Naturally the terminal gear—the leader, sinkers, swivels, and whatever—must also be rigged properly no matter whether the bait is being fished on the bottom or trolled on the surface. Obviously no single rig or hookup will meet all these conditions. And in fact no single rig will serve very well for more than the one purpose for which it was intended.

I will attempt to describe and illustrate here a few of the basic, terminal tackle rigs that are popular on both the Atlantic and the Pacific coasts for a wide variety of fishes. Obviously there are many more, but an angler with in-

genuity can begin with these and vary them to
suit his own specific fishing conditions.

Let's start with the common eel, which is
known by many names, but which by any name
is a great bait for surf-casting and trolling.

The easiest way to obtain eels is to buy them
from commercial fishermen who trap them during annual spawning migrations. However, if
you have to catch them for yourself, the best
method is to use an eelpot. This is simply a
large, wire-mesh minnow trap with a small
opening. It should be set in a bay or inlet in the
evening and then baited with chopped fish,
clams, crabs, or even pieces of beef neck. It's a
good idea to attach a float to the trap so that
you can locate it easily the next morning.

An eel is a favorite bait for striped bass,
bluefish, school tuna, cobias, and quite a number
of other big game species. And of course there
are many ways to rig and to fish eels. For surf-
casting from a beach or for shallow-water troll-
ings, a good method is to hook the eel both in
the head and about two thirds of the way back
toward the tail. The two hooks are connected
by using a long wire needle to pull the leader
entirely through the eel as shown in the diagram.

For deeper trolling, the head of the eel is
skinned out and an egg sinker is laid over the
wire leader. Then the skin is pulled back over
the sinker and sewn shut. Eels are almost always
used dead since a live eel will only twist and
turn enough to tangle tackle into a hopeless
mess.

Since it's quite a problem to cast a whole eel
with surf-casting gear, many beach fishermen
use only the skin, rigged with a weighted sinker
head. This eel-skin rig is also deadly for trolling,
as it has far more wiggle than a whole eel. The
skins are usually from 6 to 20 inches long,
depending upon the species of fish.

For fishing the bottom of the sea, whether it
be in a bay or above the reefs, the use of two
hooks will often help the angler land more fish
during the period when they're biting well and
fast. It will also double the opportunity for fish
to find the bait.

The most popular device for multiple bait
fishing is called a spreader rig. (See illustrations
below.) This is a section of spring steel or heavy
wire with a loop at each end through which
leaders and hooks are attached. The spreader bar
itself is attached to the line at the center; to sink

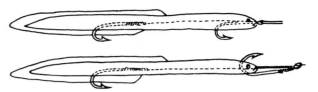

*Alternate eel rigs for trolling or casting. A long
wire needle pulls the leader through the eel's
body.*

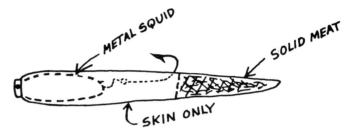

*An eel tail made by slipping eel skin (with a bit
of meat left in the tail) over a metal squid or an
egg sinker and hook.*

*Eel skin slipped over a metal squid or lead-head
jig.*

it rapidly to the proper depth a heavy sinker is
tied just below the point where the main line ties
on to the spreader bar. All kinds of spreader-rig
variations are possible, depending upon the type
of bottom to be fished and the species of fish in
question.

Tuna fishermen have devised a method to rig
herring for bait. It's called the "Wedgeport
Teaser," and it's valuable because it can be applied to many other baitfishes to catch many
other game fish.

This lure is made up by stringing several
whole herring together on a heavy line to imitate a small school of them surfacing. With
backbones removed, the herring are threaded
through the lips and each one is knotted so that
it will maintain a separate position on the line,
about 6 or 8 inches from the other herring.

Since herring used for the teasers are usually
frozen, they tend to be rather stiff and wooden
until the backbone is removed and the fish is
completely thawed. Of course, it's necessary to

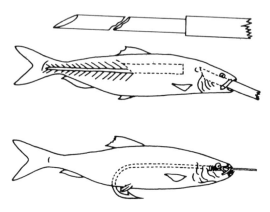

How to debone a herring, using a hollow steel tube sharpened at an angle. The technique is like coring an apple. With the backbone removed— to make the bait more flexible, lifelike—insert the hook and sew the mouth to the eye as shown.

resew the back after removing the backbone to keep the herring from falling apart. The "Teaser" is trolled behind a boat.

Following are ten of the most effective and popular saltwater rigs in use today:

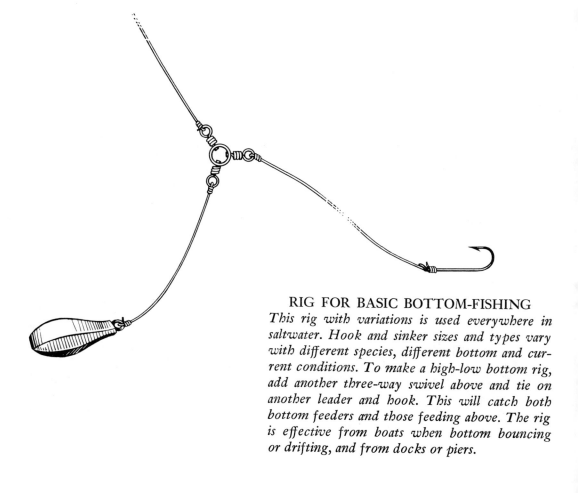

RIG FOR BASIC BOTTOM-FISHING
This rig with variations is used everywhere in saltwater. Hook and sinker sizes and types vary with different species, different bottom and current conditions. To make a high-low bottom rig, add another three-way swivel above and tie on another leader and hook. This will catch both bottom feeders and those feeding above. The rig is effective from boats when bottom bouncing or drifting, and from docks or piers.

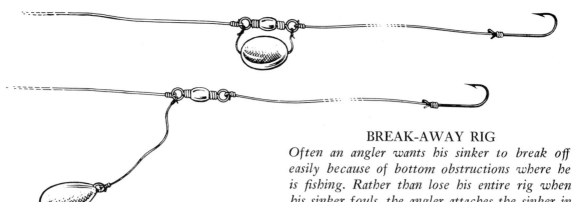

BREAK-AWAY RIG

Often an angler wants his sinker to break off easily because of bottom obstructions where he is fishing. Rather than lose his entire rig when his sinker fouls, the angler attaches the sinker in one of the ways shown here, using very light fishing line which will break off under pressure or wire wrapped in such a way that it will easily come loose. Some anglers dislike fighting fish with a heavy chunk of lead on their lines. Rigged as here, the weight will soon break off under the stress of battle.

SLIDING SINKER RIG

A simple, effective, and popular bottom rig for use from boats, bridges, and docks. The line runs through a hole in the sinker. The swivel keeps the sinker from sliding all the way to the hook. When a fish picks up bait, the line slides through the hole in the sinker and fish cannot feel the weight of the sinker. An additional hook may be added above the sinker on a three-way swivel.

FLOAT-POPPER RIG

A float with a hole through the center. Run the line through before tying on your hook. Fishing in the standard way, watch for the bobber to pop under and you know a fish is eating. It is also effective when drifting or casting. A sharp snap of the rod tip causes the dish-faced float to "pop" and calls fish to the bait.

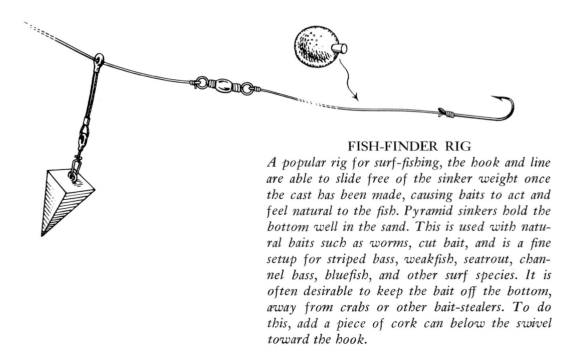

FISH-FINDER RIG

A popular rig for surf-fishing, the hook and line are able to slide free of the sinker weight once the cast has been made, causing baits to act and feel natural to the fish. Pyramid sinkers hold the bottom well in the sand. This is used with natural baits such as worms, cut bait, and is a fine setup for striped bass, weakfish, seatrout, channel bass, bluefish, and other surf species. It is often desirable to keep the bait off the bottom, away from crabs or other bait-stealers. To do this, add a piece of cork can below the swivel toward the hook.

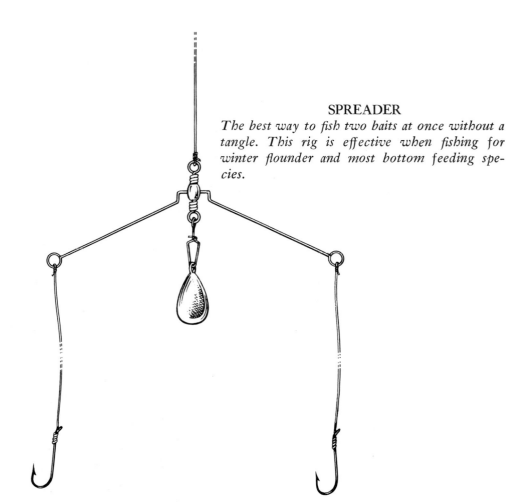

SPREADER

The best way to fish two baits at once without a tangle. This rig is effective when fishing for winter flounder and most bottom feeding species.

BOTTOM TROLLING RIG

This is a popular rig when trolling for bottom feeders from a boat. Jigs, feathers, spoons, and tubes can be used effectively. Either an in-line torpedo sinker or keel sinker go with this rig. Beads before and after the sinker prevent excessive line twist. The leader length varies from 3 feet up to 30 feet. Lead core and wire lines will also help trolled lures get deep, as will the use of planers and downriggers.

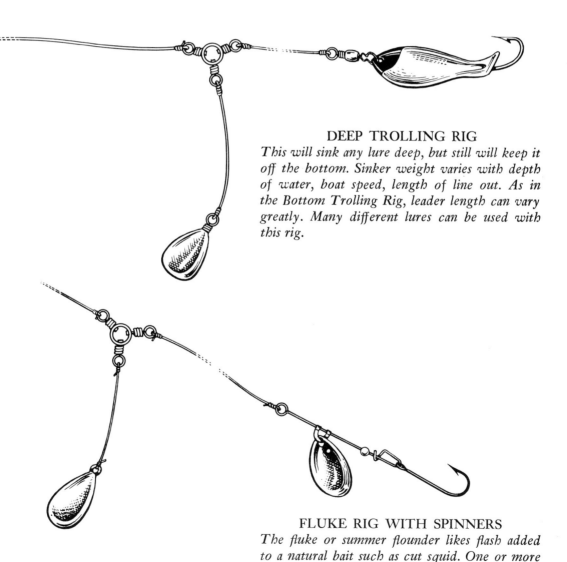

DEEP TROLLING RIG

This will sink any lure deep, but still will keep it off the bottom. Sinker weight varies with depth of water, boat speed, length of line out. As in the Bottom Trolling Rig, leader length can vary greatly. Many different lures can be used with this rig.

FLUKE RIG WITH SPINNERS

The fluke or summer flounder likes flash added to a natural bait such as cut squid. One or more spinners should do the trick.

THE EXPERTS' FAVORITE BAITS AND METHODS

Following is a list of favorite saltwater baits for twenty species of game fish obtained by interviewing two hundred fishing guides, pier operators, charter-boat captains, and well-known sport fishermen in North Carolina. Many of these men (whose total number of years of experience is an extraordinary 4,207) operate seasonally both in Florida and in North Carolina waters. Generally speaking, however, any charter-boat captain, guide, or pier operator will recommend the best baits for his particular area and will probably have an ample supply on hand.

Here are the popular game fishes and the experts' consensus:

Albacore Split mullet, whole mullet, strip squid, and cut fish are preferred, in that order. Among artificials recommended, the No. 3½ Drone spoon or a No. 4 Hopkins lure, followed by the Reflecto spoon and white or yellow feathers.

METHOD: Skip bait on top of the water; if this doesn't work, troll slower, letting the bait go deeper; if still no luck, let it sink to the bottom. When albacore move inshore to feed, fly-fishing, bait-casting, and spinning from a pier, a boat, or the surf present a real challenge.

Amberjack Live pinfish are best, followed by live mullet and squid, in that order. Drone spoons top the artificials with white and yellow feathers next.

Barracuda Whole squid, whole mullet, and strip mullet (live mullet are best). The ½-ounce feather is first among artificials, with several anglers swearing by the Loon Bone.

METHOD: Trolling on an incoming tide; use 7/0 or 8/0 hook. Troll near the bottom. Sometimes large spoons or jigs prove effective.

Black Drum Shrimp leads the list. Squid and cut mullet are next, trailed by sand fiddlers and clams. Pier fishermen recommend Sea Hawk plugs and Clark spoons.

Bluefish Bait for blues varies with the size of the fish. In the Wilmington and Southport areas of North Carolina, cut mullet was the choice for 3- to 6-pounders, while around Morehead City, Harkers Island, and Atlantic, where 10- to 14-inch fish are routinely landed, shrimp predominates; ¼-ounce to ½-ounce feathers and Sea Hawk plugs prove excellent choices among artificials. Also the Limper spoon.

METHOD: Troll fast with a spoon. Bounce Bomber Red Head jig off the bottom from a pier or drifting boat. The latter has proved most satisfactory where Shackleford Banks drops off into the channel.

Bonito Cut squid, cut mullet, Drone spoon, generally the same as for albacore.

Channel Bass Surf-casters prefer fresh mullet, salt mullet, crabs, and fatback (pork). Puppy drums may be taken on shrimp. Plugs and flies take small ones. Use swivel leader. Channel bass mouth their bait before taking. Always let the fish run about 4 yards before setting the hook. Pfleuger Record spoon is deadly.

Cobia Live pinfish on a free line. Live shrimp on a free line. Spoons, Mirrolure, Pfleuger Mustang, Bomber Jerk Plug. Monofilament is the best bet for landing these.

Dolphin Strip mullet, strip mackerel, shrimp from piers; jigs and feathers in artificials. Leaving one dolphin hooked and in the water until the next dolphin is hooked as you troll, will usually take the entire school.

King Mackerel (Kingfish) Whole mullet win hands down. Squid come next. Artificials in order: No. 3½ Drone spoon, Big Bomber jig, feathers.

Mako Shark Whole mullet, whole mackerel, whole squid—or anything you can troll. Live bait generally proves best.

Marlin Spanish mackerel, 2 to 3 pounds. Small bonitos next.

METHOD: With the aid of a special piece of copper pipe, the mackerel's spine may be removed and the hook placed in the tail from inside without breaking the external skin except where the hook protrudes. Meat inside should be mutilated. The bait is very lively when trolled just beyond the boat's wake, some 50 to 75 feet astern. Troll with skip motion. Do not split the baitfish.

Sheepshead Sand fiddlers are always effective, then sand fleas, clams, and shrimp.

METHOD: Put 5 quarts of oysters in a sack. Tie the top with one end of a long line, then beat them up thoroughly, shells and all. Drop this over the side of the boat or pier and make your line fast. Sheepshead will suck the sack when it is lowered to the proper depth. This "controlled

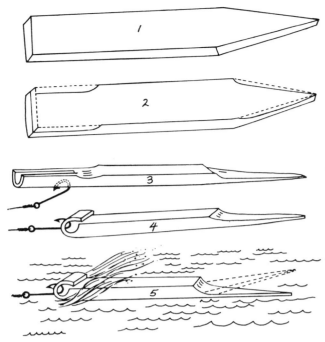

The Cannon Skip-strip bait designed to look like a flying fish about to fly. It was invented by Ray Cannon, western saltwater fishing authority of Los Angeles, and author of How to Fish the Pacific Coast.

Although the "Skip-strip" has already proved an electrifying bait for a dozen species in the Gulf of California, its full potential is yet to be learned in southern California waters. Some game fishes, on seeing this bait, rise to the surface and dash as much as 200 or 300 feet to nail it. It could be great in the Atlantic, too.

Although the drawings suggest a number of complicated operations, the whole business can be done in thirty seconds or less, with a sharp knife and a little practice. After a large slab is cut from the fish (mackerel, ocean whitefish, black skipjack, sierra, or bonito are preferred), the work is done with the skin side down; the flesh is left flat enough on top to maintain balance. Here's how Cannon describes the rig:

"In order to give a simple, clear picture of the design and proportions, I am describing a 7½-inch strip, as for a dolphinfish, roosterfish, or large yellowfin tuna. A 12-to-14-inch strip would, in some areas, be better for billfish—on down to a 4-inch strip for needlefish. Again, different sizes should be tried out according to locality and the size of baitfish being pursued at the time by the game fish.

"Fig. 1. A 7½-inch strip. This fillet is cut from the freshest fish possible. Start at the tail of the fish, cut forward, place the slab skin down and tailor it to an inch wide and slightly over ¼ inch thick. This thickness can be varied according to the weight desired—thin for slow troll, thick for faster movement.

"Fig. 2. Dotted lines show where the fish is cut from 'head' end and 'tail.' Thus half of the thickness is removed. The front cut is 1¾ inches long, the tail end about 2 inches.

"Fig. 3. The edges of the 'head' end are pinched up into a fold so that the hook can be inserted completely through the lower part of the fold and about 1 inch back of the front end. The position of the hook is important in establishing balance and to produce 'rooster-tail' sprays.

"Fig. 4. The completed sled-shaped 'Skip-strip' with the front end folded upward from the hook.

"Fig. 5. Illustrates the bait being trolled or retrieved on surface. The 'rooster-tail' sprays shooting up from the front end are indicated. This gives the illusion of flying-fish wings. The dotted lines suggest the flipping up-and-down of the 'tail.'

"After the bait has been trolled for some time, or has been hit by fish repeatedly, some of the flesh may get stripped off and throw it out of balance, causing it to revolve or lose the 'rooster-tail' spray action.

"A fast troll against a strong current will often cause the bait to dive. A smooth sledding on the surface is desirable. If the water is very smooth, the bait will function a greater distance from the boat than when water is rough. For billfish, a slow-trolled bait 40 feet back of the stern is best. For dolphin the distance may vary from 50 to 150 feet, and speeds from 3 to 8 knots. For yellowfin tuna, 100 yards at 6 to 8 knots; for bluefin and yellowtail, 4 to 7 knots; for needlefish, 3 to 5. (These trolling speeds are not specific.) Fish will take this bait at a much slower pace than a lure. When a fish makes a pass and misses, pay out the line at once, allowing the bait to remain near the spot of the strike. In all cases allow the fish time for one long run with free spool and added time for it to swallow the bait. This cannot be overstressed for billfish."

chumming" will allow you to take them on sand fiddlers. Count ten when you feel a fish hit bait, then strike. Monofilament line is best here.

Sailfish Six- to 7-inch live mullet are best, but don't split them out. Troll skip. Use free-line drift with tail-out rig in bait. Monofilament leader.

Snapper and *Grouper* Squid, cut mullet. Wire line and lead for control.

Spanish Mackerel Spoon, Reflecto 00 up to No. 1. Same as for bluefish.

Tarpon Live blue crab or stone crab. Pull off one claw, hook tail end, but don't kill. Use big popper-cork, fish about 4 feet deep.

Wahoo Live mullet, strip mullet, and in the artificials, Bomber Jerk, Mirrolure, spoons, and feathers. Monofilament line.

METHOD: Same as for king mackerel.

Weakfish (Spotted Trout, Gray Trout, etc.) Shrimp, minnows, cut bait, Mirrolure, Sea Hawks, Pal-O-Mine plug.

Whiting (Sea Mullet, Virginia Mullet) Shrimp, cut bait, and Sea Hawk plugs and jigs.

HOW TO CHUM

Saltwater fishing is completely unpredictable, but when fishing from an anchored boat, you're almost certain to have better luck if you use chum.

If you've ever awakened on a cool morning to smell coffee brewing and bacon frying, you can understand the theory of chumming. Oil, blood, or other scented matter seeps through the water and is carried along with the tide. Hungry fish become aroused and follow the "stream" of chum to its source. Small fish dart in first, followed by the big ones. By chumming you can sometimes turn a seemingly dead spot into an area alive with fish.

A number of chumming techniques are used. Party boats collect unwanted fish from the docks, or the entrails left from dressing fish, and grind them into a mush. They carry the mush in buckets and toss it over by the cupful to attract many species for their customers.

Occasionally, when a party boat anchors, the mate takes a burlap bag of ground fish and ties it to the anchor line. The liquor or chum then seeps out and keeps up an automatic stream as long as the boat is anchored in that place.

Another common method is to shape ground-up fish mixed with sand into balls. This is a good method for deep-sea fishing, especially over reefs. Plain chum would drift away on the surface, but the sand balls, which cling together for some time, have enough weight to get down where the fish are concentrated. The farther it falls, the more the sand falls apart, thereby releasing chum at a productive depth. This is especially effective on snappers, groupers, and yellowtails.

The following method of chumming used in Bermuda is quite effective: Hog-mouthed fry-tiny minnows measuring no more than an inch or so in length are seined into shallow water, then frozen in buckets until ready for use. After thawing out en route to the fishing grounds, they are mixed with sand and tossed overboard to attract snappers, porgies, and groupers.

All the methods mentioned so far require considerable preparation, and most are very messy, especially for small-boat fishermen. However, there are simpler ways to chum.

An angler, for example, can replace buckets of ground chum with a simple meat grinder which he attaches to the gunwale of his boat. Whenever he wants to chum he simply runs a mullet or two through the grinder. As he fishes, he is bound to catch many undesirable species that give him still more material for the grinder.

Just as a party boat ties a chum bag to its anchor line, a small-skiff fisherman can punch some holes in a can of sardines and then tie this can to his own anchor line.

The idea is to get fish into a hungry, even a voracious mood. The more fish to appear and compete for the available food, the better the system will work. Then it's up to you and your tackle.

19
SALTWATER SPORTFISHING GLOSSARY*

A

afghan   A spinning tangle.

A-frame net   A one-man net fitted on a 6-foot-long "A" frame used to capture smelt (family Osmeridae) as the fish come inshore to spawn in the surf.

algae   Primitive chlorophyl-bearing water plants.

anadromous   Fish that live most of their lives in saltwater but ascend freshwater rivers to breed.

B

back down   Engines in reverse, to move stern first toward a fish.

backing   Line used behind the main line as a reverse for playing fish, or for building up the line level to aid casting and retrieving.

* Compiled by and reprinted courtesy of the International Game Fish Association.

backlash   Tangle of line on a conventional reel caused by overrun of the spool.

bag net   A landing net that ends in a U-shape at the base when suspended from the frame.

bait   1. Any natural substance used to entice fish. 2. The act of presenting a lure or prepared bait to a fish. 3. Any of a large group of small fishes on which larger fish regularly feed.

bait-casting   Throwing a lure or bait with a one-handed rod and a conventional turning reel.

balling the bait   Describes the method by which game fishes herd bait species into a tight ball and then charge through the packed masses to feed.

ballyhoo   Also balao. A small baitfish widely used as a skipping bait.

balsa   A soft buoyant wood used in float making.

banana boat   Derogatory term used by some professional charter and party boat skippers to describe privately owned and operated vessels.

bar spoon   A spinning lure on which a spoon or

willow leaf–shaped blade revolves around a wire bar when pivoted from its front end.

beach buggy   A motor vehicle rigged for on-sand travel. Primarily used for transportation to and from surf-fishing locations and the carrying of equipment.

bearing   The compass direction of an object viewed by an observer.

belt socket   A belt with cup to hold butt of rod in position at the waist.

bill   Sword or spike of a billfish.

billfish   Any marlin, sailfish, spearfish, or swordfish.

biological clock   Innate reactive behavior of some fish that seems to be regulated by an inner time-sensitive nervous mechanism.

bird's nest   A backlash.

bite   The act of a fish nibbling a bait.

blank   1. A glass-fiber or carbon-fiber tapered rod, hollow or solid, from which a fishing rod is constructed. 2. A day's fishing during which no fish are caught.

blind casting   Casting where fish have not been sighted.

blitz   A hectic flurry of successful angling.

bloodworm   Any of various segmented worms of the genera *Polycirrus* and *Enoplobranchus*, having bright-red bodies and often used for bait.

boatcaster   A rod made for casting from an anchored boat.

boat pool   Also called "jackpot" or simply "the pool." Anglers contribute money to a pool and the largest fish boated takes the cash.

boat trail   Narrow channel possibly deepened by constant boat traffic.

boom   1. A rigid bar from which a hook link or trace is fished so as to help avoid tangling with the main line. 2. An attachment for a lead which runs on the line as in tope or skate fishing.

bottom-fishing   Fishing at anchor or drifting, using sinkers to carry baited hooks to the bottom.

bowing   When an angler bows to a fish, he bends forward to give quick slack.

break-off   Line breakage while casting or when fighting a fish.

breakwater   Man-made bulwark against the sea. Is usually rock and may or may not be connected to land.

breezers   A school of fish moving rapidly.

bronzed hook   A steel hook protected by a bronze-colored lacquer.

bucktail   Generic term for many lead-headed jigs armed with a single upriding hook.

bulge   A gentle swell pushed up by a fish.

buggy whip   A very light and extremely flexible fishing rod.

bulldogging   Rapid head-swinging of a fish while hooked, sending repeated shocks up the fishing line.

butt   Lower extremity of a fishing rod below the reel seat.

C

Caged drum reel   A reel with a centerpin revolving spool usually enclosed in a two-sided frame with connecting crossbars.

candying   Being overly cautious with a fish when it's hooked.

cast   The act of throwing out a bait or a lure by using the rod as a lever to give motion to the bait and achieve distance.

cast net   A one-man circular net weighted at the rim with small sinkers and designed to be flung over the water so that it falls face down or dishlike over schools of fishes, entrapping them as it sinks to the bottom. Also called throw net and hand casting net.

cattle boat   Uncomplimentary slang denoting an open-party sport-fishing boat.

charter boat   Fishing boat that may be hired by the day or for longer periods, charging a fixed fee for the trip.

check   The audible ratchet mechanism on a reel that clicks as line is drawn off the spool.

chicken   Very large feather streamer.

Chinese fire drill   Confused scrambling for position by skipper, crew, and anglers as a game fish appears behind trolled baits.

chopper   A bluefish.

Christmas tree   A string of artificial lures on a single leader.

chum   Ground, chopped, or whole bait that is doled overboard to attract fish.

chumline   The stream of chum which falls behind the boat from either the boat's movement or the action of the wind or the current.

ciguatera   An illness with symptoms such as diarrhea and paralysis caused by eating certain fishes living in tropical and subtropical regions.

click   A device that signals reel spool movement.

closed creek   Tidal creek with tree branches linked together across a channel.

clutch Braking mechanism on a reel, also called a drag.

cockpit The open protected afterdeck of a sport-fishing boat.

coffeegrinder Vernacular, often disparaging, term for the spinning reel.

commercial Anyone who sells fish for a living, but often applied to the rod-and-line angler who sells part or all of his catch.

continental shelf Undersea plain extending from shore to ocean abyss.

conventional guide Small diameter guide for use with revolving spool reel.

conventional reel Reel with revolving spool.

cow A large striped bass.

crab ring A crab trap made of coarse mesh webbing attached to two iron hoops, designed to lie flat on the bottom but to form a basket when raised.

crash the bait Sudden strike with no inspection of trolled lure or bait.

crimp Describes the act of crushing a metal ferrule onto a wire-to-hook joint or wire loop with a special pair of pliers.

crowding a catch Working the hooked fish very hard.

cruiser A fish that moves steadily, traveling rather than feeding.

custom-built rod A rod that is made by a craftsman to the special order and specification of a customer.

D

daisy chain 1. A string of baits on a single leader. Usually only the terminal bait is armed with a hook. 2. Fish which spawn in a sort of parade with the eggs being fertilized by males following females in a procession similar to a circle.

deck The floor of a boat.

deep jigging Refers to working a jig nearly straight up and down. It is retrieved in a variety of movements.

demersal Pertaining to fish that live on or near the bottom.

dip net A conical small-mesh net attached to a rigid frame on a long handle and used to catch fish and other marine animals. Also called a hand net or scoop net.

double line That portion of the fishing line that is doubled back at the outer end for greater strength.

downrigger An underwater outrigger for carrying lures down deep.

drag A feature of a reel that acts as an adjustable brake.

dragging The act of trolling a lure or bait.

drail Trolling sinker shaped like a torpedo or cigar, with an offset towing neck.

dressing Describes style and materials such as feathers, hairs, and tinsel used in the manufacture of flies.

drift fishing Trailing a weighted or unweighted line with live or dead baits behind a drifting boat.

dropback Freespooling a bait or lure to a fish before engaging the drag.

drop-off Precipitous underwater cliff or bank; edge of the continental shelf.

dropper Term used to describe a hook on a short piece of nylon fixed above the terminal hook and usually projecting at a right angle from the line or leader.

drum Cylinder holding the line, usually on a centerpin reel. On multipliers and fixed-spool reels the term used is spool.

E

ecology Study of relationship of living species to their habitats.

estuary Bay, sound, or large river mouth forming a meeting place of saltwater and freshwater.

F

fast tip Generally means a tip that moves considerably before the loading affects the rest of the rod.

fathom Nautical measure equal to 6 feet.

fathometer Electronic sounder.

feathering 1. Term used to describe catching fish, such as mackerel or pollack, on traces bearing a number of feather-decorated hooks. 2. A method of slowing down the rate of line leaving the spool of a fixed-spool reel by letting a fingertip just touch the coils as they come over the front lip.

feather lure Trolling lure dressed with or made from feathers.

feather merchant A fly-caster, derogatory only in the way it is used.

ferrule Male and female metal parts forming a fishing rod joint.

fight The duel between angler and hooked fish.

fighting chair Large, strong, swiveling chair equipped with footrest, used for fighting large fish.

finger islands Narrow rows of mangrove trees forming elongated islands.

finning fish Fish swimming with dorsal and/or tail fin exposed.

fire in the water Refers to light-emitting dinoflagelates which often handicap night fishermen.

fish box Fixed or portable deck box for storing the day's catch.

fishfinder 1. A sliding sinker bottom rig. In theory allows the fish to take bait without feeling the anchoring weight. 2. An electronic sounder.

fishing belt An adjustable belt supporting a leader or metal cup into which is thrust the butt end of the rod to assist the angler while fishing standing up.

fishing chair Light version of the fighting chair without footrest.

fish trap A portable trap for fish and shellfish usually made of wire mesh fitted over a rigid frame with an opening on one side.

fish well Fish box under boat's deck, covered with flush hatch.

flat line Trolling line fished directly off the boat's stern, without the aid of an outrigger.

flats 1. Term used to describe flatfish (i.e., flounder) as opposed to other species. 2. Very shallow, sandy or muddy areas of sea.

Florida whip A method of retrieve in light-tackle casting, particularly spinning. The retrieve is rapid and the rod tip is periodically snapped down nearly horizontal to give a jig or plug greater action in the water.

flushed fish Fish that leaves hurriedly.

flying bridge Open, elevated control station atop the deckhouse of a boat.

Flying gaff Large gaff with detachable head and safety rope.

fly-lining The casting of a live or dead bait without added sinker weight.

fly rod Light casting rod that operates by casting a heavy, tapered line instead of a weighted lure.

football A small bluefin tuna.

forged hook Hook on which the area of the bend has been hammered flat to better resist distortion when a fish is hooked.

foul-hook The act of hooking a fish elsewhere than in the mouth.

free-spool Allowing line to pay out with no reel clutch or drag engaged.

full bore High speed on a boat.

full house Complete set of trolling rods and teasers as used by fully equipped sport fishermen.

G

gaff A curved, sharp-pointed, and usually barbless hook positioned at the end of a handle to land game fishes.

gaffers Early fishing skippers who had no mates aboard and personally gaffed the fish for their patrons.

galley The kitchen on a boat.

game fish Any species of fish that is valuable primarily because of its fighting characteristics when caught by rod and reel.

ganglion A bottom fishing rig in which a number of short droppers are armed with lures or baits.

gentle swell Water pushed up by a cruising fish.

gill net A curtainlike net suspended in the water with mesh openings large enough to permit only the heads of the fish to pass through, ensnaring them around the gills when they attempt to escape.

gimbal 1. Single- or double-pivoted metal cup on belt or fighting chair, into which a rod butt may be thrust to aid angler. 2. Pivoted double ring for a compass.

gimbal belt A rod belt.

gin pole Vertical wooden or metal pole equipped with rope fall for hoisting large fish on board.

giant tuna A bluefin tuna weighing more than 300 pounds.

greyhounding Term used to describe the action of a fast-moving fish leaping forward at a low angle from the water. Usually applied to sailfish and marlin.

ground Term used to describe the seabed configuration relative to the types of fish sought, i.e., rough ground, smooth ground.

guide 1. Person who takes anglers fishing for hire. 2. Metal ring or roller on rod through which fishing line is led.

Saltwater Sportfishing Glossary
179

H

handlining Fishing with a line held in the hand, without using a rod or reel.

hangup A snagged hook.

harbor Calm, protected area. Usually behind a breakwater or jetty.

harness Cloth, leather, or other vest or heavy belt worn around the back or shoulders to take the weight of the rod via adjustable straps, leaving the hands free to manipulate the fishing rod and reel.

hauling In fly-fishing this term refers to line manipulation with the hand that doesn't hold the rod.

head The bathroom on a boat.

head boat A party boat carrying many anglers.

high surf Heavy surf on an open ocean beach.

hold Term used to indicate whether the leaded tackle will remain in position on the seabed.

hook 1. A fishhook. 2. An anchor (slang).

hookup The setting of a hook into a fish.

I

ichthyologist Fish scientist.

inlet A narrow passage of water connecting the open sea with protected coastal and inland water.

J

jackpot Money put into a pool for the largest fish.

jetty Man-made rock breakwater protruding into the sea.

jetty fishing Fishing from any man-made structure constructed of rock, stone, or the like, which projects out into the sea or other body of water.

jetty jockey The shore-based angler who does most of his fishing from jetties and breakwaters.

jig Any small heavy metal lure for casting, trolling, or jigging.

jigging Manipulating a jig to imitate a live bait, thus attracting the fish to the hook.

K

keeper 1. A fish large enough to take home. 2. A fish that breaks your line.

keg-lining Use of a float-keg, thrown overside after a large fish has been harpooned.

knockdown Act of pulling an outrigger line clear of release pin by either a fish or the angler.

knot One nautical mile per hour, or about 1⅛ statute m.p.h.

L

lead The molded piece of lead used to sink, project, anchor, or otherwise help present a bait or lure to a fish.

leader Section of wire or synthetic material placed between the hook or lure and the fishing line.

leading a fish Casting ahead of a moving fish so that the fish and lure will intercept each other.

leger To fish a bait anchored to the seabed by a lead. (Chiefly British)

line The connection between the angler and the fish; that which is on the reel.

line capacity The amount of line a reel will properly hold.

line class A term used by IGFA to classify fishing lines.

line slough The backlash in spinning, usually caused by line twist or an overfilled spool when the line comes off in a bunch and jams in the rod's guides.

lining a fish Frightening a fish by casting a line across it or very near to it.

lip-hook The method of using a live or dead fish, hooked through the lips, as a bait.

littoral Pertaining to a shore or coastal region.

live-lining Fishing a live or sometimes a dead bait from shore or boat with little or no sinker weight.

longline Type of commercial fishing gear featuring many separate hooks suspended from shorter branch lines.

long release Refers wryly to a fish that escapes some distance out.

looker Fish that inspects lure but does not strike.

loran Electronic navigation system.

lucky Joe A light ganglion with small, sharp hooks equipped with yarn or feathers. Used to catch bait such as mackerel or squid.

lure An artificial bait.

M

mark Location at sea where there is good fishing; found either by radar navigation systems or by lining up on landmarks.

meatball   A dense school of baitfish, driven to the surface and preyed upon by such fish as tuna or albacore, many times accompanied by large flocks of birds, sometimes called "bird schools."

memory   Quality of a line which enables it to stretch, then return to its former position.

mincing machine   Slang name for a fixed-spool reel, used mainly by those who do not like using it.

monofilament   Line made of a single continuous synthetic fiber.

monel metal   A malleable, noncorrodible material, used to make wire fishing lines.

monster fishing   Almost always employed to describe angling for big sharks.

mooching   A term to describe trolling on a dead drift, usually with live or fresh-cut bait presented in the depths.

mosquito fleet   Privately owned small craft often in competition with larger charter boats on inshore and offshore grounds.

motor trail   Groove caused by a propeller in the bottom of a flat.

mudder   A fish, usually a bonefish on tropical flats, grubbing and causing a cloud of visible mud in otherwise clear water.

muscle man   A term used by light-tackle enthusiasts to describe big game anglers.

Mylar   A bright plastic material, resembling shiny metal; often made into a braided tube and used to make flies.

N

neap tide   A tide where the rise and fall between high and low is at a minimum.

nervous water   Aptly describes an indistinct surface commotion caused by unseen fish.

Nantucket sleigh ride   When a small boat is dragged by a large fish.

nodding nudnik   North Atlantic surf-caster's term for anyone who watches other anglers and does not cast until he sees neighbors catching fish.

O

offshore   Open ocean as opposed to inshore, i.e., close to beaches, in estuaries or sheltered bays.

old gaffer   Retired skipper.

on the reel   Playing a fly-rod catch from the reel itself as opposed to running line through the "line hand." When loose line has been "picked up" the fish is said to be "on the reel."

outrigger   Long pole or shaft fastened to boat's side and extended outboard at a lift angle of 45 degrees to give lift and separation to lines trolled behind the boat.

overhang   The amount of leader or line extending from rod tip to lure or bait when making a cast.

overrun   Line coming from the spool too fast (usually on a multiplier or fixed-spool reel) then getting caught up by winding itself around the spool the wrong way.

P

Palm Beach release   A fish that is released or escapes without being boated. Often associated with sailfish that are balling the bait.

panfish   Any small, edible fish.

party boat   A fishing boat carrying large groups of anglers for a fee and operating on a scheduled basis.

pelagic   Term used to describe fish and other sea animals that are more or less independent of the bottom. They are characteristically active swimmers, spending much of their time in midwater or near the surface.

pickup   The act of a fish picking up a bait or lure.

pier fishing   Fishing from any private or public structure set on pilings that extends over a body of water.

pilgrim   Description of a first-time angler or one who fishes infrequently.

pirk   A heavy metal or plastic/metal lure fished up and down, usually from a boat; used for predatory fish, such as cod, pollack, and coalfish.

plankton   Tiny plant or animal life floating freely in water.

play   To exhaust a hooked fish by allowing it to pull on the line.

plug   A nonspecific term for any artificial lure with a distinct "body" made of wood or plastic and having one or more sets of single, double, or treble hooks attached.

pod   A small group of shallow-water fish.

Poke-poling   A unique method of rocky-shore fishing for blennies and other crevice-seeking animals that inhabit deep tide pools. The gear is essentially homemade. A long bamboo pole of about 9 to 12 feet is fitted with a semiflexible wire tip to which a nylon-cord leader and hook are attached. The bait, usually mussel or shrimp, is poked into crevices under and between large boulders in rocky areas at low tide, then retrieved quickly after the first sharp tug of a fish. This is mainly a British technique.

pole The same as the rod except that no reel is attached, nor are there any guides. As in cane pole, lift pole, etc.

popped line A broken line.

popper A lightweight artificial lure made of cork or plastic having a concave face that produces a popping sound when twitched on the water's surface.

pulpit Railed platform extending forward from a vessel's bow, primarily a platform from which to harpoon big game fish.

pump The action of lifting a fish by raising the rod, then winding in slack line rapidly as the rod is lowered again.

pushing water Describes a wave pushed by fish cruising close to or on the surface.

R

radar A system of electronic detecting and ranging.

range Imaginary line between two objects on shore, as a base of a triangle, projected to the observer in a boat.

rat Derogatory term for a small fish.

recovery rate The amount of line rewound on the spool or drum of a reel in one turn of the handle.

reel Any mechanical device for storing fishing line on a fixed or revolving metal or plastic spool.

reelseat Metal sleeve attached to rod shaft to receive the reel.

regular A highly advanced angler specializing in one or more disciplines; an expert on a given ground.

retrieve ratio Gear ratio of a reel, i.e., a 3 to 1 ratio causes the spool to turn three times faster than the reel handle.

rig Name for terminal tackle.

ringer Entry of an expert in an area fishing tournament.

rings Fittings on the rod through which line runs and is supported.

rocket launcher Special type of multiple rod holder for trolling.

rod Any flexible, tapered shaft arranged to carry a reel and line, and used in manipulating the bait or lure, and in handling the fish after it has been hooked.

rod belt A belt with socket to hold the butt of a rod.

rod blank The blank of fiberglass, graphite, split bamboo, or other material. Also often called a "stick."

rod holder Metal or plastic tube arranged to receive and hold the butt end of the rod in a standby condition.

roller 1. Revolving part in the pickup arm of a fixed-spool reel to reduce friction. 2. Rotating part of a rod guide over which line passes.

roller guide Guide with revolving roller(s) used to decrease friction and wear on line.

rolling When a fish comes up and its back periodically breaks the surface of the water.

roughing him up Playing a fish with a heavy hand.

run 1. The action of a hooked fish swimming away from the angler. 2. The movement of migratory fish to and from a region at a particular season of the year.

rushing bait Term used when a school of game fish are attacking massed bait on the surface.

S

salinity Percentage of salt in water.

sand spike A device used to hold a rod upright in shoreside sand, mud, or clay.

school A group of fish that travels as one; scattered fish are also called schools if they travel fairly close together.

school tuna A bluefin tuna under 300 pounds.

seine Form of commercial fishnet.

set 1. Bend that remains permanently in a rod after stress. 2. The action of sinking the hook in a fish's mouth.

shiver Surface water that seems to vibrate over a large fish.

shoal Shallow area.

shock line Also called shock leader or shocker. A heavy trace or leader of strong monofilament which extends from overhand back to a few turns around the reel's spool and thus absorbs heavy stresses at the beginning of a cast.

shooting head   Specially weighted head line for distance fly-casting.

shopper   Fish that inspects a bait or lure, but does not take. Also called a "looker."

short   Any fish shorter than a legal limit.

short strike   When a fish strikes short of the lure.

sight casting   Casting of lures or bait to fish seen schooling close to the surface.

sink and draw   Lift and fall action of fishing a lure or bait.

sinker   A weight, usually of lead, used to take the bait or lure to a desired depth.

skiff fishing   Recreational fishing from a relatively small private or rented boat.

skimmer   The surf or bait clam.

skunked   A term used to describe an angler who has caught no fish.

slab bait   A fillet of fish with the skin on.

slick   Layer of oil on water.

slider   Surface fly-rod bug that does not pop but darts from side to side.

slough   A backwater out of the current of a creek or river.

smokers   A word often used to describe powerful, fast-running king mackerel.

snagging   Foul-hooking a fish.

snakes   1. Small eels or small mackerel. 2. The light wire guides used on fly rods.

snarl   A tangle in the line.

snazzle   A term used to describe a batch of monofilament that has come off a spinning reel.

sneak   Snook smaller than the legal limit.

soft rod   A rod that bends easily.

sound   1. To measure the depth of water. 2. Also refers to a fish diving deep from the surface.

sounder   Device for measuring depth.

spade-end   A hook with a spade-shaped, flattened end to its shank which holds a whipping knot firmly.

spear fishing   Impaling fish with a spear from either above or below the water's surface.

species   Scientific term for a specific group of life forms which belong to the same genus. The species is indicated by the second half of the scientific Latin name.

spinner   An artificial lure with metal or plastic blades that whirl on a shaft or a swivel as the lure is retrieved.

spinning   A method of rod-and-reel fishing distinguished by the use of a fixed-spool reel or "spinning" reel. When casting, the line slips off the end of the reel spool, which does not revolve as does a conventional bait-casting reel spool. The line is laid on the spool by a revolving metal arm or bail.

spinning reel   A reel with a fixed spool (one which does not revolve), which allows the line to "spin" directly off the spool without the friction of a revolving spool.

splice   Method of joining two pieces of rope, cable, or wire by interweaving strands without knots.

spooked   Refers to a fish that is frightened by you or your boat.

spool   Portion of a reel on which the line is stored.

spoon   Metal lure shaped like the bowl of a spoon.

spread   The placement of several trolled baits or lures, perhaps two from outriggers and two on flat lines.

spreader   A two-armed rig with a single hook attached to each arm.

spring tide   A tide where the rise and fall between high and low is at a maximum; the opposite of neap tide.

squidding   Surf-casting with lures, originally with block-tin squid; now often refers to plug-casting as well.

star drag   The adjustment piece on the reel that controls the amount of drag.

steep-to   Description of a beach that slopes steeply from the water level.

stern door   Opening in boat's stern for admitting large fish.

stick boat   Any craft used to harpoon game fishes.

sticking   The harpooning of large fishes; also called "ironing."

still-fishing   Fishing natural baits from shore, pier, or anchored boat. Usually the bait is fished on or near the bottom, although it is sometimes held off the bottom with a float.

stinger   1. A secondary hook placed well back toward the tail of a lure or bait. 2. A line running from the tip of an outrigger to the trolling line.

stop   A knot or some other device by which a lead or a sliding float is fixed on the line at the correct fishing depth.

stranger   A baitfish used in an area where it is not indigenous.

strike 1. The act of a fish attacking or biting a bait or lure. 2. The act of an angler hooking a fish with hook and line.

striking drag Amount of tension to which a reel drag is preset.

string Fishing line (slang).

strip bait Bait made from a strip of fish, pork rind, or fish belly.

structure Bottom formations or obstructions.

suds Boiling surf, very close to the beach. Also called the "wash."

surfboat A light craft either manhandled into the surf or launched by means of a prime mover such as a four-wheel-drive beach buggy. A surfboat is launched and recovered in surf.

surf-netting A unique type of fishing using special one- or two-man nets to catch smelt along sandy beaches.

surgical tubing Round, hollow, soft plastic tubing often used in the manufacture of lures.

surround net A beach seine, typically a long net with floats along the upper edge and weights along the bottom, used to capture an assortment of fishes in shallow, protected water.

swash The shallow water left to recede after a wave has run up a shallow-surf beach and expended its energy.

swash channel Shallow channel, sometimes formed or deepened by boat traffic.

swirl An eddy around your lure.

swivel Metal device placed between leader and fishing line to form a connection counteracting twisting.

T

tag Metal or plastic device attached to a fish to identify it for scientific purposes.

tail rope A rigged rope or cable to secure a large fish by its tail.

tailer A fish, usually a bonefish or permit, feeding on a shallow flat so that the upper part of its tail lobe is above the surface.

tailing fish A fish such as marlin or bonefish that frequently exposes its tail while swimming.

tail walking A fish moving along above the surface with its tail working in the water.

take Action of a fish grabbing a bait or lure.

teaser Artificial lurelike device without hooks, to entice fish.

terminal tackle Any part of fishing tackle used at the lower end of the line, such as sinkers, hooks, leaders, etc.

test The amount, expressed in pounds, kilograms, or newtons, to which a line will resist linear elongation.

test curve Optimum bend in a rod for safety, by which safe casting weight and safe line test to be used can be evaluated.

thermocline Transition layer of temperature change between warm surface water and deep cold water.

thin water Shallows such as flats, now often called "skinny water."

throwing iron Slang for casting a jig.

thumb Action of braking a multiplier reel spool, when casting and fighting a fish.

thumb stall A woven thumb protector used for braking a reel spool.

tidal river One that is controlled by tidal movement.

tide rip Visible wave condition or clash of water caused by a swift current flowing over a shallow reef or by two opposing currents rubbing against each other.

tin squid A relatively heavy, spoon-shaped, thin lure used in surf-casting; also called "block-tin" or simply "tin."

tip The top end of the rod.

tip-top The end guide at the tip of the rod.

torch fishing Locating or attracting marine animals at night with a light held above the surface of the water.

touch An unhooked strike that doesn't make much fuss.

tournament Any fishing contest operated according to accepted rules of fishing behavior.

tournament casting Casting on a field for distance and accuracy.

tournament tackle High-quality tackle meeting tournament rules as to type and method of construction.

tower Elevated metal structure, usually equipped with steering and motor controls, used as a fishing lookout.

transducer Device that changes electric pulses into sound pulses, and vice versa.

troll To drag lures or baits behind a moving boat.

trolley line A device which employs one rod and reel to anchor another line streamed from a second outfit via a release snap.

tuna door A door in the transom of a boat used to facilitate boating of large fish.

U

umbrella   Spreader rig, often with a number of armed lures and teasers attached.

W

waist gimbal   A rod belt.

washing   The action of a fish, such as shad, rolling gently.

water column   Refers to qualities of a vertical section of water from surface to bottom.

weed line   A line of floating seaweed on the surface of the water.

weekend admiral   An inexperienced skipper.

weepy rod   One that bends too easily.

wetland   Coastal intertidal area, wet at high tide, dry at low tide.

whelm   The disturbance visible on the surface caused by a fish moving fast deep down and changing direction.

whip   An erratic retrieve with rod-tip motion.

wire a fish   To take a leader in hand and land a fish.

wire line   Any metallic fishing line.

wobble plate   Also called "wiggle lip" or "wiggle plate." A metal lip device attached to the fore-end of a lure to ensure action in the water.

work-harden   Means by which the molecular construction of a metal (such as wire line) is altered and made brittle by constant friction over another unresistant surface.

Y

yo-yo   1. The up-and-down motion imparted to a lure jigged almost directly under a boat. 2. A slang term for spinning tackle.

20

THE INTERNATIONAL GAME FISH ASSOCIATION

A SHORT HISTORY

Until 1940, there was no universal code of sporting ethics to guide ocean anglers in their pursuits. Some rules pertaining to gentlemanly and sporting conduct in marine game fish angling were in effect at certain well-established fishing clubs, but they varied according to the dictates of each club. To quote angler/writer Philip Wylie, ". . . good competition requires precise rules; but ocean fishing was full of quirks and inequities. It was somewhat the way you'd find football if you put a squad of eleven men on the field and learned that the opposing team played with fifteen men—but nothing could be done about it."

The idea of a worldwide association of marine anglers had been brewing for some time in England, Australia, and the United States. The first steps in this direction were taken in the late 1930s by members of the British Tunny Club, who hoped to establish headquarters in England to formulate rules for ethical angling. The threat of war, however, interrupted their plans.

At the same time, Michael Lerner, a renowned American angler, was busy organizing a fishing expedition to the waters of Australia and New Zealand in conjunction with the American Museum of Natural History in New York. He had heard something of the British Tunny Club's plans, and when he arrived in Australia, he immediately looked up one of the country's finest anglers, Clive Firth, to discuss the idea with him.

"It was Mr. Firth's suggestion that the Americans should devise and administer the rules. For the Australian noted a long-standing tendency of the colonies and the mother country to quarrel about everything—even about rules for fishing. Mr. Firth, aware of the feats of the Californians, Floridians, Long Islanders, and others, felt that England, her colonies and dominions would accept American judgment as sporting and impartial . . ."

When Dr. William King Gregory, a member

Bob Stearns, Miami, with a world-record 117½-pound Pacific sailfish taken on a fly rod, Bahía Pez Vela, Costa Rica, 13 August 1979.

of the Australia–New Zealand expedition, heard that it might be possible to headquarter a world-wide sport-fishing association in the United States, he became enthusiastic about the idea. As head of the departments of ichthyology and comparative anatomy at the American Museum of Natural History, "he immediately suggested that it might be possible to affiliate such an organization with the museum. His interest in such an association and the information it could provide to scientists was the beginning of IGFA's long-lasting connection with scientists and scientific institutions."

At that time there were very few opportunities for game fish research, as very few vessels were outfitted for scientific exploration on the open seas. The best-known vessels in the United States were owned by the Woods Hole Oceanographic Institution and the Scripps Institution of Oceanography. "There were, of course, commercial fishing boats, . . . but their cargo . . . in the case of the very large fishes, was usually minus parts of the body not edible or saleable, but important for scientific work."

Thus, the angler was, and still is, an important source of game information; and Michael Lerner's funding and leadership of early expeditions to Cape Breton, Bimini, Australia and New Zealand, Ecuador, Peru, and Chile provided specimens of immense value to ichthyologists. Such large fishes as sailfish, tuna, marlin, and swordfish were not easy to come by, and Mr. Lerner's catches provided much initial information on biology, concentrations, breeding grounds, and more.

On June 7, 1939, the International Game Fish Association was formally launched in a meeting held at the American Museum of Natural History. Present were Dr. Gregory (who became the first president of the association), Mr. Lerner, angler/writer Van Campen Heilner, and Francesca LaMonte, associate curator of fishes for the museum and science leader of several expeditions.

The officers immediately set to the task of establishing angling guidelines and requirements for world record catches. Records of a sort had been issued jointly by *Field & Stream* magazine and the museum for some eighteen years. According to the minutes of the first IGFA meeting in June 1939: "Miss LaMonte reported that she had talked with Mr. Dan Holland, the fishing editor of *Field & Stream* . . . , and that Mr. Holland was in full accord with and enthusiastic about the idea of the association." Thus it was that a new system of world record-keeping with specific angling rules and regulations was launched.

Another immediate task was to notify scientific institutions and fishing clubs throughout the world about the IGFA, its activities and intentions. By January 1940, only a few months after the inception of the association, there were two associated scientific institutions, ten member clubs, and twelve overseas representatives. By 1948, the numbers had grown to ten scientific institutions, eighty member clubs, and IGFA representatives in forty-one areas of the world.

Clive Firth of Australia was elected IGFA's first overseas representative, and others were chosen in Nigeria, New Zealand, Bermuda, the Bahamas, Chile, Costa Rica, the Canal Zone, Cuba, Hawaii, Mexico, and Puerto Rico.

Among the first associated clubs were the Catalina Tuna Club, the Miami Beach Rod and Reel Club, the Cape Breton Big Game Anglers Association, the Long Island Tuna Club, the Atlantic City Tuna Club, the Freeport Tuna Club, and the Liverpool and Wedgeport divisions of the Lunenburg Tuna Club.

As news of the IGFA spread, other noted sportsmen and scientists were drawn to its administration. Among the early officers were fisherman and novelist Ernest Hemingway, who served as a vice-president from 1940 until his death in 1962; Philip Wylie, elected field representative in 1941 and a vice-president in 1948; B. Davis Crowninshield, elected an officer in 1948; and Charles M. Broder, Jr., who served as chairman of the Committee on Scientific Activities.

Michael Lerner took responsibility for financing the International Game Fish Association from the very beginning, and when Dr. Gregory retired from the museum staff in 1944, Mike took responsibility for the presidency as well.

During the following years, IGFA's promotional and record-keeping activities earned it growing esteem around the world. By 1960 IGFA angling rules and ethics were being adopted by fishing clubs and tournaments worldwide. It was evident that the IGFA was here to stay, and that serious thought must be given to its future funding and goals.

In the early 1970s, veteran saltwater angler Elwood K. Harry, elected vice-president of IGFA in 1962, proposed that opening the organization to individual public membership would not only insure its funding but would also help unite international anglers and provide a greater awareness of the problems threatening fishery resources.

Times had changed for the sport fisherman, and it was now up to the IGFA to address these changes. A telling passage from a 1945 edition of IGFA's *Organization and Rules* booklet read, "Fish, like the waters of the sea themselves, are the common property of all the people of the earth." Life, at least for the angler, was simpler then, and 200-mile limits and fishery management programs did not disturb the tranquility of the seas.

By the 1970s, however, such legislation and programs were becoming essential to preservation of the ocean's resources. The IGFA, under the leadership of Mr. Harry, would soon begin to play a vital role both in increasing the recreational angler's importance in fishery management decisions and in making anglers more aware of how they could contribute to conservation and management of game fish stocks.

In March 1973, IGFA was rechartered as a broadly based nonprofit and tax-exempt organization with responsibilities for educational, scientific, and charitable contributions. Under this status, donations to the association became tax deductible to the extent allowed by law. At this same time, an IGFA membership campaign was launched through mailings to anglers worldwide and promoted by a network of outdoor writers.

Not only had times changed for the sport fisherman since the early years of the IGFA, the nature of saltwater angling itself had changed. No longer was it necessary to be able to afford a large offshore boat and expensive equipment to enjoy the leisure and excitement of recreational fishing. Hundreds of thousands of people were taking to coastal waters in small outboards, or fishing from shore and pier.

The new breed of angler necessitated changes in world record-keeping procedures, and in the early 1970s a lighter (6-pound) line class was added to the record categories. Along with this change, IGFA began to add more of the smaller coastal fishes to its list of species. Anglers fishing inshore waters now had more opportunity to set international records along with deep-sea fishermen, and the rules were no less stringent.

The need for worldwide standardization of sport-fishing equipment also prompted IGFA officials to establish closer ties with tackle manufacturers. With the advent of universal acceptance of the metric system, for example, metric line classifications had to be established which would comply with current manufacturing technology.

In 1976, the IGFA established a liaison committee with the American Fishing Tackle Manufacturers Association (AFTMA) in order to keep IGFA fishing equipment regulations within the realistic abilities of the industry. Thus, when metric line classifications for world record purposes were announced by IGFA in September 1976, they were not without the sanction of tackle manufacturers in the United States and abroad.

Opening the IGFA to active individual membership also offered advantages in the field of game fish research. Just as Michael Lerner and the IGFA had provided invaluable assistance to scientists in the early years of the association, the efforts of anglers of the seventies would prove essential to assessment of certain fishery stocks for conservation purposes. Through its membership communications, the IGFA could now relay to anglers the needs and results of scientific tag and release and data collection programs, and inform anglers of how they could participate.

IGFA's efforts to "save" the Atlantic bluefin tuna, for example, or to establish viable management plans for billfish, were and are being aided by many of the association's member anglers and fishing clubs who actively participate in legislative and data collection processes.

LOOKING AHEAD

The establishment of a world fishing library and the many new programs undertaken by the association pointed up the need for a permanent building for the organization. By 1978, IGFA was quickly outgrowing its leased offices in Fort Lauderdale, and a committee was appointed to research site selection for a permanent structure.

A new home for IGFA would house all of the administration and publication offices, the International Library of Fishes, meeting rooms for symposiums, seminars, and educational forums, and an exhibition hall where angling artifacts, photographs, and art would be displayed. In a sense, it would be an angler's hall of fame where those who had contributed to the sport and conservation would be honored for their achieve-

ments. Though the IGFA has come a long way since its founding in 1939, it has never strayed from its original precepts.

MAJOR OBJECTIVES

1. To encourage and further the study of game fish angling, the related game species, and the habitat requirements of such species.

2. To work at all levels of government and industry for the preservation of the species and the protection of their natural habitats.

3. To compile and distribute game fish information to all IGFA members, the general public, and scientific and legislative government bodies for the furtherance of education in the wise use and conservation of the species.

4. To ensure that the recreational angler is adequately represented at all meetings where the future of the game fish population and the angling sport is being determined.

5. To assist and participate in domestic and international game fish seminars and symposiums where the expertise, data, and purposes of this organization may be helpful in assisting other organizations with similar objectives.

6. To develop and support game fish tagging programs and other scientific data collection efforts, and to aid scientific data collection efforts, and to aid scientific and educational institutions which provide vital instruction and

Record-breaking angler Stu Apte with a wahoo taken on plug-casting tackle with a surface plug.

research in ichthyology, the fishery sciences, and related studies.

7. To maintain and promote fair, uniform, and ethical international angling regulations, and to compile and maintain world record data for game fish caught according to these regulations.

8. To develop and maintain an international reference library on game fish, the angling sport, and related subjects.

9. To accumulate and maintain a worldwide history of game fishing for the use and benefit of the public.

INTERNATIONAL ANGLING RULES

The following angling rules have been formulated by the International Game Fish Association to promote ethical and sporting angling practices, to establish uniform regulations for the compilation of world game fish records, and to provide basic angling guidelines for use in fishing tournaments and any other group angling activities.

The word "angling" is defined as catching or attempting to catch fish with a rod, reel, line, and hook as outlined in the international angling rules. There are some aspects of angling that cannot be controlled through rulemaking, however. Angling regulations cannot insure an outstanding performance from each fish, and world records cannot indicate the amount of difficulty in catching the fish. Captures in which the fish has not fought or has not had a chance to fight do not reflect credit on the fisherman, and only the angler can properly evaluate the degree of achievement in establishing the record.

Only fish caught in accordance with IGFA international angling rules, and within the intent of these rules, will be considered for world records.

Following are the rules for saltwater fishing and a separate set of rules for fly-fishing.

Rules for Fishing in Saltwater
(Also see *Rules for Fly-fishing*)

Equipment Regulations
A. LINE
1. Monofilament, multifilament, and lead core multifilament lines may be used. For line classes, see *World Record Requirements*.
2. Wire lines are prohibited.

B. LINE BACKING
1. Backing attached to the fishing line is permissible provided that the line closest to the hook or double line (if one is used) is a minimum of 50 feet (15.24 meters) in length.
2. Backing not attached to the fishing line is permissible with no restrictions as to size or material.

C. DOUBLE LINE
The use of a double line is not required. If one is used, it must meet the following specifications:
1. A double line must consist of the actual line used to catch the fish.
2. Double lines are measured from the start of the knot, braid, roll, or splice making the double to the farthermost end of the knot, splice, snap, swivel, or other device used for securing the trace, leader, lure, or hook to the double line.

The double line on all weights of tackle shall be limited to 30 feet (9.14 meters). The combined length of the double line and leader shall not exceed 40 feet (12.19 meters).

D. LEADER
The use of a leader is not required. If one is used, it must meet the following specifications:
1. The length of the leader is the overall length including any lure, hook arrangement, or other device. The leader must be connected to the line with a snap, knot, splice, swivel, or other device. There are no regulations regarding the material or strength of the leader.

The leader on all weights of tackle shall be limited to 30 feet (9.14 meters). The combined length of the double line and leader shall be limited to 40 feet (12.19 meters).
2. The combined overall length of the double line and the leader shall not exceed 40 feet (12.19 meters).
3. The leader must be connected to the line with a knot, splice, snap, swivel, or other device.
4. There are no regulations regarding the material or strength of the leader.

E. ROD
1. Rods must comply with sporting ethics and

customs. Considerable latitude is allowed in the choice of a rod, but rods giving the angler an unfair advantage will be disqualified. This rule is intended to eliminate the use of unconventional rods.

2. The rod tip must be a minimum of 40 inches (101.6 cm) in length. The rod butt cannot exceed 27 inches (68.58 cm) in length. These measurements must be made from a point directly beneath the center of the reel. A curved butt is measured in a straight line. (The above measurements do not apply to surf-casting rods.)

F. REEL

1. Reels must comply with sporting ethics and customs.

2. Power-driven reels of any kind are prohibited. This includes motor, hydraulic, or electrically driven reels, and any device which gives the angler an unfair advantage.

3. Ratchet handle reels are prohibited.

4. Reels designed to be cranked with both hands at the same time are prohibited.

G. HOOKS FOR BAIT-FISHING

1. For live- or dead-bait-fishing no more than two single hooks may be used. Both must be firmly embedded in or securely attached to the bait. The eyes of the hooks must be no less than a hook's length (the length of the largest hook used) apart and no more than 18 inches (45.72 cm) apart. The only exception is that the point of one hook may be passed through the eye of the other hook.

2. The use of a dangling or swinging hook is prohibited.

3. A two-hook rig for bottom fishing is acceptable if it consists of two single hooks on separate leaders or drops. Both hooks must be embedded in the respective baits and separated sufficiently so that a fish caught on one hook cannot be foul-hooked by the other.

4. All record applications made for fish caught on two-hook tackle must be accompanied by a photograph or sketch of the hook arrangement.

H. HOOKS AND LURES

1. When using an artificial lure with a skirt or trailing material, no more than two single hooks may be attached to the line, leader, or trace. The hooks need not be attached separately. The eyes of the hooks must be no less than an overall hook's length (the overall length of the largest hook used) apart and no farther than 12 inches (30.48 cm) apart. The only exception is that the point of one hook may be passed through the eye of the other hook. The trailing hook may not extend more than a hook's length beyond the skirt of the lure. A photograph or sketch showing the hook arrangement must accompany a record application.

2. Gang hooks are permitted when attached to plugs and other artificial lures that are specifically designed for this use. Gang hooks shall be limited to a maximum of two hooks (either single, double, or treble, or a combination of any two). These hooks must be permanently and directly attached to the lure and must be free-swinging. A photograph or sketch of the plug or lure must be submitted with record applications. If the picture is not satisfactory, the plug or lure itself may be requested.

I. OTHER EQUIPMENT

1. *Fighting chairs* may not have any mechanically propelled devices which aid the angler in fighting a fish.

2. *Gimbals* must be free-swinging, which includes gimbals that swing in a vertical plane only. Any gimbal that allows the angler to reduce strain or to rest while fighting the fish is prohibited.

3. *Gaffs and nets* used to boat or land a fish must not exceed 8 feet (2.43 meters) in overall length. (When fishing from a bridge, pier, or other high platform or structure, this length limitation does not apply.) In using a flying or detachable gaff, the rope may not exceed 30 feet (9.14 meters). The gaff rope must be measured from the point where it is secured to the detachable head to the other end. Only the effective length will be considered. If a fixed head gaff is used, the same limitations shall apply and the gaff rope shall be measured from the same location on the gaff hook. Only a single hook is permitted on any gaff. Harpoon or lance attachments are prohibited.

4. *Floats* are prohibited with the exception of any small flotation device attached to the line or leader for the sole purpose of regulating the depth of the bait. The flotation device must not

in any way hamper the fighting ability of the fish.

5. Entangling devices, either with or without a hook, are prohibited and may not be used for any purpose, including baiting, hooking, fighting, or landing the fish.

6. Outriggers, downriggers, and kites are permitted to be used provided that the actual fishing line is attached to the snap or other release device, either directly or with some other material. The leader or double line may not be connected to the release mechanism either directly or with the use of a connecting device.

7. A safety line may be attached to the rod provided that it does not in any way assist the angler in fighting the fish.

Angling Regulations

1. From the time that a fish strikes or takes a bait or lure, the angler must hook, fight, and bring the fish to gaff without the aid of any other person, except as provided in these regulations.

2. If a rod holder is used and a fish strikes or takes the bait or lure, the angler must remove the rod from the holder as quickly as possible. The intent of this rule is that the angler shall strike and hook the fish.

3. In the event of a multiple strike on separate lines being fished by a single angler, only the first fish fought by the angler will be considered for a world record.

4. If a double line is used, the intent of the regulations is that the fish will be fought on the single line most of the time that it takes to land the fish.

5. A harness may be attached to the reel or rod, but not to the fighting chair. The harness may be replaced or adjusted by a person other than the angler.

6. Use of rod belt or waist gimbal is permitted.

7. When angling from a boat, once the leader is brought within the grasp of the mate, or the end of the leader is wound to the rod tip, more than one person is permitted to hold the leader.

8. One or more gaffers may be used in addition to persons holding the leader. The gaff handle must be in hand when the fish is gaffed.

9. A fish is considered caught when it is presented to the weighmaster for weighing.

The following acts will disqualify a catch:

1. Failure to comply with equipment or angling regulations.

2. The act of persons other than the angler in touching any part of the rod, reel, or line (including the double line) either bodily or with any device during the playing of the fish, or in giving any aid other than that allowed in the rules and regulations. If an obstacle to the passage of the line through the rod guides has to be removed from the line, then the obstacle (whether chum, floatline, rubber band, or other material) shall be held and cut free. Under no circumstances should the line be held or touched by anyone other than the angler during this process.

3. Resting the rod in a rod holder, on the gunwale of the boat, or any other object while playing the fish.

4. Handlining or using a handline or rope attached in any manner to the angler's line or leader for the purpose of holding or lifting the fish.

5. Shooting, harpooning, or lancing the fish being played (including sharks) during any stage of the catch.

6. Chumming with or using as bait the flesh, blood, skin, or any part of mammals other than hair or pork rind used in lures designed for trolling or casting.

7. Using a boat or device to beach or drive a fish into shallow water in order to deprive the fish of its normal ability to swim.

8. Changing the rod or reel while the fish is being played.

9. Splicing, removing, or adding to the line while the fish is being played.

10. Intentionally foul-hooking a fish.

11. Catching a fish in a manner that the double line never leaves the rod tip.

12. Using sizes or kinds of bait that are illegal to possess.

The following situations will disqualify a catch:

1. When a rod breaks in a manner that reduces the length of the tip below minimum dimensions or severely impairs its angling characteristics.

2. Mutilations to the fish caused by sharks, other fish, mammals, or propellers that remove or penetrate the flesh. (Injuries caused by leader

or line, scratches, old healed scars or regeneration deformities are not considered to be disqualifying injuries.) Any mutilation on the fish must be shown in a photograph and fully explained in a separate report accompanying the record application.

3. When a fish is hooked on more than one line.

Rules for Fly-fishing

Equipment Regulations
A. LINE
Any type of fly line and backing may be used. The breaking strength of the fly line and backing are not restricted.

B. LEADER
Leaders must conform to generally accepted fly-fishing customs.

A leader includes a class tippet and, optionally, a shock tippet. A butt or taper section between the fly line and the class tippet shall also be considered part of the leader, and there are no limits on its length, material, or strength.

A class tippet must be made of nonmetallic material and attached directly to either the fly or the shock tippet, if one is used. The class tippet must be at least 15 inches (38.10 cm) long (measured inside connecting knots). There is no maximum-length limitation. The breaking strength determines the class of the tippet.

A shock tippet, not to exceed 12 inches (30.48 cm) in length, may be added to the class tippet and tied to the lure. It can be made of any type of material, and there is no limit on its breaking strength. The shock tippet is measured from the eye of the hook to the single strand of class tippet and includes any knots used to connect the shock tippet to the class tippet.

In the case of a tandem hook fly, the shock tippet shall be measured from the eye of the leading hook.

C. ROD
Regardless of material used or number of sections, rods must conform to generally accepted fly-fishing customs and practices. A rod shall not measure less than 6 feet (1.82 meters) in overall length. Any rod that gives the angler an unsporting advantage will be disqualified.

D. REEL
The reel must be designed expressly for fly-fishing and cannot be used in casting the fly other than as a storage spool for the line. There are no restrictions on ratio of retrieve or type of drag employed except where the angler would gain an unfair advantage. Electric or electronically operated reels are prohibited.

E. HOOKS
A conventional fly shall contain only one single hook. A maximum of two single hooks may be used in a tandem fly if both hooks are firmly tied into the fly material. The eyes of the hooks must be no less than an overall hook's length (the overall length of the largest hook used) apart and no farther than 12 inches (30.48 cm) apart. The hooks must not extend beyond the fly material.

F. LURES
The lure must be artificial and designed for fly-casting, and must be of a type which can be false-cast in the generally accepted fashion. The use of any type of natural bait on the lure is expressly disallowed. In the case of a weighted lure, the fact that it can be cast is not evidence, in itself, that the lure was designed for fly-fishing. It must be light enough to permit repeated false casts without causing undue strain on the angler or his equipment. The use of any lure designed to entangle or foul-hook a fish is prohibited.

G. GAFFS AND NETS
Gaffs and nets used to boat or land a fish must not exceed 8 feet (2.48 meters) in overall length. (When fishing from a bridge, pier, or other high stationary structure, this length limitation does not apply.) When using a flying or detachable gaff, the rope may not exceed 30 feet (9.14 meters) in length. The gaff rope must be measured from the point where it is secured to the detachable head to the other end. Only the effective length will be considered. If a fixed head gaff is used, the same limitations shall apply and the gaff rope shall be measured from the same location on the gaff hook. Only a single hook is permitted on any gaff. Harpoon or lance attachments are prohibited.

Angling Regulations

1. The angler must cast, hook, fight, and bring the fish to gaff unaided by any other person. No other person may touch any part of the tackle during the playing of the fish or give aid other than taking the leader for gaffing purposes.

2. Casting and retrieving must be carried out in accordance with normal customs and generally accepted practices. The major criteria in casting is that the weight of the line must carry the lure rather than the weight of the lure carrying the line. Trolling a lure behind a moving water craft is not permitted. The craft must be completely out of gear both at the time the fly is presented to the fish and during the retrieve.

3. Once a fish is hooked, the tackle may not be altered in any way, with the exception of adding an extension butt.

4. Fish must be hooked on the lure in use. If a small fish takes the lure and a larger fish swallows the smaller fish, the catch will be disallowed.

5. One or more gaffers may be used. The gaff handle must be in hand when the fish is gaffed.

6. A fish is considered caught when it is presented to the weighmaster for weighing.

The following acts will disqualify a catch:

1. Failure to comply with equipment or angling regulations.

2. The act of persons other than the angler in touching any part of the rod, reel, or line either bodily or with any device during the playing of the fish, or in giving any aid other than that allowed in the rules and regulations. If an obstacle to the passage of the line through the rod guides has to be removed from the line, then the obstacle shall be held and cut free. Under no circumstances should the line be held or touched by anyone other than the angler during this process.

3. Resting the rod on any part of the boat, or on any other object while playing the fish.

4. Handlining or using a handline or rope attached in any manner to the angler's line or leader for the purpose of holding or lifting the fish.

5. Intentionally foul-hooking or snagging a fish.

6. Shooting, harpooning, or lancing the fish being played (including sharks) during any stage of the catch.

7. Chumming with the flesh, blood, skin, or any part of mammals.

8. Using a boat or device to beach or drive a fish into shallow water in order to deprive the fish of its normal ability to swim.

The following situations will disqualify a catch:

1. When a rod breaks in a manner that reduces its length below minimum dimensions or severely impairs its angling characteristics.

2. When a fish is hooked on more than one line.

3. Mutilations to the fish caused by sharks, other fish, mammals, or propellers that remove or penetrate the flesh. (Injuries caused by leader or line, scratches, old healed scars or regeneration deformities are not considered to be disqualifying injuries.) Any mutilation on the fish must be shown in a photograph and fully explained in a separate report accompanying the record application.

WORLD RECORD REQUIREMENTS

Game fish catches can only qualify for world record status if they are caught according to International Angling Rules. Following is information on world record categories, requirements, and procedures for filing claims, effective January 1, 1980.

World Record Categories

GENERAL INFORMATION

IGFA maintains world records for both freshwater and saltwater game fishes. In order to be eligible for a world record, a fish must be caught according to IGFA angling rules, must be of legal limit size, and must have been caught within the legal open season. No applications will be accepted for fish caught in private club waters, controlled private bodies of water, hatchery waters, or sanctuaries. The catch must not be in variance with any laws or regulations governing the species or the waters in which it was caught.

In order to qualify for a record, a catch must outweigh the existing record by the required amount or meet the minimum weight requirements for vacant records.

When an additional species of game fish is made eligible for IGFA world records, the effective date will be announced. Fishes caught on or after the effective date will be eligible for records. Catches made prior to the effective date will not be considered.

SALTWATER RECORDS
All Tackle and Line Class

Saltwater all-tackle records are kept for the heaviest fish of each of the species listed below caught by an angler in any line class up to 60 kg (130 lb). Fish caught on lines designed to test over the 60 kg (130 lb) class will not be considered.

Saltwater line class records are maintained according to the wet testing strength of the line used by the angler. Records are kept for both men and women in the following line class categories, which are limited for certain species:

Metric	*U.S. Customary*
3 kg	6 lb
6 kg	12 lb
10 kg	20 lb
15 kg	30 lb
24 kg	50 lb
37 kg	80 lb
60 kg	130 lb

With the exception of all-tackle claims, line classes are limited for certain smaller and medium-sized species of saltwater fish. Listed below are the maximum line classes acceptable for world record purposes in each species category.

Species	*Maximum Line Class*
Albacore	37 kg (80 lb)
Amberjack, greater	60 kg (130 lb)
Barracuda, great	37 kg (80 lb)
Bass, black sea	15 kg (30 lb)
Bass, giant sea	60 kg (130 lb)
Bass, striped	37 kg (80 lb)
Bluefish	24 kg (50 lb)
Bonefish	15 kg (30 lb)
Bonito, Atlantic	15 kg (30 lb)
Bonito, Pacific	15 kg (30 lb)
Cobia	37 kg (80 lb)
Cod	37 kg (80 lb)
Dolphin	37 kg (80 lb)
Drum, black	37 kg (80 lb)
Drum, red	37 kg (80 lb)
Flounder, summer	15 kg (30 lb)
Halibut, Atlantic	60 kg (130 lb)
Halibut, California	37 kg (80 lb)
Halibut, Pacific	60 kg (130 lb)
Jack, crevalle	24 kg (50 lb)
Jack, horse-eye	24 kg (50 lb)
Jewfish	60 kg (130 lb)
Kawakawa	15 kg (30 lb)
Mackerel, king	37 kg (80 lb)
Marlin, black	60 kg (130 lb)
Marlin, blue (Atlantic)	60 kg (130 lb)
Marlin, blue (Pacific)	60 kg (130 lb)
Marlin, striped	60 kg (130 lb)
Permit	24 kg (50 lb)
Pollack	24 kg (50 lb)
Pollock	24 kg (50 lb)
Pompano, African	24 kg (50 lb)
Roosterfish	60 kg (130 lb)
Runner, rainbow	24 kg (50 lb)
Sailfish (Atlantic)	37 kg (80 lb)
Sailfish (Pacific)	60 kg (130 lb)
Seabass, white	37 kg (80 lb)
Seatrout, spotted	15 kg (30 lb)
Shark, blue	60 kg (130 lb)
Shark, hammerhead	60 kg (130 lb)
Shark, porbeagle	60 kg (130 lb)
Shark, shortfin mako	60 kg (130 lb)
Shark, thresher	60 kg (130 lb)
Shark, tiger	60 kg (130 lb)
Shark, white	60 kg (130 lb)
Skipjack, black	15 kg (30 lb)
Snook	24 kg (50 lb)
Spearfish	37 kg (80 lb)
Swordfish	60 kg (130 lb)
Tanguigue	37 kg (80 lb)
Tarpon	60 kg (130 lb)
Tautog	15 kg (30 lb)
Trevally, giant	60 kg (130 lb)
Trevally, lowly	60 kg (130 lb)
Tuna, bigeye (Atlantic)	60 kg (130 lb)
Tuna, bigeye (Pacific)	60 kg (130 lb)
Tuna, blackfin	24 kg (50 lb)
Tuna, bluefin	60 kg (130 lb)
Tuna, dogtooth	60 kg (130 lb)
Tuna, longtail	37 kg (80 lb)
Tuna, skipjack	24 kg (50 lb)
Tuna, southern bluefin	60 kg (130 lb)
Tuna, yellowfin	60 kg (130 lb)
Tunny, little	15 kg (30 lb)

Wahoo	60 kg (130 lb)
Weakfish	15 kg (30 lb)
Yellowtail, California	37 kg (80 lb)
Yellowtail, southern	60 kg (130 lb)

Fly Rod

Saltwater fly-rod world records are maintained according to tippet strength. Records are kept for the same species listed for all-tackle and line class saltwater records in the following tippet classes:

Metric	*U.S. Customary*
3 kg	6 lb
5 kg	10 lb
6 kg	12 lb
7 kg	15 lb

LINE TESTING

IGFA tests all line and tippet samples submitted with world record claims in accordance with the metric line class designations, which vary slightly from the standard U.S. customary designations. For example, the U.S. customary equivalent of 6 kilograms is 13.22 pounds. Thus, line designated by the manufacturer as 12-pound class line may test up to 13.22 pounds (6 kg) to qualify for a 12-pound line class record. The U.S. customary equivalents in pounds for the metric line classes are as follows:

Metric	*U.S. Customary Equivalent*
1 kg	2.20 lb
2 kg	4.40 lb
3 kg	6.61 lb
4 kg	8.81 lb
5 kg	11.02 lb
6 kg	13.22 lb
7 kg	15.43 lb
8 kg	17.63 lb
10 kg	22.04 lb
15 kg	33.06 lb
24 kg	52.91 lb
37 kg	81.57 lb
60 kg	132.27 lb

Line and tippet samples submitted with record claims are uniformly tested in a nationally recognized laboratory in accordance with government specifications which have been modified and supplemented by IGFA.

Note: IGFA only tests lines and tippets submitted for world record claims.

Regulations Governing Record Catches

GENERAL INFORMATION

1. Protested applications or disputed existing records will be referred to the IGFA Executive Committee for review. Its decisions will be final. IGFA reserves the sole right to either grant or reject any record applications. All IGFA decisions will be based upon the intent of the regulations.

2. In case of a disputed species identification, photographs of the catch will be submitted to two qualified ichthyologists for their decisions. When a question of identification arises, the angler will be notified and given ample opportunity to submit further evidence of identification.

3. In some instances, an IGFA officer or member of the International Committee or a deputy from a local IGFA member club may be asked to recheck information supplied on a claim. Such action is not to be regarded as doubt of the formal affidavit, but rather as evidence of the extreme care with which IGFA investigates and maintains its records.

WITNESSES TO CATCH

Fly-rod catches must be witnessed to qualify for a world record. It is important that the witness can attest to compliance with the international fly-fishing rules and regulations.

On all other record claims, witnesses to the catch are highly desirable.

WEIGHTS NEEDED TO DEFEAT OR TIE EXISTING RECORDS

1. To replace a record for a fish weighing less than 10 pounds (4.53 kg), the replacement must weigh at least 2 ounces (65.69 gm) more than the existing record.

2. To replace a record for à fish weighing from 10 pounds (4.53 kg) to under 20 pounds (9.07 kg), the replacement must weigh at least 4 ounces (113.39 gm) more than the existing record.

3. To replace a record for a fish weighing from 20 pounds (9.07 kg) to under 100 pounds (45.35 kg), the replacement must weigh at least

8 ounces (226.7 gm) more than the existing record.

4. To replace a record for a fish weighing 100 pounds (45.35 kg) or more, the replacement must weigh at least one half of 1 percent (.005%) more than the existing record weight. Examples: At 200 pounds (90.71 kg) the additional weight required would be 1 pound (.45 kg); at 400 pounds (181.43 kg) the additional weight required would be 2 pounds (.90 kg).

5. Any catch which matches the weight of an existing record or exceeds the weight by less than the amount required to defeat the record will be considered a tie. In case of a tie claim involving more than two catches, weight must be compared with the original record (first fish to be caught). Nothing weighing less than the original record will be considered.

6. Estimated weights will not be accepted. (See *Weighing Requirements.*)

TIME LIMIT ON CLAIMS

Claims for record fish caught in U.S. continental waters must be received by IGFA within sixty days of the date of catch. Claims for record fish caught in other waters must be received by IGFA within three months of the date of catch.

If an incomplete record claim is submitted, it must be accompanied by an explanation of why certain portions are incomplete. An incomplete claim will be considered for a record if the following conditions are met:

1. The incomplete claim with explanations of why portions are incomplete must be received by IGFA within the time limits specified above.

2. Missing data must be due to circumstances beyond the control of the angler making the record claim.

3. All missing data must be supplied within a period of time considered to be reasonable in view of the particular circumstances.

Final decisions on incomplete claims will be made by IGFA's Executive Committee.

WEIGHING REQUIREMENTS FOR RECORD FISH

The fish must be weighed by an official weighmaster (if one is available) or by an IGFA official or by a recognized local person familiar with the scale. Disinterested witnesses to the weight should be used whenever possible.

The weight of the sling, platform, or rope (if one is used to secure the fish on the scales) must be determined and deducted from the total weight.

At the time of weighing, the actual tackle used by the angler to catch the fish must be exhibited to the weighmaster and weight witness.

No estimated weights will be accepted. Fish weighed only at sea or on other bodies of water will not be accepted.

All record fish should be weighed on scales that have been checked and certified for accuracy by government agencies or other qualified and accredited organizations. All scales must be regularly checked for accuracy and certified in accordance with applicable government regulations at least once every twelve months.

If at the time of weighing the fish, the scale has not been properly certified within twelve months, it should be checked and certified for accuracy as quickly as possible, and an official report stating the findings of the inspection prior to any adjustments of the scale must be included with the record application.

If there is no official government inspector or accredited commercial scales representative available in the area where the fish is weighed, the scales must be checked by weighing objects of recognized and proved weight. Objects weighed must be at least equal to the weight of the fish. Substantiation of the correct weight of these objects must be submitted to IGFA along with the names and complete addresses of accredited witnesses to the entire procedure.

IGFA reserves the right to have any scale recertified for accuracy if there are any indications that the scale might not have weighed correctly.

SPECIES IDENTIFICATION

If there is the slightest doubt that the fish cannot be properly identified from the photographs and other data submitted, the fish should be examined by a qualified scientist or retained in a preserved or frozen condition until a qualified authority can verify the species or until notified by IGFA that the fish need no longer be retained.

Preparation of Record Claims

To apply for a world record, the angler must submit a completed IGFA application form, the mandatory length of line or fly leader used to catch the fish, and acceptable photographs of the fish, the tackle used to catch the fish, the scale used to weigh the fish, and the angler with the fish.

APPLICATION FORM

The official IGFA world record application form must be used for record claims. This form may be reproduced as long as all items are included.

The angler must fill in the application personally. IGFA also recommends that the angler personally mail the application, line sample or fly leader, and photographs.

When making any record claim, the angler must indicate the specified strength of the line or tippet used to catch the fish. In the cases of line class and tippet class records, this will place the claim in an IGFA line or tippet class category (see *World Record Categories*). If the line or tippet overtests its particular category, the application will be considered in the next highest category; if it undertests into a lower line or tippet class category, the application will not be considered for the lower line class. The heaviest line class permitted for both freshwater and saltwater records is 60 kg (130 lb) class. The heaviest tippet class permitted for saltwater records is 7 kg (15 lb) and for freshwater records the maximum is 8 kg (16 lb). If the line or tippet overtests these maximum strengths, the claim will be disqualified.

Extreme care should be exercised in measuring the fish, as the measurements are often important for weight verification and scientific studies. See the measurement diagram on the record application to be sure you have measured correctly.

The angler is responsible for seeing that the necessary signatures and correct addresses of the boat captain, weighmaster, and witnesses are on the application. If an IGFA officer or representative, or an officer or member of an IGFA club is available, he or she should be asked to witness the claim. The name of a boatman, guide, or weighmaster repeated as witness is not acceptable.

The angler must appear in person to have his application notarized. In territories where notarization is not possible or customary, the signature of a government commissioner or resident, a member of an embassy, legation, or consular staff, or an IGFA officer or International Committee member may replace notarization.

Any deliberate falsification of an application will disqualify the applicant for any future IGFA world record, and any existing records will be nullified.

LINE OR TIPPET SAMPLE

All applications for fly-fishing records must be accompanied by the lure, the entire tippet, and the leader along with 1 inch of the fly line beyond the attachment to the leader. These components must be intact and connected. The lure will be returned to the angler on request.

All applications for freshwater and saltwater line class records must be accompanied by the entire leader, the double line, and at least 40 feet (15.24 meters) of the single line closest to the double line, leader or hook. All line samples and the leader (if one is used) must be submitted in one piece. If a lure is used with the leader, the leader should be cut at the eye attachment to the lure.

Each line sample must be in one piece. It must be submitted in a manner that it can be easily unwound without damage to the line. A recommended method is to take a rectangular piece of stiff cardboard and cut notches in two opposite ends. Secure one end of the line to the cardboard and wind the line around the cardboard through the notched areas. Secure the other end, and write your name and the specified strength of the line on the cardboard. Do not submit the line in a hank.

PHOTOGRAPHS

Photographs showing the full length of the fish, the rod and reel used to make the catch, and the scale used to weigh the fish must accompany each record application. A photograph of the angler with the fish is also required.

So that there can be no question of species identification, the clearest possible photos should be submitted. This is especially important in the cases of marlin, bass, salmon, trout, sharks, tuna, and other fishes that may be confused with similar species. Shark applications should also include

IGFA Fishing Contests—Application Form

FORM FOR RECORDING SALTWATER AND FRESHWATER ENTRIES

Read all IGFA angling rules and contest regulations before completing and signing this application. The angler's signature on the completed form must be witnessed by a notary. This application must be accompanied by line or tippet samples and photographs as specified in the World Record Requirements.

I AM SUBMITTING THIS CONTEST APPLICATION FOR A FISH CAUGHT IN

☐ Fresh water

☐ Salt water

USING THE FOLLOWING LINE:

Line class _____

Tippet class _____

SPECIES

Common name: _____

Scientific name: _____

WEIGHT

lbs, oz: _____ kg: _____

LENGTH (See measurement diagrams)

inches: x to x _____ xx to xx _____

cm: x to x _____ xx to xx _____

GIRTH (See measurement diagrams)

inches: _____ cm: _____

DATE OF CATCH: _____

PLACE OF CATCH: _____

_____

METHOD OF CATCH (trolling, casting, fly fishing, etc.): _____

FIGHTING TIME: _____

ANGLER (Print name as you wish it to appear on contest certificate):

_____

Permanent address
(Include country and address code):

_____

_____

_____

Angler's fishing club affiliation (if any):

_____

EQUIPMENT

Rod
Make: _____

Tip length (center of reel to end of tip): _____

Butt length (center of reel to lower end of butt):

_____

Reel
Make: _____ Size: _____

Line or tippet
Make: _____ Size: _____

SPECIES MEASUREMENTS

Measure as indicated below, taking lengths from X to X and XX to XX.
Take girth around the fish on line marked G or at largest dimension location.

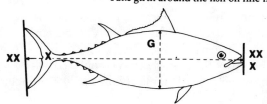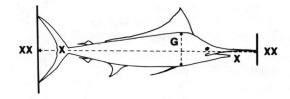

Length of double line: _____

Make of backing: _____ Size: _____

Other equipment:

Type of gaff: _____ Length: _____

Length of trace or leader: _____

Number of hooks: _____

Name of lure, fly or bait: _____

BOAT (if used)

Name: _____

Make: _____ Length: _____

Captain's name: _____

Signature: _____

Address: _____

_____

Mate's name: _____

Signature: _____

Address: _____

_____

SCALES

Location: _____

Type: _____

Manufacturer: _____

Date last certified: _____

Person and/or agency that certified scales:

_____

Weighmaster: _____

Signature: _____

Address: _____

WITNESSES

Witness to weighing (other than angler, captain or

weighmaster): _____

Address: _____

_____

Witnesses to catch (other than captain). List two names and addresses if possible. On fly rod records a witness is mandatory.

1. _____

_____

_____

2. _____

_____

_____

Number of persons witnessing catch: _____

AFFIDAVIT

I, the undersigned, hereby take oath and attest that the fish described in this application was hooked, fought, and brought to gaff by me without assistance from anyone, except as specifically provided in the regulations; and that it was caught in accordance with IGFA angling rules; and that the line submitted with this application is the actual line used to catch the fish. I further declare that all the information in this application is true and correct to the best of my knowledge.

Signature of angler: _____

Sworn before me this _____ day of _____ 19_____

Notary signature and seal: _____

When completely filled out and signed, mail this application with photos and line sample by quickest means to: INTERNATIONAL GAME FISH ASSOCIATION, 3000 East Las Olas Boulevard, Fort Lauderdale, Florida 33316 U.S.A.
(This application may be reproduced.)

a photograph of the shark's head and the front teeth.

Photographs should be taken of the fish in hanging position and also lying on a flat surface on its side. In both types of photographs no part of the fish should be obscured.

When hanging, the fish should be broadside to the camera with the fins fully extended and with the tip of the jaw and sword or spear clearly shown. Do not hold the tip of any fin. Do not stand in front of the fish. Do not hold the fish in your hands. A sky background for the fish is most desirable. Background cluttered with objects and people many times complicate identification and detract from the photograph.

When photographing a fish lying on its side, the surface beneath the fish should be smooth and a ruler or marked tape should be placed beside the fish if possible. Photographs from various angles are most helpful.

An additional photograph of the fish on the scale with actual weight visible helps to expedite the application.

Photos taken by daylight are highly recommended if at all possible.

Note: Now that IGFA has a bimonthly newsletter to keep anglers up to date on world record catches, it is more important than ever that we have clear, publishable photographs of the fish and the angler. If you have action shots of the catch, we would like to see them also.

IGFA SALTWATER ALL-TACKLE WORLD RECORDS

All-tackle records are kept for the heaviest saltwater fish of each species caught by an angler in any line class category up to 60 kg (130 lb). Following are the all-tackle records granted as of January 1, 1980.

SPECIES	SCIENTIFIC NAME	WEIGHT	PLACE	DATE	ANGLER
Albacore	*Thunnus alalunga*	40.00 kg 88 lb 2 oz	Mogan Port, Gran Canaria, Canary I.	Nov. 19, 1977	Siegfried Dickemann
Amberjack, greater	*Seriola dumerili*	67.58 kg 149 lb	Bermuda	June 21, 1964	Peter Simons
Barracuda, great	*Sphyraena barracuda*	37.64 kg 83 lb	Lagos, Nigeria	Jan. 13, 1952	K. J. W. Hackett
Bass, black sea	*Centropristis striata*	3.96 kg 8 lb 12 oz	Oregon Inlet, North Carolina, USA	Apr. 21, 1979	Joe W. Mizelle, Sr.
Bass, giant sea	*Stereolepis gigas*	255.60 kg 563 lb 8 oz	Anacapa Island, California, USA	Aug. 20, 1968	James D. McAdam, Jr.
Bass, striped	*Morone saxatilis*	32.65 kg 72 lb	Cuttyhunk, Massachusetts, USA	Oct. 10, 1969	Edward J. Kirker
Bluefish	*Pomatomus saltatrix*	14.40 kg 31 lb 12 oz	Hatteras, North Carolina, USA	Jan. 30, 1972	James M. Hussey
Bonefish	*Albula vulpes*	8.61 kg 19 lb	Zululand, South Africa	May 26, 1962	Brian W. Batchelor
Bonito, Atlantic	*Sarda sarda*	6.00 kg 13 lb 3 oz	Fuerteventura Island, Canary Islands	Aug. 22, 1979	Renate Reichel
Bonito, Pacific	*Sarda spp.*	10.65 kg 23 lb 8 oz	Victoria, Mahe, Seychelles	Feb. 19, 1975	Mrs. Anne Cochain
Cobia	*Rachycentron canadum*	50.03 kg 110 lb 5 oz	Mombasa, Kenya	Sept. 8, 1964	Eric Tinworth
Cod	*Gadus morhua*	44.79 kg 98 lb 12 oz	Isle of Shoals, New Hampshire, USA	June 8, 1969	Alphonse J. Bielevich
Dolphin	*Coryphaena hippurus*	39.46 kg 87 lb	Papagallo Gulf, Costa Rica	Sept. 25, 1976	Manuel Salazar
Drum, black	*Pogonias cromis*	51.28 kg 113 lb 1 oz	Lewes, Delaware, USA	Sept. 15, 1975	Gerald M. Townsend
Drum, red	*Sciaenops ocellata*	40.82 kg 90 lb	Rodanthe, North Carolina, USA	Nov. 7, 1973	Elvin Hooper

SPECIES	SCIENTIFIC NAME	WEIGHT	PLACE	DATE	ANGLER
Flounder, summer	*Paralichthys dentatus*	10.17 kg 22 lb 7 oz	Montauk, New York, USA	Sept. 15, 1975	Charles Nappi
Halibut, California	*Paralichthys californicus*	17.01 kg 37 lb 8 oz	San Diego, California, USA	July 22, 1979	William E. Williams
Jack, crevalle	*Caranx hippos*	23.13 kg 51 lb	Lake Worth, Florida, USA	June 20, 1978	Stephen V. Schwenk
Jack, horse-eye	*Caranx latus*	9.66 kg 21 lb 5 oz	Arcus Bank, Bermuda	June 24, 1979	Tom Smith
Jewfish	*Epinephelus itajara*	308.44 kg 680 lb	Fernandina Beach, Florida, USA	May 20, 1961	Lynn Joyner
Kawakawa	*Euthynnus affinis*	9.52 kg 21 lb	Kilauea, Kauai, Hawaii, USA	Aug. 21, 1975	E. John O'Dell
Mackerel, king	*Scomberomorus cavalla*	40.82 kg 90 lb	Key West, Florida, USA	Feb. 16, 1976	Norton J. Thornton
Marlin, black	*Makaira indica*	707.61 kg 1560 lb	Cabo Blanco, Peru	Aug. 4, 1953	Alfred C. Glassell, Jr.
Marlin, blue (Atlantic)	*Makaira nigricans*	581.51 kg 1282 lb	St. Thomas, Virgin Islands	Aug. 6, 1977	Larry Martin
Marlin, blue (Pacific)	*Makaira nigricans*	522.99 kg 1153 lb	Ritidian Point, Guam	Aug. 21, 1969	Greg D. Perez
Marlin, striped	*Tetrapturus audax*	189.37 kg 417 lb 8 oz	Cavalli Islands, New Zealand	Jan. 14, 1977	Phillip Bryers
Marlin, white	*Tetrapturus albidus*	79.00 kg 174 lb 3 oz	Vitória, Brazil	Nov. 1, 1975	Otavio Cunha Reboucac
Permit	*Trachinotus falcatus*	23.35 kg 51 lb 8 oz	Lake Worth, Florida, USA	Apr. 28, 1978	William M. Kenney
Pollack	*Pollachius virens*	21.06 kg 46 lb 7 oz	Brielle, New Jersey, USA	May 26, 1975	John Tomes Holton
Pompano, African	*Alectis ciliaris*	18.82 kg 41 lb 8 oz	Fort Lauderdale, Florida, USA	Feb. 15, 1979	Wayne Sommers
Roosterfish	*Nematistius pectoralis*	51.71 kg 114 lb	La Paz, Baja, Mexico	June 1, 1960	Abe Sackheim
Runner, rainbow	*Elagatis bipinnulatus*	15.25 kg 33 lb 10 oz	Clarion Island, Mexico	Mar. 14, 1976	Ralph A. Mikkelsen
Sailfish (Atlantic)	*Istiophorus platypterus*	58.10 kg 128 lb 1 oz	Luanda, Angola	Mar. 27, 1974	Harm Steyn
Sailfish (Pacific)	*Istiophorus platypterus*	100.24 kg 221 lb	Santa Cruz Island, Ecuador	Feb. 12, 1947	C. W. Stewart
Seabass, white	*Cynoscion nobilis*	37.98 kg 83 lb 12 oz	San Felipe, Mexico	Mar. 31, 1953	L. C. Baumgardner
Seatrout, spotted	*Cynoscion nebulosus*	7.25 kg 16 lb	Mason's Beach, Virginia, USA	May 28, 1977	William Katko
Shark, blue	*Prionace glauca*	198.22 kg 437 lb	Catherine Bay, N.S.W., Australia	Oct. 2, 1976	Peter Hyde
Shark, hammerhead	*Sphyrna spp.*	318.87 kg 703 lb	Jacksonville Beach, Florida, USA	July 5, 1975	H. B. "Blackie" Reas
Shark, porbeagle	*Lamna nasus*	210.92 kg 465 lb	Padstow, Cornwall, England, U.K.	July 23, 1976	Jorge Potier
Shark, shortfin mako	*Isurus oxyrinchus*	489.88 kg 1080 lb	Montauk, New York, USA	Aug. 26, 1979	James I. Melanson
Shark, thresher	*Alopias spp.*	335.20 kg 739 lb	Tutukaka, New Zealand	Feb. 17, 1975	Brian Galvin
Shark, tiger	*Galeocerdo cuvieri*	807.40 kg 1780 lb	Cherry Grove, S. Carolina, USA	June 14, 1964	Walter Maxwell
Shark, white	*Carcharodon carcharias*	1208.38 kg 2664 lb	Ceduna, South Australia	Apr. 21, 1959	Alfred Dean
Skipjack, black	*Euthynnus lineatus*	6.57 kg 14 lb 8 oz	Cabo San Lucas, Baja, Mexico	May 24, 1977	Lorraine Carlton

SPECIES	SCIENTIFIC NAME	WEIGHT	PLACE	DATE	ANGLER
Snook	*Centropomus undecimalis*	24.32 kg 53 lb 10 oz	Río de Parasmina, Costa Rica	Oct. 18, 1978	Gilbert Ponzi
Spearfish	*Tetrapturus spp.*	36.00 kg 79 lb 5 oz	Madeira Islands	May 25, 1979	Ronald Eckett
Swordfish	*Xiphias gladius*	536.15 kg 1182 lb	Iquique, Chile	May 7, 1953	L. Marron
Tanguigue	*Scomberomorus commerson*	38.75 kg 85 lb 6 oz	Rottnest Island, Western Australia	May 5, 1978	Barry Wrightson
Tarpon	*Megalops atlantica*	128.36 kg 283 lb	Lake Maracaibo, Venezuela	Mar. 19, 1956	M. Salazar
Tautog	*Tautoga onitis*	9.69 kg 21 lb 6 oz	Cape May, New Jersey, USA	June 12, 1954	R. N. Sheafer
Trevally, lowly	*Caranx ignobilis*	53.61 kg 116 lb	Pago Pago, American Samoa	Feb. 20, 1978	William G. Foster
Tuna, bigeye (Atlantic)	*Thunnus obesus*	170.32 kg 375 lb 8 oz	Ocean City, Maryland, USA	Aug. 26, 1977	Cecil Browne
Tuna, bigeye (Pacific)	*Thunnus obesus*	197.31 kg 435 lb	Cabo Blanco, Peru	Apr. 17, 1957	Dr. Russell V. A. Lee
Tuna, blackfin	*Thunnus atlanticus*	19.05 kg 42 lb	Bermuda	June 2, 1978	Alan J. Card
Tuna, bluefin	*Thunnus thynnus*	679.00 kg 1496 lb	Aulds Cove, Nova Scotia, Canada	Oct. 26, 1979	Ken Fraser
Tuna, dogtooth	*Gymnosarda unicolor*	85.80 kg 189 lb 2 oz	Dar es Salaam, Tanzania	Nov. 12, 1978	Luke John Samaras
Tuna, longtail	*Thunnus tonggol*	29.50 kg 65 lb	Port Stephens, N.S.W., Australia	Apr. 20, 1978	Michael James
Tuna, skipjack	*Katsuwonus pelamis*	18.11 kg 39 lb 15 oz	Walker Cay, Bahamas	Jan. 21, 1952	F. Drowley
Tuna, skipjack (tie with above)	*Katsuwonus pelamis*	18.14 kg 40 lb	Baie du Tambeau, Mauritius	Apr. 19, 1971	Joseph R. P. Caboch
Tuna, southern bluefin	*Thunnus maccoyii*	116.50 kg 256 lb 13 oz	Hippolyte Rock, Tasmania, Australia	May 29, 1979	Rodney James Bean
Tuna, yellowfin	*Thunnus albacares*	176.35 kg 388 lb 12 oz	San Benedicto I., Mexico	Apr. 1, 1977	Curt Wiesenhutter
Tunny, little	*Euthynnus alletteratus*	12.24 kg 27 lb	Key Largo, Florida, USA	Apr. 20, 1976	William E. Allison
Wahoo	*Acanthocybium solandri*	67.58 kg 149 lb	Cay Cay, Bahamas	June 15, 1962	John Pirovano
Weakfish	*Cynoscion regalis*	8.84 kg 19 lb 8 oz	Trinidad, West Indies	Apr. 13, 1962	Dennis B. Hall
Yellowtail, California	*Seriola lalandi dorsalis*	32.65 kg 71 lb 15 oz	Alijos Rocks, Mexico	June 24, 1979	Michael Carpenter
Yellowtail, southern	*Seriola lalandi, lalandi*	50.34 kg 111 lb	Bay of Islands, New Zealand	June 11, 1961	A. F. Plim

THE SALTWATER ANGLER'S GALLEY

Nearly every nation in the world is touched by saltwater and everywhere the gifts of the sea are, in some manner, prepared for the table. Here are just a few of the favorite recipes of cooks beyond our borders. All have been adapted to the American kitchen where necessary.

FROM CARIBBEAN KITCHENS

Martinique, northernmost of the Windward Islands

Poisson en Blaff (Poached Fish)

Prepare a marinade of ⅓ cup lime juice, 1 fresh red-hot pepper, seeded and pounded in a mortar, 3 cloves of garlic, crushed, and 1 tablespoon salt. Combine in a shallow dish and add 2 cups water and 2 whole, cleaned one-pound red snappers (or other white-fleshed fish). Marinade should cover fish; add more water if necessary. Marinate 1 hour.

Remove fish and discard marinade; halve fish crosswise and set aside. In skillet just large enough to hold fish, mix 2 cups each water and dry white wine, 1 onion finely chopped, 1 garlic clove, crushed, 1 tablespoon lime juice, 2 cloves, 2 allspice berries, 2 bay leaves, 1 fresh whole red-hot pepper, 1 sprig thyme, and salt and pepper to taste. Bring the liquid to a boil and simmer 5 minutes. Add fish and simmer uncovered 10 to 12 minutes or until they flake easily. Serve fish portions in an oval platter. Spoon cooking liquid over each portion and serve with steamed rice and fried bananas. Serves 2.

Puerto Rico

Mero en Escabeche (Pickled Halibut)

Cut 3 pounds halibut fillets into 1¼-inch squares and sprinkle with salt. Heat 3 tablespoons olive oil in a large skillet and cook fish 2 minutes. Spoon fish into glass or ceramic bowl. Prepare pickling liquid in saucepan using 2 garlic cloves, peeled, 2 thinly sliced onions, 1 cup vinegar, 1 tablespoon salt, and ¼ teaspoon peppercorns. Slowly cook mixture until onions are tender. Cool marinade to room temperature and add 1 cup small pitted green olives and ¾ cup olive oil. Pour mixture over fish and chill, covered, for at least 24 hours. Serves 6–8.

British West Indies

Sole with Bananas

Sprinkle four sole fillets with salt and pepper. Mince 2 or 3 shallots (or 4 scallions with green tops) and spread evenly in the bottom of skillet just large enough to hold fish in single layer; lay fish in skillet. Add 1 cup fish stock (or bottled clam juice), 2 cups dry white wine, and ¾ cup lime juice and simmer covered for 7 minutes or until fish is just opaque. Remove the fillets and keep warm. Into the liquid in the skillet, stir 2 teaspoons curry powder and boil until reduced to ½ cup. Add 1 cup heavy cream and again reduce over high heat to ½ cup. Off heat stir in 2 egg yolks, beaten with ½ cup heavy cream, and cook over low flame (heat) 2 minutes. Do not boil. Divide 2 cups cooked rice among 4 shallow baking dishes, top rice in each dish with banana slices (one or two bananas will do) and arrange a fillet on each dish. Spoon sauce over fish and slide under preheated broiler 3 minutes or until tops are lightly browned. Serves 4.

The Grenadines

Fried Fish Puffs

Marinate 2½ cups chopped fillets of sole or halibut in the juice of 3 limes for 15 minutes, turning occasionally. With slotted spoon transfer fish to bowl. To juice add 1 chopped onion, 1 cup evaporated milk, and 1 cup flour, ¾ cup chopped cooked parsnips, 2 tablespoons soy sauce, and ½ teaspoon each salt, pepper, and Worcestershire sauce. Stir well, add the chopped fish, and puree mixture half at a time in blender. Drop puree by rounded tablespoons into hot (360° F.) oil in a deep fryer. Fry for 30 seconds or until browned on all sides. Remove puffs with slotted spoon and drain on paper towels. Makes about 36 puffs.

Haiti

Haitian Fish Stew

Heat ¼ cup peanut oil in large, heavy kettle, add 3 minced garlic cloves and 1 diced large onion, and cook until onion is soft. Add 1 minced green pepper, 1 chili pepper, seeded and minced, and sauté mixture 5 minutes. Add 1½ cups dry white wine, 1 cup white fish stock (or bottled clam juice), 1 cup peeled and diced yam, 1 cup peeled, seeded, and diced acorn squash, ¼ teaspoon crushed cumin seed, ⅛ teaspoon crushed saffron threads, soaked in 1 tablespoon water, 2 bay leaves, and salt to taste. Bring to a boil over high heat, reduce heat to moderate, and cook mixture for 10 minutes. Add 4 large tomatoes, peeled, seeded, and chopped, and ¼ pound mushrooms, sliced, and return the liquid to a boil over high heat. Add ½ pound each red snapper fillets, dolphinfish fillets or swordfish steaks, and tuna steaks, all cut into 1-inch pieces, and cook the whole over moderate heat for 6 minutes. Add the meat from an 8-ounce lobster tail, cut into ½-inch rounds, and ½ pound small shrimp, shelled and deveined, and cook the mixture for 3 to 4 minutes, or until the fish and shrimp are just cooked. Add ½ cup each of cooked crabmeat, minced parsley, and minced scallion, including the green tops and salt to taste and heat the stew for 2 minutes. Do not cook longer or fish will get tough.

Leeward Islands

Steamed Fish Fillets

Marinate 6 thick fillets of sole in the juice of 3 lemons for 15 minutes, turning several times. Pat fish dry and sprinkle with salt and pepper. Roll up white side out and place rolls in a buttered baking dish just large enough to hold them. Peel, seed, and thinly slice 3 tomatoes; thinly slice a large onion and scatter onion and tomato slices over the fish. Sprinkle the top with 2 tablespoons chopped fresh basil (or 2 teaspoons dried) and ⅛ teaspoon nutmeg. Cover with foil and bake in 350° F. oven for 10 to 15 minutes, or until they flake easily when pierced with a fork.

SOUTH AMERICA

Brazil

Fish in Tangerine Sauce

Clean a 3-pound red snapper or bass leaving the head and tail on. Sprinkle with 2 tablespoons lemon juice and salt and pepper. Place the fish in a greased baking dish just large enough to hold it and dribble 1 tablespoon each melted butter and olive oil over it. Strew over the top ¼ pound mushrooms, sliced, 1 tablespoon minced parsley, 1 scallion including the green top, chopped, 1 cup dry white wine, and ½ cup tangerine juice. Bake the fish in hot (400° F.) oven for a half hour or until fish flakes easily when tested with a fork. Serves 4.

Salt Cod with Eggs

Soak ½ pound salt cod in a glass or ceramic dish in cold water for 24 hours, changing water frequently. Drain and rinse cod and poach it in a saucepan in just enough water to cover at low heat for 15 to 20 minutes, or until it flakes easily when tested with a fork. Drain and flake the fish.

In a small bowl combine 2 tablespoons cornstarch with ¼ cup milk. In a saucepan combine the cornstarch mixture with 1¾ cups milk, add 1 tablespoon butter, and cook the mixture over moderate heat, stirring, until it is smooth and slightly thickened.

In another saucepan sauté 1 onion, grated, in a half stick (⅛ cup) butter until it is softened. Add 2 tomatoes, peeled, seeded, and chopped, and cook until most of the liquid has evaporated. Add the cod, the sauce, 2 tablespoons drained capers, and salt and pepper to taste. Let the mixture cool for 5 minutes. Butter 6 small ramekins and break an egg into each. Divide the cod mixture among the ramekins and sprinkle the top of each with ½ tablespoon freshly grated Parmesan cheese. Bake the ramekins in a hot (400° F.) oven for 8 minutes. Serves 6 as a first course.

Stuffed Crabs

Remove and pick over the meat from 6 steamed hard-shelled crabs and measure it. You'll need 1½ cups in all. Add extra canned crabmeat if necessary. Wash and dry top crab shells, brush insides with oil. Discard other shells. To crabmeat in bowl add 2 tablespoons lime (or lemon) juice, 2 garlic cloves, crushed, salt and pepper to taste.

In a skillet sauté 1 onion grated, 2 scallions including green tops, chopped, and 2 tomatoes, peeled, seeded, and chopped, in 2 tablespoons olive oil until mixture is soft and well blended. Let mixture cool to room temperature and combine it with crab mixture. Add 1 cup fresh bread crumbs, 2 tablespoons chopped fresh coriander or Chinese parsley, and 1 red-hot chili pepper, seeded and chopped, and stir to blend. Stuff the reserved shells with crab mixture, brush tops with beaten egg, and sprinkle each with ¼ teaspoon fine bulgur (cracked wheat). Put the stuffed crabs on a baking sheet and bake them in a moderate (350° F.) oven for 30 minutes or until lightly browned. Place crabs on serving plates and garnish with lettuce leaves and green and black olives. Serves 6 as a first course.

SOUTH OF THE BORDER

Baja California

Garlic Shrimp

Clean and devein 2 pounds shrimp. Melt 1 stick (¼ pound) butter in a cast-iron skillet and add 8 or more cloves of finely diced garlic, garlic salt or powder to taste, and ½ cup white wine. When very hot, add shrimp and cook, stirring gently and slowly until shrimp curl and turn pink but are still tender. Serve over plain white rice with frosty *cervesa* (Mexican beer).

Mainland Mexico

Pickled Fish

The day before serving, wash 2 pounds sole or haddock fillets and dry on paper towels. Melt ¼ cup butter in skillet and sauté fish on each side for 1 minute. Arrange in 12″ × 8″ × 2″ shallow glass or ceramic dish. Remove outer peel from 2 oranges with peeler or grate with coarse grater (you'll need about 1 cup). Squeeze juice from oranges to measure about ⅓ cup. In medium bowl combine orange juice, ¼ cup olive oil, 3 tablespoons tarragon vinegar, 1 teaspoon dried tarragon leaves, 1 teaspoon salt, ⅛ teaspoon pepper, ¼ cup chopped scallion, and 1 clove garlic; mix well. Stir in 2 bay leaves, the orange peel, and green pepper strips ⅛ inch wide from one pepper. Spoon the mixture over the fish, cover tightly with foil, and refrigerate at least 12 hours, basting occasionally with the marinade. Makes 8 servings.

NORTH OF THE BORDER

French Canada

Salmon and Potato Pie

Prepare dough for double pie shell (Bisquick Baking Mix is an acceptable short cut). Wrap dough in waxed paper and chill while preparing filling.

In a large skillet sauté ½ cup chopped salt pork until browned. Pour off all but 2 tablespoons of fat from the pan and in the fat remaining sauté 1 onion, coarsely chopped, until soft. Cut enough peeled potatoes into ½-inch cubes to measure 2 cups and add to the pan. Coat potatoes with fat and add enough boiling water to cover them. Simmer covered, for 10 to 15 minutes or until potatoes are tender. Remove the pan from heat and add a 1-pound salmon steak, boned, skinned, and cut into small pieces. Let the mixture cool.

Divide dough in half, roll out one half to a ¼-inch thickness and line a 9″ round dish. Fill with salmon mixture. Roll out the remaining half of the dough to a ¼-inch thickness and place it over the filling. Seal the edges by pressing them together with tines of a fork. Cut several slits in the top crust. Bake in a hot (400° F.) oven for 15 minutes, reduce the heat to moderate (350° F.), and continue to bake the dish for 25 to 30 minutes, or until the crust is golden. Serve the pie hot.

EUROPE

Switzerland

Baked Stuffed Trout

Chop 1 cup mushrooms finely and squeeze in a double thickness of cheesecloth to extract excess moisture. In a skillet melt ¼ pound butter and add the mushrooms, ⅔ cup each finely chopped carrots and celery, ¼ cup finely chopped onion, ¼ teaspoon thyme, and salt and pepper to taste. Cover the vegetables with foil and steam over moderately low heat until tender.

Clean and remove backbones from 2 trout, each weighing about ¾ pound. Season the fish lightly with salt and pepper, stuff the cavities with the vegetable mixture, and secure with skewers. Arrange the trout in a well-buttered shallow baking dish, dot with generous amount of butter, and bake in very hot (450° F.) oven, basting occasionally with the butter, for 15 to 18 minutes. Cover the trout with ½ cup heavy cream, lightly whipped and salted, and put them under the broiler until lightly brown. Serves 2.

Greece

Fish Plaki

In a skillet, sauté 1 pound freshly sliced tomatoes, 2 tablespoons oregano, 3 chopped scallions, 1 cup chopped parsley, and 1 clove minced garlic in ½ cup olive oil. Pour mixture into a baking dish and add 3 pounds baking fish—bluefish, striped bass, or sea bass will do. Lightly brush oil mixture onto top side of fish and salt and pepper to taste. Sprinkle fish with 4 tablespoons breadcrumbs, dot with butter, and cover with 2 large onions and 2 lemons that have both been sliced into rings. Add 1 cup water to baking dish. Bake at 350 degrees for 45 minutes. Serves 6.

Sicily, Italy

Pasta with Tuna Sauce

Heat ¼ cup each butter and olive oil in a saucepan and sauté 2 chopped onions and 2 garlic cloves until golden. Remove and discard the garlic cloves. Add to the pan ¼ cup each diced roasted sweet red pepper and diced green pepper and cook the mixture over moderate heat, stirring 2 or 3 times, for 20 minutes. Add one 7-ounce can tuna, drained, 6 anchovy fillets and 6 stuffed green olives, both chopped. Simmer the mixture for 3 to 4 minutes, or until the tuna is hot, and add salt and pepper to taste. Serve the sauce over 1 pound cooked pasta. Serves 4.

Lake Como, Italy

Perch with Italian Rice

Soak 2 tablespoons dried mushrooms in warm water, chop finely, and sauté until tender. Steam 1 cup short-grain Italian rice until done (follow directions on box), stir in ¼ cup butter, softened and cut into small pieces, ⅔ cup freshly grated Parmesan cheese, and the mushrooms. Cover and keep warm.

Sprinkle 4 perch or flounder fillets with salt and pepper and dust lightly with flour. Sauté in ½ cup clarified butter on both sides until lightly brown. Spoon rice into warm serving dish and arrange fillets on top. Sprinkle with minced fresh sage. Serves 4.

Belgium

Scallop Brochettes

In a saucepan blanch 24 very small white onions, peeled, in boiling salted water to cover for 2 minutes. Remove onions with a slotted spoon and set aside. In a skillet sauté 8 slices of bacon until translucent and cut into thirds. Sprinkle 24 small sea scallops with thyme and tarragon. Wrap each scallop in a piece of bacon and thread them on four 10-inch skewers, alternating scallops and onions. Arrange the skewers on the rack of a hot grill or a preheated broiler and broil them 2 to 3 inches from the heat, turning them, until the bacon is crisp and the onions are tender. Serve the brochettes with tartar sauce. Serves 4.

Finland

Smelts with Potatoes and Bacon

Clean and remove the backbones from 1 pound smelts, dry, and sprinkle with salt and pepper. Peel and thinly slice 1½ pounds potatoes and 1 onion. Grease well a 10″ × 6″ baking dish and place half the potato slices, slightly overlapping, on the bottom. Sprinkle with salt and pepper. Add half the smelts, half the onions, and 2 slices bacon, cut into 1-inch pieces. Add half the remaining potatoes, the remaining smelts and onions, 2 more slices of bacon; top with a layer of potatoes. In a bowl combine 1 cup milk, ½ cup heavy cream, 1 egg, and salt and pepper to taste. Pour over the smelt mixture and top with 2 more slices of bacon cut into 1-inch pieces and 2 tablespoons softened butter, cut into bits. Bake in a moderate (350° F.) oven for 1 hour, or until the potatoes are browned. Serves 4.

France

Baked Fish with Soufflé Sauce

Cut 1 pound fish fillets into serving-size pieces, coat with Shake 'n Bake (for fish), and bake as directed on package. Combine ½ cup mayonnaise, 2 tablespoons sweet relish, 2 tablespoons chopped parsley, ¼ teaspoon salt, and dash of cayenne; fold in 2 egg whites, stiffly beaten. Place hot baked fish on an ovenproof serving dish and top with sauce. Broil a minute or two until sauce is golden brown. Serves 4.

France (Brittany)

Breton Fish Soup

Cut 4 pounds of striped or channel bass or bluefish into 3-inch pieces and in a large, deep skillet quickly sauté them in a small amount of olive oil. Scoop browned pieces into a kettle as they are done. When all are browned, add 2 chopped onions and 1 crushed clove of garlic to the skillet and lightly brown in a bit more oil, if necessary. Transfer to the kettle and add 2 leeks, chopped, 2 tomatoes, chopped, 1 cup tomato sauce, 6 sprigs parsley, ¼ teaspoon cayenne, salt to taste, and 2 quarts dry white wine and simmer 15 minutes, or until the vegetables are soft. Add 4 pounds assorted fish bones and trimmings and 3 quarts of water and simmer the stock for 1 hour. Strain the broth through a fine sieve, pressing down hard on the solids, into the kettle. Simmer gently for 10 minutes, or until the fish is cooked and the soup is hot. Serve with hot croutons.

INDIA, CHINA, AND THE PACIFIC

India

Shrimp Curry

Heat 2 tablespoons butter and 1 tablespoon vegetable oil in a large skillet; sauté 1 cup chopped onion until soft and stir in 4 teaspoons curry powder. Cook, stirring constantly, 2 minutes longer. Add 1 can condensed chicken broth, ½ teaspoon salt, and 1 package (1½ pounds) frozen shelled and deveined shrimp. Bring to boil and simmer 5 minutes.

Blend 2 tablespoons cornstarch, ½ teaspoon ground ginger, 1 tablespoon lime juice, and 2 tablespoons water in a small bowl. Stir into shrimp mixture; continue cooking and stirring until it thickens and bubbles 1 minute. Stir in 1 tomato cut into wedges, 1 cup shredded lettuce, and cover. Simmer 3 minutes longer or until tomatoes are hot, but still firm. Serve over hot cooked rice. Serve with chutney, shredded coconut, and peanuts, if you wish. Serves 6.

China

Szechuan Bass or Perch

In a preheated nonstick skillet or wok, lightly brown over medium heat in ¼ cup oil (peanut oil is good) 1 pound bass or perch fillets, cut in 1-inch pieces, 2 ounces scallions including tops, cut in ¼-inch slices, and 2 cloves garlic, minced. Add 1 cup beef bouillon, 2 tablespoons soy sauce, 2 teaspoons minced gingerroot, 2 teaspoons sherry extract, 2 teaspoons cider vinegar, ¼ teaspoon crushed red or Szechuan pepper, or hot-pepper sauce to taste, cover, and cook over low heat 5 to 7 minutes or until fish flakes easily, basting several times. Serves 2.

Polynesia

Mahi-Mahi

For the batter, beat 2 eggs, add 2 teaspoons light soy sauce, 1 teaspoon baking powder, salt, pepper, and ¼ teaspoon Accent until blended. Add 4 tablespoons flour or enough to thicken mixture to the consistency of pancake batter.

Dip 4–6 ounce pieces of white flesh fillets (or about 1 small dolphin) in batter and deep-fry 3–4 minutes in hot oil until golden. Remove and place on large serving platter.

For the sauce, place 4 cups chicken stock in a saucepan over medium-high heat; add 2 tablespoons finely chopped mushrooms, 2 tablespoons finely chopped water chestnuts, 2 tablespoons finely chopped bamboo shoots, ½ teaspoon Accent, and ½ teaspoon sesame seed oil, and salt and pepper to taste. As mixture begins to heat, add enough cornstarch (about 4 tablespoons) to bring to consistency of good gravy. Reduce heat, add oyster sauce (8 teaspoons) and ¼ cup chopped green onion. Stir well and let thicken again. Pour over platter of deep-fried fish fillets. Serve immediately. Serves 4.

Hawaii

Teriyaki from Dolphin, Snook, Grouper or Snapper

Combine ⅔ cup soy sauce, ¼ cup brown sugar, 1 clove garlic, crushed, ¼ teaspoon powdered ginger, 2 tablespoons salad oil, ¼ teaspoon monosodium glutamate (Accent), 2 tablespoons toasted sesame seed and mix well. Marinate 2 pounds fish fillets for an hour or more. Broil 5 inches from broiler unit for 15 to 20 minutes. Serves 6.